Demystifying Virtual Private Networks

Michael Busby

Wordware Publishing, Inc.

Library of Congress Cataloging-in-Publication Data

Busby, Michael
    Demystifying virtual private networks / by Michael Busby.
      p. cm.
    ISBN 1-55622-672-1 (pbk.)
    1. Extranets (Computer networks).   2. Business enterprises—Computer networks.
    3. Internet.   4. Computer networks—Security measures.   5. Computer network protocols.
    I. Title.

    TK5105.875.E87 B79   2000
    650'.0285'46--dc21   00-060031
                                            CIP

ISBN 1-55622-672-1

10 9 8 7 6 5 4

0009

All inquiries for volume purchases of this book should be addressed to Wordware Publishing, Inc.,
at the above address. Telephone inquiries may be made by calling:

(972) 423-0090

Dedication

For some special people: my loving wife, Alethea, and my best friends, Michael, Marty, Shane, Drew, and Stuart.

For a special family: J.D., Gail, Johnny, Jimmy, and sweet Caroline Carlson. Semper Fi.

For a special group: the former and current enlisted men of the United States Marine Corps.

And for a special place: Dixie's Corner. . . I remember.

Contents

Contents

Contents

Introduction

VPNs—virtual private networks—suddenly appeared upon the communications scene recently. VPNs serve a useful purpose within the realm of business communications. Until VPNs came along, corporations were limited in their ability to connect remote users to their internal local area networks. Now, VPNs connect remote users, regardless of their geographical location, to all manner of corporate computing resources.

VPNs exist and serve a useful purpose primarily because of the existence of the Internet and its enabling protocols, TCP/IP. This book is intended to help those individuals with little or no understanding of internetworking to understand VPNs. If you are already familiar with the world in which VPNs exist, that is TCP/IP, then you will find the material in this book of little use. However, if you are unfamiliar with TCP/IP, and wish to understand how VPNs fit into the overall networking environment, this book is for you.

The material is presented in a logical fashion, taking you from the basic business reasons for selecting VPNs as a communications solution to the fundamentals of networking and the complexities of VPNs. Due to such mundane concerns as page count, not every possible topic is covered in great detail; such an endeavor would require many thousands of pages. I have included those topics of general interest to those with limited exposure to networking communications.

While networking technologies may seem daunting to the uninitiated, many thousands of individuals have successfully mastered them, and so can you. Just remember, at the most fundamental level, everything is either a zero or a one, and everything else is just a question of what the zero and one mean. Have fun!

Chapter 1 Introduction to Virtual Private Networking

Questions answered in this chapter:

- What is a virtual private network?
- What is the history of VPNs?
- What remote access solutions are available?
- Why are VPNs the best solution?
- What benefits do VPNs provide?

Introduction

What exactly is a VPN? A VPN is nothing more, or less, than a private network *connection* configured within a public network.

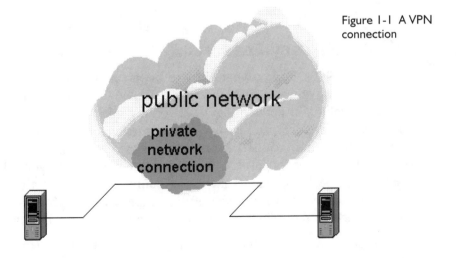

Figure 1-1 A VPN connection

public network

private network connection

That is, the VPN appears as a private national or international network connection to the using company's premises, but physically shares backbone trunks and additional physical resources with other customers of the transporting enterprise. From the perspective of an enterprise, a VPN is nothing more than a public network connection indistinguishable from a dial-up connection. From the perspective of a remote access user, a VPN connection is identical to a dial-up connection.

VPNs are not limited to any particular networking transport technology. Transport technologies VPNs have utilized include TCP/IP, frame relay, X.25, and ATM. The interest today, due to the significant cost savings that can be realized over such conventional technologies as leased lines, is building VPNs over the Internet and using TCP/IP as the transport technology. The focus of this book will therefore be using VPNs over TCP/IP-based networks.

Figure 1-2 VPNs equal cost savings

A Short (VPN) History Lesson

In the late 1960s, a somewhat obscure Department of Defense group called the Defense Advanced Research Projects Agency (DARPA) started the network ball rolling by sponsoring a networking initiative among the various campuses where defense research was occurring. For some time, networking was the domain of the Department of Defense. As time passed, personal computers began propagating faster than the proverbial bunny rabbit. High-tech companies saw the wisdom of interconnecting their computing resources in order to share those expensive resources, such as file servers and printers. Then we discovered something called e-mail.

The impetus to interconnect computing resources changed from sharing an expensive laser printer to sending and receiving e-mail. But e-mail required a different networking approach to enable communications among the computing resources. To share a printer, each computer required a primarily one-way communication path to the printer. For the typical setup, there was no need for a printer to talk to a computer, other than to send a simple signal indicating the print job was received.

But to send e-mail, each computer needed some communications path to every other computer. Thus was born the local area network. And the world began networking with a vengeance, installing local area networks (LANs) as fast as the company management could be convinced of the utility, and cost savings, of a LAN.

Then, high-tech companies with widespread campuses decided they wished to connect the geographically diverse campus LANs into something called wide area networks (WANs). The road was thus paved to add but one additional element to the web of networking sites spreading across the globe. So was born the World Wide Web and something called the Internet.

Initially, the World Wide Web was the supreme domain of the geeks, high-tech companies, college research centers, and the Department of Defense. But low-tech companies began connecting to the World Wide Web in the early 1990s, spreading the gospel of networking down the NASDAQ food chain. By the mid-1990s, every periodical in the United States seemed to be hyping the World Wide Web. Companies and individuals of all descriptions began to connect to the web. It seemed like "virtual gold fever" swept the nation and no one wanted to be left out of the Internet "gold rush." Very much like the 1849 California gold rush, the 1995 Internet "virtual gold rush" made a few millionaires almost overnight. Eventually, a few even became billionaires.

While all the networking fuss was going on, telephone companies were reaping billions from leasing lines to companies that needed a means of transporting their data from campus to campus in the 1980s and 1990s. Then someone determined that if the Internet, whose presence, as manifested by a local Internet service provider (ISP), was in every American city and many international cities, could be used to transport secure data for these companies, a great cost savings over leasing lines would result as the ISP would only be a local telephone call away over the twisted copper line or an ISDN connection.

In the interest of capitalizing on the ubiquitous Internet presence, several companies that manufactured networking products sponsored an initiative, something called a VPN, and introduced a new communications method to the commercial world. Virtual private networks (VPNs) burst upon the communication scene just a couple of years ago (1998). While still not in everyone's vocabulary, they are becoming more and more well known as companies look for more competitive ways to conduct their business.

A Reason for Being

Why the interest in VPNs? Corporations have a financial interest in providing easy, cost-effective, remote network access solutions for the growing number of employees requiring remote access to corporate data, such as:

- Electronic mail
- Corporate database/database applications
- Document/data warehousing
- Sales force automation applications
- File/data/document replication
- Intranet access and productivity
- Multimedia presentations/teleconferencing
- Voice connectivity
- Electronic data interchange

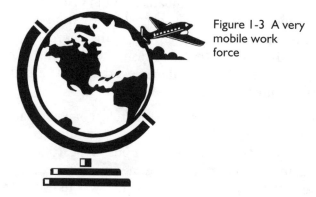

Figure 1-3 A very mobile work force

Corporate interests, of course, do not operate in a vacuum, although we may occasionally think so. The factors driving the corporate interest in remote access solutions are:

- The role of information management in an increasingly competitive society
- Technology that makes remote network access simple, secure, and practical

- Organizational and work force changes such as telecommuters and roaming users
- Corporations have several choices available to connect their remote users to the corporate LAN

The remote access solutions available for corporate users to connect to the corporate LAN are:

- Public switched telephone networks (PSTN)
- Integrated Services Digital Network (ISDN)
- DSL modems
- Cable modems
- Wireless data networks
- Bulk data transport technologies (ATM/frame relay/SMDS)
- Internet and VPN technologies

The available remote access solutions come with various advantages and disadvantages. The advantages of any particular remote access solution outweigh its disadvantages only in specific circumstances. However, an Internet-based solution utilizing VPN technology is the only cost-effective solution.

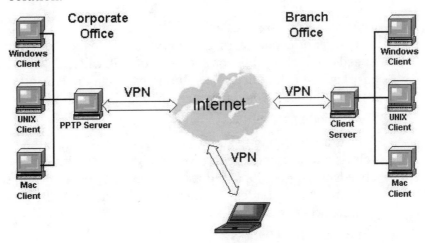

Figure 1-4 A typical corporate application for VPNs

Remote Access Options

VPNs are designed to accommodate the increasing demand for tele-commuting, which is related to the distributed operations of companies and the need to share information in real time over large distances. VPNs are not the only remote access solution. There are several remote access options available to companies that need to add remote network access capability. Each option has its own set of advantages and disadvantages, of course. The options vary considerably in availability, cost, service coverage, throughput, and suitability for various applications. The options are:

- Public switched telephone network (PSTN) solutions

  These solutions include modem banks, (copper wire) telephone lines, 800 numbers, and remote access servers, typically transporting voice and data over one or more leased lines, either locally, nationally, or internationally.

- Integrated Services Digital Network (ISDN)

  ISDN is a digital multiplexing upgrade to PSTN, offering up to 128 Kbps of channel capacity on a single Basic Rate Interface (BRI) line. ISDN is another leased line solution, albeit a faster data rate.

- Digital subscriber line (DSL)

  DSL is a technology designed to leverage the existing telephone infra-structure, or copper wiring, to provide high-bandwidth data access at speeds up to 1.5 Mbps for a version of DSL called ADSL. While DSL is just beyond its infancy, it is still not available in all locations, is not nec-essarily reliable even when available, and can be expensive.

- Cable modems

  This is an emerging technology designed to leverage the existing cable television infrastructure to provide high-bandwidth data access at speeds up to 400 Kbps. It does not appear to be a reliable solution at this time and just adds another layer of cost, the CATV provider, to a remote access solution.

- Wireless data networks

  This is a still-emerging technology that uses wireless (RF) technology. Wireless is always subject to interference, and sunspot activity can wreak havoc with data throughput.

- ATM/Frame relay

  ATM and frame relay are viable options only for those companies transporting large amounts of data on an almost 24-hour basis. Frame relay is an older transmission technology that will be eventually replaced by ATM in the marketplace. Both ATM and frame relay require dedicated ISDN lines from the corporate ATM/frame relay switch and the remote access ATM/frame relay switch to the local exchange. ATM/frame relay service must be available via the local service provider in the service area.

- SMDS

  Switched Multimegabit Data Service is an almost extinct dodo bird. Like the dodo bird, it never flew over any nest. Only one company stubbornly continues to try to market the arcane technology. Do you want to sign a four-year contract with a company that has no competitors in the technology?

- Internet access and virtual private network (VPN) solutions

  VPNs leverage the global, public Internet to provide secure remote access via Internet service providers (ISPs) at an economical rate.

While a simple PSTN and modem-based solution for remote access may have a low entry cost, expenses rapidly escalate as the volume of users and their geographic mobility increases, driving up the associated toll charges. Corporate remote access solutions based on Internet and VPN technologies are highly cost effective, especially when remote access is required from Europe, Asia, South America, and third world countries. Each remote access choice and their relative advantages and disadvantages are described in the following sections.

Public Switched Telephone Networks (PSTN)

PSTN technology has been around ever since Alexander Graham Bell uttered the famous "come hither" sentence to Dr. Watson. The age of the technology is both its advantage and its disadvantage.

- Advantages

  The PSTN approach consists of a bank of modems, some number of telephone lines, and a remote access server. Also, a toll-free 800 number to provide remote access to domestic roaming users may be utilized. The main advantage of the PSTN solution is the entry cost for a small-scale deployment is very low. For the lowest entry cost, all an organization needs is a Windows NT server, a modem, and a telephone line. The Windows NT has remote access service built into the machine. The age of the technology says, "I am reliable," and it is.

▶ Disadvantages

Supporting remote access users quickly becomes problematic as the number of users exceeds a small threshold. A remote access support staff plus the purchase and deployment of multiple dedicated remote access servers, modem banks, and telephone lines is required when the number of users exceeds just a few.

Costs of the PSTN solution are not as flexible as other solutions. Leased line costs are fixed regardless of the amount of traffic. And toll-free 800 lines are fixed price per some unit of measure (typically seconds of use).

The age of the technology also says, "I am slow, but I will get there, sooner or later," and today it most likely is later. The speed of the connection is limited to the speed of the newest analog modem design, currently at 56.6 Kbps and expected to stagnate at that speed due to technical limitations of the technology. In the period of 100 Mbps Ethernet LANs, 56.6 Kbps seems as slow as cold molasses tightly gripping the sides of an upturned bottle.

Accommodating all users during peak usage hours requires sufficient resource capacity. The additional capacity required to support peak hours represents inefficiency, as the resource cost is fixed even when the capacity is idle during low usage hours.

Connection costs for users who roam across international boundaries becomes increasingly problematic as the distance from home base increases. Also, toll quality connections in many other areas of the world are not comparable to toll quality connections in the United States. The data may need to be retransmitted numerous times, resulting in dramatically increased toll charges.

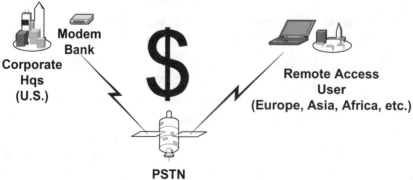

Figure 1-5 Typical PSTN remote access solution

Integrated Services Digital Network (ISDN)

ISDN technology has been available since the early 1980s, and represents an end-to-end digital upgrade to PSTN. A typical solution involves lines and equipment supplied by an ISDN service provider, a remote access server with ISDN support, and an ISDN bridge/router. Like PSTN, ISDN users are only charged for the duration of their connection.

▶ Advantages

ISDN's primary advantage is its improved bandwidth over PSTN. A Basic Rate Interface (BRI) can reliably carry data at 128 Kbps without the use of data compression technology (as opposed to a maximum of 56.6 Kbps for PSTN solutions). With the use of data compression technology, throughput can be even higher.

▶ Disadvantages

Cost, cost, cost. ISDN has many of the same cost disadvantages as PSTN solutions for remote access. Organizations must purchase and administer phone lines and remote access equipment. Plus, adding capacity to serve additional users can be expensive. In addition, ISDN is not available in all areas and cannot be used reliably across service provider boundaries. As a result, ISDN can provide a satisfactory solution for telecommuters living in an ISDN service area, but is not suitable for the roaming user.

Digital Subscriber Line (DSL)

DSL is an emerging modem technology that leverages the existing PSTN copper wire transmission infrastructure. The DSL technology makes use of an "asymmetric" channel, meaning that downstream and upstream access rates are different. DSL uses the standard twisted-pair telephone lines to provide high-speed connectivity to the Internet (through a participating Internet service provider and local telephone company) and/or corporate LANs. DSL generally provides downstream data rates from 1.544 Mbps to 9 Mbps. Upstream rates are 16 Kbps to 640 Kbps. An example of a DSL service is Verizon's (formerly GTE) FasTrack DSL service, which provides customers in limited service areas with 1.544 Mbps downstream and 384 Kbps upstream. To connect directly to the corporate LAN, businesses must connect to Verizon's switched data network.

▶ Advantages

DSL's cost per bit is competitive with PSTN and analog modems, even though its bit throughput is much greater than analog modems. DSL is also easy to install.

▶ Disadvantages

DSL's main disadvantage is that it is a relatively new technology, and therefore unproven in the marketplace. DSL also has some of the same disadvantages as PSTN such as DSL modem banks for multiple subscribers. Its access is limited to installed service areas, and may not be an actual option for you.

DSL is an emerging technology. Not all areas are served by DSL. A convenient way to determine if your area is DSL enabled is to visit http://www.dslreports.com.

Cable Modems

Cable modems are another emerging modem technology that leverages the existing cable television shielded coaxial cable transmission infrastructure. Cable modems also make use of an "asymmetric" channel, meaning that downstream and upstream access may be at different rates. Because of the bandwidth demands upon the local cable television network, cable modem services provide variable downstream performance, typically in the 1.5 to 3 Mbps range, depending on how much traffic is on the network. The availability of the bandwidth can be used in conjunction with VPN technology to provide a secure corporate remote access solution.

Cable modems use the currently installed cable television plant and transmission infrastructure to get the signal from the cable office to the intended destination, your place of business or your home. However, the link must still be connected somehow between the cable office and the PSTN network, as cable transmission systems do not form a homogeneous network covering the country, continent, and world.

▶ Advantages

Cable modem has a high bandwidth and low entry cost.

▶ Disadvantages

The disadvantages of cable modem are similar to DSL, in that both are relatively new technologies, and thus are unproven in the marketplace. Having a single service provider in any particular community eliminates competition, and the addition of another service provider layer, the

CATV company, adds cost. Additionally, some of the same disadvantages exist as with analog modems, such as the need for data banks to provide multiple access.

ADSL and cable modems are promising as a cost-effective means of providing high-speed corporate remote access to telecommuters and remotely located workers who are in fixed and known locations and comprise a limited number of access nodes. However, both solutions require special lines and equipment at the remote site and are very limited in terms of service area. As a result, these two approaches to remote access do not represent a practical solution for roaming corporate users.

Wireless Data Networks

Wireless data networks allow roaming users, connecting with laptop computers, WindowsCE machines, or PDAs, to have continuous untethered access to messages and limited amounts of corporate data. A corporate customer connects to a wireless network service provider through a leased line to implement a wireless corporate remote access solution. The end-user computing device must be equipped with a compatible wireless modem, which allows it to send and receive data over the wireless network.

▶ Advantages

The primary advantage wireless solutions offer is the high degree of mobility they provide users. Users can connect anywhere, even where no telephone lines are available. However, this mobility comes at a handsome cost.

▶ Disadvantages

Coverage and reliability for wireless solutions is problematic. A company offering a wireless solution usually cannot provide coverage in all locations. For example, one service provider offers service coverage only for the top 100 metropolitan areas in the United States. Also, the ability to roam across national boundaries and maintain connectivity is very limited. Buildings, geographical characteristics such as mountains, and other natural and man-made obstructions affect the robustness of the connection. Applications using wireless services must be able to tolerate frequent dropouts and data errors.

The cost for wireless solutions is higher than wireline solutions. As a result, wireless remote access solutions are suitable for specialized users and applications. They are not really suitable for broad groups of telecommuters, people who have to travel across national borders, or applications with high bandwidth requirements (such as file transfer and database transactions).

However, the socialization of humankind being what it is, and especially in the United States, most mobile workers will probably clamor for wireless connectivity, elevating them to some higher plane in the social strata of the work environment, offering some small compensation for the wretched cubicles they are forced to endure.

ATM/Frame Relay

ATM/frame relay are bulk data carrying services and are usually associated with large trunking networks. In other words, an ATM or frame relay trunking network is the transport technology used by large network players to move tremendous amounts of data. It is hardly cost effective as a remote access solution for a mobile work force.

► Advantages

The main advantage ATM/frame relay provides is that it can move huge amounts of data.

► Disadvantages

However, only the rich and famous can afford it.

ATM and frame relay are for the really big players in the networking game, such as the U.S. government, telecommunications companies providing the trunking backbone of the nation, and perhaps certain businesses that deal with terabytes/hour transmission rates.

Internet and VPNs

VPNs leverage the accessibility of the ubiquitous Internet to provide a remote access solution virtually in any city in the world at an economical price.

► Advantages

VPNs are easy to set up and very cost effective. They are also easy to maintain and secure.

► Disadvantages

VPN coverage can be lacking in some areas.

An Internet-based solution with VPN technology is a practical solution for companies that must provide remote access to the corporate network.

When Summer is Over, or A Reason to Migrate

The differences and similarities between leased lines and virtual private networks are described in this section. A thorough grasp of the nuances of the two technologies is essential for convincing usually deaf management to change to a better way of accomplishing the goals of the company. Good luck.

In the traditional leased line solution, the data is transported from the customer's premises to the local or trunking office over standard lightwave telephone lines. There is no Internet service provider involved in getting data from one customer premises to another via leased lines. The customer's data is considered "safe" since the transport path does not go through an ISP. The physical transmission path from server to server, or server to remote user, is a dedicated connection that is "nailed up" all the time. That is, no other user shares the connection and the connection is hard-wired from customer premise to customer premise.

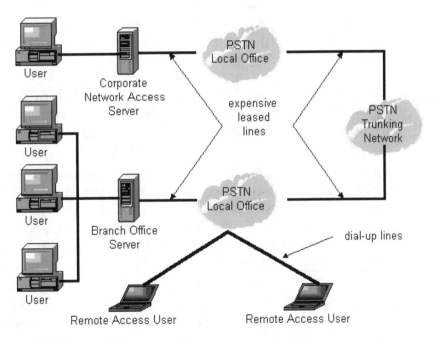

Figure 1-6 A leased line perspective of remote access

In the old days, which still exist for many companies, a company leased a digital line or lines capable of transporting the volume of data necessary to perform the company's business from point A to point B from a common carrier. Common carriers made a lot of money off these leased lines, as the leasing company paid a goodly sum for the line regardless of the amount of traffic carried on it.

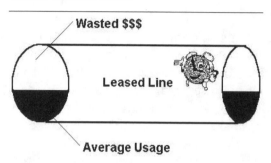

Figure 1-7 The cost of leased lines and the "Happy Telco"

That is, if the company only used the leased line at 50% capacity, the company still paid for 100% utilization. And telcos encouraged companies to lease lines, as the approach for solving enterprises' communication needs was a virtual pot of gold for the greedy telephone companies. In the 1970s and '80s, time-division multiplexing (TDM) T1 solutions over leased lines were adopted by many corporations in the U.S. in an almost fruitless attempt to reduce bandwidth costs by consolidating voice and data applications over common facilities. Telcos simply raised the price of leased lines.

Regardless of the cost, the leasing company was assured some degree of privacy on a public transport system, as no other company had easy physical access to the leased line and the data it carried. Therefore, the leasing company assumed its transported data was entirely safe, an assumption that those who have worked on government electronic warfare programs know to be false. However insecure, at least the leasing company thought its data was safe.

Then the World Wide Web and the Internet burst forth on the communications stage in the early to mid-1990s, offering opportunities to develop new communication methods. Leveraging the opportunities presented by the Internet, a couple of companies in the networking business developed VPN technology.

VPNs offer cost savings for voice networks as well as data networks. VPN services deliver lower cost and simpler voice networking topologies than private leased line network solutions. The opportunity to leverage the Internet and save money is causing a migration from TDM-based voice networks to VPNs.

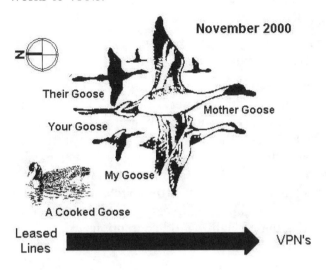

Figure 1-8 A wise bird migrates

So far, we have focused on remote access needs and solutions. However, VPN technology can be applied to enterprise voice networks for significant cost savings. Enterprise voice networks traditionally use analog and digital leased lines between corporate locations served by local PBX switches. In a typical enterprise PBX implementation, call routes are hard coded using fixed call routing tables in each PBX. Routes are specified for each destination with various alternate routes specified for use during peak traffic periods on each route. Of course, the alternate routes must accommodate the bandwidth needs of the user. The costs and problems associated with this approach are:

▶ High operational costs

    Maintaining multiple hard-coded PBX routing tables and reconfiguring network bandwidth assignments when traffic patterns change is very expensive for any network that can be classified as anything greater than small.

▶ Inefficient bandwidth usage

    The bandwidth allocated is dedicated to the route, and utilization determines efficiency. Anything less than 100% is inefficient and no longer cost effective.

15

▸ Quality of service degradation

Compression techniques in multiple hop configurations degrade the quality of the transmission.

▸ Unnecessarily blocked calls

When a route cannot accept any more calls, the new calls must overflow to PSTN links, which can be costly.

VPNs automatically configure the call routing as appropriate. Each PBX is connected to a service provider's network via a VPN, which interprets the PBX signaling and routes the calls to the appropriate remote PBXs. With voice VPN-based services, there is no need for pre-specifying trunk routes on a per-PBX basis. Each PBX in the voice network is logically just a single hop away from any other PBX in the network. A new PBX is added to the voice network by making an entry in the database resident on the service provider's network. This approach makes use of existing enterprise infrastructure. For bulk data freighting, other solutions exist that use a combination of ATM, DSL, and VPNs.

A Detailed Description of VPNs

VPNs incorporate key technologies that permit private networking over public intranetworks and internetworks. A VPN connects the physical components and resources of two networks, or a network and a remote user, over another network, such as the Internet. VPNs accomplish this by providing a means for the user to "tunnel" through the Internet or other public networks in such a way that the tunnel participants may enjoy the same network security and user features available in private networks.

When VPNs are utilized as the data transport protocol, the data is transported from the customer's premises to the Internet service provider over standard lightwave or copper wire telephone lines. Depending upon the data volume, the lines may be leased or they may be dial-up. The data is transported over the lightwave or copper wire to the local office. From the local office, the data is transported to the ISP. The Internet service provider transports the data to the common carrier trunking office over standard lightwave telephone lines. The customer's data is considered "safe" since it is encrypted and provided with access controls. The physical connection from ISP server to ISP server is not a dedicated circuit and is considered connectionless switching, that is, the connection is a shared resource with many other users.

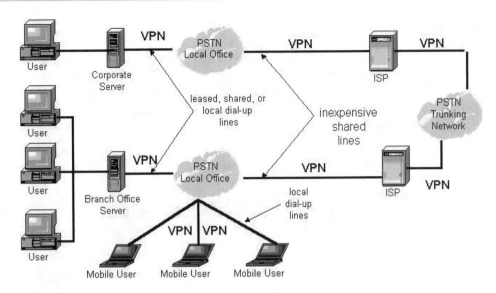

Figure 1-9 A virtual private network perspective of remote access

VPNs allow remote employees such as marketing and sales, field engineering, branch offices, or telecommuters of any description to connect to the corporate local area network (LAN) edge server using the trunking infrastructure provided by a public network such as an ISP. And the connection is a "secure" connection. Just what the configuration of the public network is remains immaterial to the remote user. For all practical purposes, the interconnection appears the same as a private, dedicated connection. The interconnection performs the same logical role as a wide area network (WAN) connection. It is <u>virtually</u> the same as a *private network*; therefore it is called virtual private network by the enterprises that created it. However, the name is a misnomer. Since a network is usually thought of in terms of many users connected together in some manner with the intent of sharing common resources, an individual remote user connecting into a LAN hardly fills the role of a *network*. It is really a virtual private network *connection*.

VPN Implementation

There are several ways to implement VPNs. These are described in the following sections.

Remote Access Over the Internet

VPNs provide remote access to corporate users over the public Internet, while maintaining information privacy. Figure 1-10 shows a VPN used to connect a remote user to a corporate intranet.

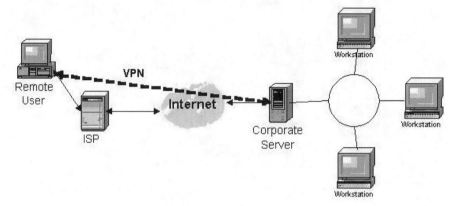

Figure 1-10 Using a VPN to connect a remote client to a corporate LAN via a public network

Rather than making a leased line, long distance, or 800 call to a corporate or outsourced network access server (NAS), the remote user first calls a local ISP phone number. Using the local connection to the ISP, the VPN software creates a virtual private network (connection) between the dial-up user and the corporate VPN server across the Internet.

Basic VPN Requirements

When a company decides to deploy a remote networking access solution, determining who will get access is an important initial consideration. A company's interest is usually best served if access to valuable company information is limited and unauthorized access is prohibited. Therefore, a company must choose a security solution wisely.

The security solution selected would ideally provide an easy method for remote offices and users to connect to corporate local area network resources while blocking all unauthorized access. However, the overriding access control concern requires any viable solution to guarantee the privacy and integrity of data as it traverses the public Internet or a corporate intranetwork.

Thoughtful consideration of numerous issues before a company implements a remote access solution is wise. What does a company expect to gain from a remote access solution? From an analysis of expectations, a company will determine what services are required to implement the decided upon solution. Any remote access solution should provide the following features and services:

- User authentication

  The solution must verify a user's identity and restrict VPN access to authorized users only. In addition, the solution must provide audit and accounting records to show who accessed what information and when.

- Address management

  The solution must assign a client's address on the private network, and must ensure that private addresses are kept private.

- Data encryption

  Data transmitted on the public (and even the private) network must be rendered unreadable while transiting the network.

- Key management

  The solution must generate and refresh encryption keys for both the client and server.

- Multiprotocol support

  The solution must be able to handle common protocols used in the public network. These include Internet Protocol (IP), Internetwork Packet Exchange (IPX), and similar protocols.

- Robust firewall

  The solution must be flexible enough to easily add or remove users.

- Reporting tools

  Connection status reporting and user reports by user and location are necessary to effectively manage the solution.

- Remote management

  Remotely managing VPN connections allows for a centralized management function including installation, fault reporting, tracking, and repairing effort, all of which are essential to timely resolution of connection issues.

- Real-time alerting

  The ability to identify and report connection issues when they occur is important to maintaining a robust network.

▶ Remote user VPN

A VPN solution must allow a single remote user, such as a mobile worker, to plug in anywhere the worker may be.

▶ Remote office VPN

A VPN solution must provide for the case of a remote office solution. The remote office case is not the same as a remote user as the remote office may have many users, some of whom may be mobile and some of whom are usually in a fixed location.

A VPN solution based on the Point-to-Point Tunneling Protocol (PPTP) or Layer 2 Tunneling Protocol (L2TP) meets all of the basic VPN requirements to provide secure communications between remote users and corporate facilities. An additional feature of a PPTP or L2TP solution is the ability to utilize the low-cost and easy access to the worldwide Internet. Other solutions, including the IP Security Protocol (IPSec), only meet some of these requirements, but they may remain useful for specific and unique remote access requirements.

Companies requiring a remote access solution should carefully consider the capabilities of a prospective Internet service provider to provide remote access. All Internet service providers were not created equal. There is a wide margin of difference in the ability of the many ISPs to meet a company's remote access needs. For a successful solution, careful consideration of the following ISP issues is a must:

▶ Service area coverage

Some ISPs provide only local or regional coverage, while others offer national and international coverage.

▶ Interoperability with other ISPs

While VPN standards exist, there is always the issue of interoperability with other ISPs due to the numerous manufacturers of various equipment adding features unique to their equipment.

▶ Data security

ISPs differ in their ability to provide a secure connection.

▶ Quality of service

QOS is a significant issue, as dropped packets require retransmission, affecting the speed and throughput of data, and adversely impacting time-managed networking elements.

▶ Ease of deployment and use

If deployment and usage is not easy, such costs as maintenance and training rise proportionally.

Connecting Networks Over the Internet

There are two approaches for using VPNs to connect corporate local area networks to remote sites:

▶ Dedicated lines connect a user such as a branch office to a corporate LAN

Note that the remote user may be any authorized entity requiring access to the corporate LAN.

The branch office and the corporate hub routers use local, dedicated ISDN lines and local ISPs to connect to the Internet. The VPN software uses each local ISP connection and the public Internet transport infrastructure to create a virtual private network connection between the branch office router and corporate hub router.

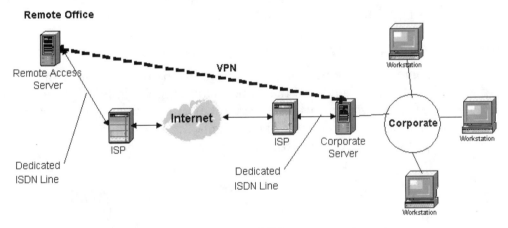

Figure 1-11 Using a VPN to connect a corporate LAN to a remote site

This solution is really a hybridized approach as a local dedicated or leased line is used to connect both the remote user and the corporate remote access server to local ISPs. However, for branch offices with high data transfer volumes, such an approach is certainly less expensive than leasing a dedicated long-haul line from source to destination, especially if the transmission path crosses several different regional exchanges.

▶ Dial-up line connects a user such as a branch office to a corporate LAN

The router at the branch office calls the local ISP over a plain old telephone line. The VPN software uses the connection to the local ISP to create a virtual private network between the branch office router and the corporate hub router via the Internet infrastructure.

The corporate VPN server may either be listening constantly for a connection request or the server may only listen during specific, pre-arranged times, depending upon the operational requirements of the remote user. In most cases, the server will probably need to listen 24 hours per day for a connection driving the need to connect the server to a local dedicated line. The local dedicated line could be a dedicated ISDN line or a plain old telephone line (copper) with or without a DSL modem. Data volume will dictate which solution is best.

In some situations, the facilities that connect a branch office and a corporate office to the Internet are local to both parties. In this model, both client/server and server-server VPN cost savings are dependent upon the use of local access to complete the connection. Cost savings are significant using POTS and DSL or cable modems.

Connecting Computers Over an Intranet

Some corporate networking applications disconnect a department's LAN from the remainder of the corporate internetwork. Perhaps the departmental data is so sensitive that the data must be protected by the disconnect to provide some guarantee of confidentiality. But such a solution may create access issues for users who are not able to connect directly to the department LAN.

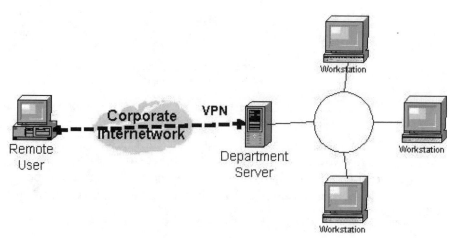

Figure 1-12 Using a VPN to connect two computers on the same LAN

Using the approach shown in Figure 1-12, a remote user may be connected to a department's LAN via the corporate internetwork by utilizing VPN technology and a VPN server at the LAN edge. The server does not perform the same function as a router, as a router would allow all internetwork users to connect to the LAN. The network administrator controls who is allowed access to the VPN server based upon some company need-to-know policy.

VPN Security

Of grave concern to most enterprises using networks is the issue of security. The concern for security arises due to the innate desire to protect property. Companies perceive all information within their organization to be the property of the company. And by extension of that philosophy, unauthorized individuals should not be able to intercept the exchange of that information among company employees. Therefore, network security is a major concern to companies. Are VPNs secure? The companies that originally developed VPN technology claim that VPNs are secure. However, at least one cryptology expert has found a way to spoof VPNs.

The enterprises that developed VPNs were made aware of the security breach, and supposedly implemented fixes. In any case, only a very sophisticated operation, such as may be found among some government entities, can breach VPN security, if at all, and within a certain degree of confidence, a user can be assured the connection is secure. How are VPNs configured to prevent unauthorized access? By using access control and data encryption.

VPNs and User Administration

Certain user administration elements are an issue with remote access via the Internet transmission path. Authorized user names and password assignments must be coordinated with the chosen Internet service provider. If the scope of the remote access is local or regional, such as a local branch office requiring remote access, then local or regional ISPs are sufficient to provide the services required. If a larger scope is necessary, such as the foreign office of a company, arrangements with multiple ISPs may be required to provide the larger geographical coverage. Or, contracting with a single national or international ISP that provides national and/or global coverage may be the answer, depending upon the specific needs of the contracting company.

Summary

The amazing growth of the Internet and its ubiquitous presence has led a few suppliers of networking products to investigate using it as a means of low-cost, secure, and reliable remote access to the corporate network. VPNs were the offspring of their efforts. Usually, all that is required to enable VPNs at the company and the remote access demarcations is connectivity to the Internet and the appropriate access control software installed on the corporate remote access server and the remote access client. The access control software must include the corporate firewall necessary to provide a secure communications link between the two users.

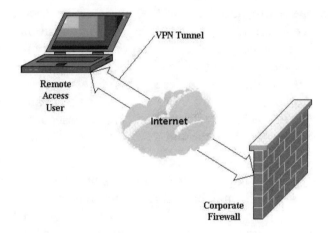

Figure 1-13 VPN remote access

An important enabling element in the use of VPNs for remote access solutions is the ability to leverage public switched telephone networks (PSTNs) and the Internet for virtual private networking connections. VPNs simplify and reduce the cost of deploying enterprise-wide, remote access solutions for remote and mobile users. VPNs are able to reduce cost because they provide secure and encrypted communications over public telephone lines and the Internet, eliminating the need for expensive leased lines and dedicated communication servers.

Incorporating a simple modem-based PSTN solution for corporate access has a low entry cost, and for a small number of users it may be extremely appealing to a company. But expenses rapidly escalate as the volume of users and their geographic mobility increase. Corporate remote access solutions based on Internet and VPN technologies are highly cost effective, easy to configure, and easy to maintain regardless of the number of users and their geographic locations.

Organizations requiring widespread remote access will find significant savings in Internet and VPN solutions versus traditional modem banks. Since many ISPs offer national and international points of presence, VPNs can provide global coverage while offering improved quality of service and data security when Internet access solutions are utilized.

Chapter 2 Networks

Introduction

A VPN is an internetworking protocol. Without networks, VPNs are homeless. Therefore, it may be impossible to completely comprehend the workings of VPNs without some degree of network knowledge. To understand what VPNs can do for you, and for society, an understanding of basic network technology is imperative. Otherwise, it is nothing more than gibberish.

This chapter seeks to give the reader a basic understanding of networking technology. In some respects, networking is very complicated if you consider every single possible technical facet of the networking environment. However, it is not the intent of this book to give the reader such a grounding in communications. Rather, we seek a fundamental networking knowledge that provides a solid foundation for understanding VPNs. If you desire a greater understanding of networks, further reading is necessary and encouraged. Hopefully, after reading this chapter, the networking novice will be able to understand the context of the remaining chapters and how VPNs fit in with other networking technologies.

Networks

Computer communication networks play an important role in military, government, and civilian environments. Seems we are inundated with the term "network." Forty years ago only television stations networked, forming the familiar NBC, CBS, and ABC television networks. Thirty years ago computers began forming networks, twenty years ago countries began networking, and ten years ago people began to network. (One wonders if people felt compelled to keep up with the computers.) Now, computer networks are networked, forming hierarchical systems of computer networks.

In a larger sense, networks, whether television, computers, countries, or people, share a common goal. Each type of network has as its primary purpose the sharing of information for the benefit of at least one of the parties involved in the sharing. The methodology for storing, retrieving, and transmitting the information is all that distinguishes one network type from another. But what exactly is a computer network?

What is a Computer Network?

Webster's New World Dictionary defines network as "any arrangement or fabric of parallel wires, threads, etc., crossed at regular intervals by others so as to leave open spaces." In the world of computing, a network is "an arrangement of interconnected computing devices." A computer network exists when two or more computing devices are electronically connected together so that the devices may share their computing resources with each other in some deterministic fashion. Of course, it must be deterministic. After all, we do know what we are doing, eh?

Figure 2-1 A simple network

A physical connection that provides an electrical path between some or all the network devices may or may not exist. If there is no physical connection, i.e., wires, cables, optical fiber, etc., then electrical continuity must be established in some other manner, usually via RF wave propagation, such as found in satellite communication links.

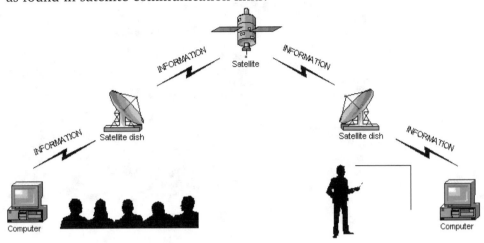

Figure 2-2 Still a simple network

The desire to move information quickly and efficiently across a network, from source to destination, is the underlying driving force behind networking computers. Of course, at the heart of the matter is economics. As we gain access to more and more information with less and less physical resources we become more cost efficient, keeping us in the race for self-preservation. Perhaps someday, as we take the physical limit of the self-preservation equation, we will know everything about nothing.

Anyone can own and operate a network. All that is required for a person to understand networking is a desire to understand and the ability to read. Who has networks and where are they? The technical junkie with two or more interconnected computers at home possesses a bona fide computer network. The small business with two or three or more computers interconnected at the office possesses a bona fide computer network. The Fortune 500 company with hundreds of interconnected computers scattered across the nation and perhaps the world possesses one or more bona fide networks. Just as there are many different tastes in the world, so are there many different sizes and types of networks.

It is easy to distinguish between two functionally different but physically similar networks. One network type is an "intranet" and the other is an "internet." Each type of network has its own special purpose and usefulness as explained in greater detail in the following sections.

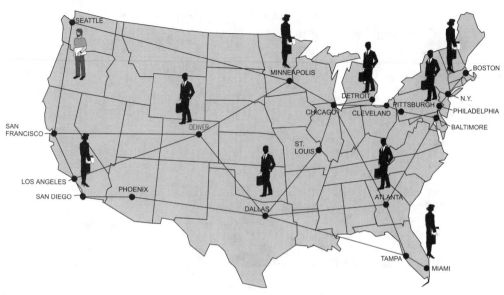

Figure 2-3 "Packet-men" and "packet-women" carrying the e-mail

Network Topologies

It is important to know how networks are built because this provides a framework for discussions about how a network operates. One way to explain how networks are built is to explore how network devices are physically connected to a common transmission medium. The idea of a common medium is fundamental to many networks. Granted this common medium may span great distances and be comprised of "different" types of media. Collectively, the medium can be considered as a whole.

Networks may consist of devices such as computers, printers, servers, etc., connected together. These devices connect to the medium directly or indirectly. The medium may consist of different types, but the common thread is the connection of these devices to the medium, thus a network is formed. The devices may be spread out physically around the world. There are various physical layouts in use. Each layout has unique characteristics that make it desirable for a particular networking application. A layout is called a *topology*. A number of topologies exist, but our focus here will include:

- ▲ Bus
- ▲ Ring
- ▲ Hub

- Switch
- Mesh

Two terms frequently used in discussions about networks are "physical" and "logical." The term physical, in networking, is used to describe the physical characteristics of the network, such as connections, wiring, equipment placement, etc. When used, physical may describe how the interconnecting network wiring snakes around and through walls, ceilings, and floors, or perhaps from business location to central office or central office to the trunking office. Accurately depicting the physical wiring of a network is very important for current and future reference. Installers and technicians must have adequate documentation to show where to place the wiring, drops, and network equipment. And when it is necessary to troubleshoot the network, adequate documentation depicting the network physical resources is almost mandatory. Granted, connecting two computers together to form a network is no big deal. But how about a hundred computers that are also connected to bridges, routers, gateways, network access servers, and/or switches that might be connected to the public switched telephone network (PSTN)? Can a person describe, in such a network, where the demarcation is between the PSTN and the customer premises equipment (CPE) without a detailed physical wiring and connection diagram? No.

However, for a network manager, such detailed network drawings are very cumbersome to use. For a network manager to manage the network, the physical placement of cables is not important, assuming the network wiring was installed correctly. But the manager must know how the equipment is connected in a particular fashion. That is, what the port assignments are. Such an overview of the network is called a logic diagram and the short-hand representations of the network connections are called logical connections. When an individual mentions logical connections, he is concerned with the two (or more) ends of interconnecting devices and ignores the intervening hardware. So, "logical" is function related where "physical" is form related.

Confused? Take a look ahead at the bus topology shown in the next section. Figure 2-4 depicting the bus topology is a logical diagram. You do not see how the interconnecting cabling connecting all of the equipment together snakes through the physical environment. What you do see is an "idealized" drawing depicting, at a high level, the interconnection of the network devices. This is a high-level logical drawing in the sense that the drawing does not show port assignments.

The Bus

In the bus topology, the bus is a cable that serves as an access point for all network devices. A bus-based network can best be understood by analogy. A bus can be thought of as a street. Each house on the street has physical access to the street. For the sake of simplicity, let us assume all driveways are connected from the garage to the street at the front of the house. It really does not matter, but the visualization may be easier if considered in this manner.

The bus topology is similar to a street because each network device has access to the bus in the same fashion that each house has access to the street. But there is a significant difference in the street/bus traffic analogy. Any number of autos may be present at any given time on the two-way street with some quantity of autos traveling in each direction. On the bus, only one device may be sending or receiving a signal at any particular moment of time. The bus may be thought of as a one-way street for each individual electrical signal transmission. If two or more electrical signals are present on the bus at the same time, they interfere with each other in a destructive way. Kind of like hitting another car head-on when traveling down the street at a high rate of speed. What is left is not pretty to look at, is probably not even recognizable as the original human, auto, or electrical signal, and is no longer of any use.

Consider Figure 2-4, which depicts a bus with computers, printers, file servers, and communication servers. The transceivers act as the interface between the bus devices such as printers and computers and the bus itself. All electrical signals to and from a bus device pass through its transceiver. Also, all electrical signals on the bus itself pass through every transceiver. The transceiver maintains the bus address of its bus device and pulls off the bus those signals that are addressed to its bus device.

The figure shows a straight line as the common link between all participating network devices. In reality this is generally not the case. Because the bus is a cable, it usually gets shaped to fit the physical environment where it is installed.

One example of a bus topology is where network devices attach to the cable via a transceiver. The transceiver serves as a connection point for network devices. Transceivers do more than serve as a connection point, but this is not the focus here. Historically, these transceivers have a cable that connects them to the network device interface card. This cable is typically called a drop cable. However, most currently manufactured network

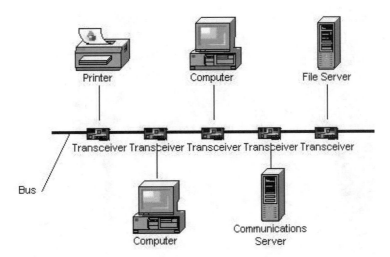

Figure 2-4 Bus network topology

interface cards integrate the transceiver onto the interface card itself. A number of computers ship from the factory with a network interface and transceiver integral to the system board. Therefore, it may not be possible to identify a separate transceiver for each piece of network equipment in a bus network.

A bus could be considered a data highway. It is the medium where data is passed from source to destination. Devices attached to the bus can access it and send or receive data. In a very real sense it is a data highway.

The Ring

When a ring topology is mentioned, token ring may come to mind. Token ring is a protocol (way of passing data) at lower layers within a network, specifically the data link layer. The ring topology uses a cable in a ring fashion and serves as the data highway for data to get from source to destination. A token ring network schematically looks like Figure 2-5.

The figure is a "logical" example of a network based on a ring topology. It does not depict how a token ring network appears physically. A token ring network is built around a device called a Media (some call it a Medium) Access Unit (MAU). If one goes looking for a token ring network, the portion of Figure 2-6 identified as the physical representation, that is, a physical piece of hardware, is an example of what will be found.

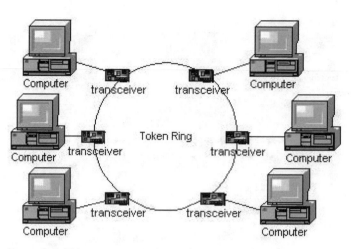

Figure 2-5 Token ring network topology

The MAU has a physical ring inside. Unfortunately, many diagrams and explanations depicting a ring network either assume the reader possesses this knowledge, or for whatever reason, it is omitted.

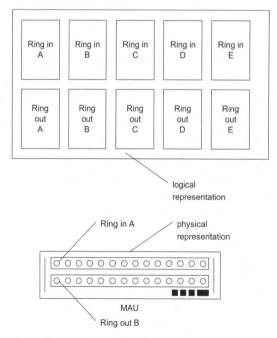

Figure 2-6 Media Access Unit

This could be funny. Can you imagine someone new to token ring networks being asked to isolate a problem with a token ring network? If nobody told the individual there is no visible "ring" to be found (outside of disassembling the MAU), they could look for days! Sort of like asking a new recruit to go to the supply shop and pick up ten yards of flight line or five gallons of prop wash.

There is an important reason for constructing the network ring with a return cable run to the MAU between every device. If a network device fails, the circuits in the MAU can isolate the defective device and continue the network operation with the remaining devices without bringing down the complete network. This reliability feature has always been a strong selling point of ring-based networks.

Other types of ring-based networks exist; however, they are based on the same fundamental premise. They have a ring (or two) used to pass data.

The Hub

A hub is like its name connotes. It is a central point of connection. Figure 2-7 shows how a hub topology appears. The circuit board backplane, also called a motherboard, is the circuit board all of the other circuit boards physically plug into. The backplane distributes electrical signals to the other circuit boards. In this case, the circuit cards are network cards.

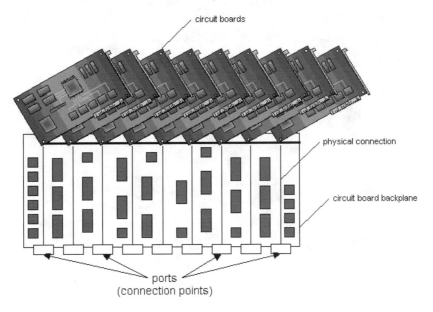

Figure 2-7 Hub network topology

A hub is the central point of the network from a physical connection perspective. In the world of Ethernet networks, the hub is typically called a *concentrator.* Historically, the physical star configuration of a token ring network, and its ability to isolate defective nodes, was a strong selling point over Ethernet, which in its original definition was based on connecting a single wire from computer to computer. The bus-topology Ethernet system was vulnerable to breaks in the cable. Any cable fault would disable all the computer systems attached to the Ethernet segment containing the fault.

The Ethernet concentrator maintains the bus topology of the Ethernet system from an electrical perspective but implements it physically as a star network where every computer connects to the concentrator via two twisted pairs of wire. Combining the low-cost manufacturing of standards-based Ethernet cards with the reliability of a hub-based cable plant allowed Ethernet to become the dominant network technology in the 1990s. Additionally, adding intelligence to the hub electronics allows the electronics to communicate with SNMP management consoles so that the network infrastructure can be centrally managed by technical support personnel.

The Switch

From the outside, you can't tell a hub from a switch. Both sit at the core of a star-shaped wiring scheme. The difference is on the inside. A network hub, or concentrator, implements a physical star wiring scheme—but an electrical bus. In the case of Ethernet, the bus operates at either 10 megabits per second (Mbps) or 100 Mbps.

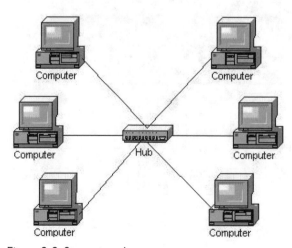

Figure 2-8 Star network

A star network was common in the 1960s and 1970s. During this time period, virtually all networks were owned by either the military or the defense-industrial complex. For military networks, distributed computing was not the mainstay of networks. A typical military network consisted of a master node (or station as they were called at the time) and one or more slave nodes. The master node would query each slave node in turn for downloads and uploads of data. The maximum data rate achievable using the star topology is not very high since each node must wait until the master node has transmitted updates and received updates from all the other nodes before it can query a particular node again. But this type of network is very reliable since each slave node is capable of assuming the role of master node if the master node is silenced—a very real possibility in real-life combat situations.

In the star network, all of the devices connected to the hub take turns sharing the single 10 megabit bus. An Ethernet switch, in contrast, provides a 10 megabit data path to each network device, allowing multiple, simultaneous connections. The limiting factor of the switch is the speed of its backplane, which in an Ethernet switch is typically in the neighborhood of 600 megabits per second.

An additional performance boost can be gained in Ethernet switching by operating the switch in full-duplex mode rather than half-duplex mode. In the original Ethernet system, at a particular point in time, a single Ethernet card could either transmit or receive—but could not do both at the same time. Once every Ethernet device has its own dedicated set of wires to the switch backplane, it is possible to configure the system so that a single card can both transmit and receive at the same time.

In considering, for example, the connection to a server, it is easy to see where the ability to receive a request from one client while simultaneously sending data to another client would provide a real performance boost. There is a small downside to full-duplex switching, however. While any Ethernet card can participate in a half-duplex switched environment, the ability to operate in full-duplex mode is a feature that is only available on premium-quality, current-technology cards. Fortunately, full-duplex switches can generally be configured to work simultaneously with a mixture of half-duplex and full-duplex devices.

Switching additionally serves as the foundation of some of our highest speed network technologies. The ATM (Asynchronous Transfer Mode) network system is based on the rapid switching of small, 53-byte data packets. Asynchronous Transfer Mode networks range from 25 megabit per second switches typically used for providing high-speed connectivity to the desktop to 2 gigabit ATM switches for exceptionally demanding high-bandwidth environments.

Mesh

Figure 2-9 depicts a partial mesh network consisting of other networks. The partial mesh network does not have a physical connection to every single other network. Hence, it is partial. A mesh network that connects to every single node in the overall network is called a full mesh network. The Internet is not a full mesh network. To achieve complete connectivity among the Internet users, routers, also called gateways or network access servers, pass the information on down the line until the information reaches a router connected to the destination network. Of course, to achieve such connectivity, routers must be able to determine which router, of possibly many routers they are connected to, is the appropriate router to forward the information to.

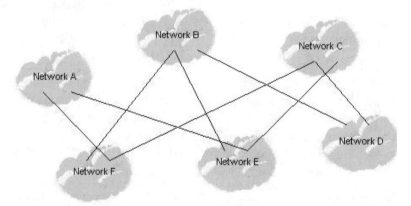

Figure 2-9 Partial mesh network

The individual networks depicted in Figure 2-9 may consist of any combination of network topologies previously defined (bus, ring, etc.) and may be either LANs, WANs, or GANs. A great example of a mesh network is the popular Internet. If Figure 2-9 represents the Internet, then the individual networks could represent Internet service providers and defense, government, university, and company intra-networks.

The salient characteristic of mesh networks is the variety of connections between networks, or nodes. Any network may connect to any other network without constraint. Well, actually, there are some constraints, such as number of ports available to use which is directly related to the financial means and perceived necessity of the owning organization. But let us assume an unlimited bank account and necessity. Then, any network may connect to any other network. The resultant mesh network may appear to be a confusing and totally unmanageable mass of interconnecting networks. In the case of the Internet, appearances are very realistic. Yet TCP/IP does manage the process quite well.

The mesh topology makes the Internet possible. What makes a mesh network possible is state-of-the-art network routers and their routing algorithms. An algorithm is the step-by-step approach used by engineers to solve a problem. For Internet routers, the routing algorithm of choice is Open Shortest Path First (OSPF) routing.

A note about routers. For high-capacity communication links, used by large organizations such as telephone companies (as part of their national commercial backbone), major corporations, and governments, routers are replaced with switches. While routers are complicated enough, switches are very complex electronic devices capable of switching data from small bit streams to massive gigabit streams.

What is an Intranet?

An *intranet* is composed of locally administered local area networks (LANs) utilizing TCP/IP for their upper layer transmission protocols. An intranet does not have all of the restrictions and requirements an internet must abide by because it is a "local" network in scope. That is, the LANs comprising intranets are physically confined to small geographical areas with access limited to those computers either connected directly together and/or to a server and those computer users authorized to "dial in" via "remote node access." An intranet may consist of a single LAN or several LANs interconnected via private or public switched network lines. Several interconnected LANs form a wide area network (WAN).

An intranet is not necessarily a geographically small network. The private networks, or intranets, maintained by multinational corporations such as Texas Instruments, IBM, EDS, and NASDAQ span the country and even the globe. While they may not have as many users as the much larger and now commercialized Internet, they are certainly global in their reach. Employees from IBM can access their company's network from any location on the globe where dial-up capabilities exist, assuming the employee has the proper authorization to use IBM's intranet. And even some individuals without permission, called hackers, occasionally penetrate a company or government's intranet and may or may not cause damage or alarm.

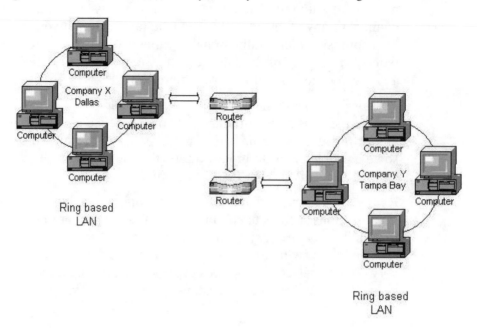

Figure 2-10 An intranet

While an intranet does not have all the restrictions of an internet, an intranet does have restrictions and requirements in order for it to be functional. One very important restriction is access, especially if the intranet is connected to an internet. Intranet owners, typically corporations, do not want unauthorized users gaining access to privileged corporate information. For intranet security, it is relatively easy for corporate Information Technology (IT) bit counters (programmers) to limit intranet access since corporate physical security methods prevent unwanted users from gaining access to the premises where the computers are located. However, when the intranet is connected to an internet, or another intranet off campus, via a gateway, physical access limitations to the company network (and the associated data) disappear. To prevent unwanted users from gaining access to the intranet via the internet, corporations erect software barriers called *firewalls*. Sometimes the existence of a corporate firewall makes it easy to determine where the internet leaves off and the intranet begins. Other times, the point of demarcation (where an "internet" begins/ends and an "intranet" ends/begins) may simply be a router that provides the connection between the company or organization and the world at large.

What is an Internetwork?

An *internetwork* consists of hosts (computers, servers, clients, etc.) connected to networks. These networks are connected together via gateways. The networks forming the internetwork may be any combination of local networks (such as Ethernets and/or Token Rings) or large networks (ARPANET, Intranetworks). It was fashionable in times gone by to limit the internetwork definition to networks based upon packet switching technology. However, with the advent of new networking and communication technologies, the packet switching limitation no longer applies. As an example, it is quite convenient to connect packet-switched networks together via cell switched backbone networks using a relatively new communications technology called Asynchronous Transfer Mode (ATM). Networks based upon the native ATM communications protocol are quite capable of replacing the packet-switched networks, resulting in faster and leaner communications. But that is really the subject of another book, such as *Demystifying ATM/ADSL*, from Wordware Publishing.

The term internet is a shortened form of internetwork. An internet in the purest sense of the term is just the interconnection of two or more networks and/or the interconnection of other computing resources that may or may not be part of a network. An example is, of course, the home computer connected to the Internet. While the home computer is connected to the Internet, it is a part of the network comprising the Internet, although by itself it is not necessarily a part of another network. But, from a purist's perspective, any two or more networks connected together form an internet.

Many globally connected intranets are connected to the Internet. Special restrictions apply to intranets connected to the Internet. Typically, the connection of individual intranets to the Internet must be accomplished by having a router or a multihomed host, a host attached to two or more LANs. A multihomed host connecting an intranet to the Internet has a local IP address and another IP address assigned to it so it can be known by both networks. Figure 2-11 depicts multiple intranets and Internet service providers connected, in a mesh topology, as the Internet. Of course, the real Internet has thousands of service providers and hundreds or perhaps thousands of intranets connected together in a mesh network. So, this is a simplified diagram of the Internet.

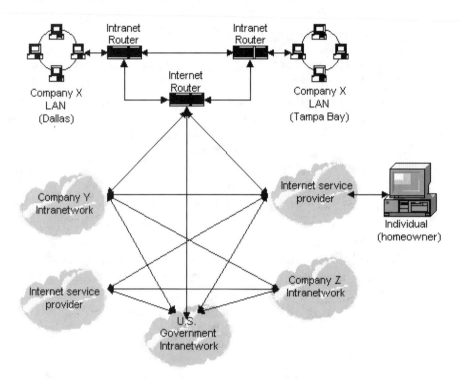

Figure 2-11 Intranets connected as an internet

Each "cloud" in Figure 2-11 represents an intranet of the type depicted at the top of the figure (see Figure 2-10) as Company X. Each of these intranets and the Internet service providers connect to the mesh through on-site routers, or switches. These intranets must be physically connected together somehow. The somehow, most often, is public switched network (the telephone companies) leased lines. However, some connections exist through privately owned telephone lines, especially when the ISP is a regional or national telephone company.

Notice the humble individual/homeowner who gets into the internet-working act through a modem connection to a commercial Internet service provider. Employees of companies with sufficient resources connect to the Internet through the service provided by their company, not through commercial Internet service providers. However, small companies without the resources may use a commercial Internet service provider to put up a web page and to send/receive e-mail.

Why is all this important to understanding VPNs? Figure 2-11 depicts the environment where VPNs are used. VPNs are designed to leverage the internetworking environment, capitalizing on the TCP/IP technology that enables the networking environment.

All those intranets, Internet service providers, and homeowners are able to communicate with each other because of TCP/IP. Each individual intranet may communicate using a proprietary communications protocol but they talk to the outside world using TCP/IP.

Multiple communications protocols were the norm in the 1980s, but more and more companies are migrating to TCP/IP for their intranet communications. TCP/IP is popular because it is a public domain protocol and no single manufacturer can hold a company hostage, price-wise. Millions of people use TCP/IP on a daily basis and soon we can boast hundreds of millions will use it. An enabling protocol for TCP/IP is Point-to-Point Protocol (PPP). And guess what? VPNs are based on Point-to-Point Tunneling Protocol (PPTP), which is a derivative of PPP. So, understanding networks, TCP/IP, and PPP are a good foundation for understanding VPNs.

What is *the* Internet?

The Internet is usually modeled as a collection of computers and "intelligent" devices interconnected with diverse switching and transmission facilities. The collection of computers and intelligent devices are called hosts, gateways, bridges, routers, and switches. Control over the Internet is distributed among the various administrative authorities that comprise the networking resources of the Internet. A domain is the network resources controlled by an authority. DARPA is an example of an administrative authority.

The word "Internet" has been a point of confusion for many people. "Internet" is the name used to refer to the worldwide network that began when ARPANET connected with other private networks, comprising mainly defense companies and educational institutions. The Internet grew, and ARPANET remained the main network of the Internet until the late '80s when it was replaced by the National Science Foundation Network (NSFNET). The primary purpose for the change was the need to incorporate high-speed links in various places, or so we are told. Who thinks of the Department of Defense as the center of the Internet "web" now?

Although the Internet is no longer a government sponsored project, it is not owned by any single company or entity. However, many of the collaborative structures, including the Internet Engineering Task Force (IETF), that established the initial rules for the operation of the Internet are still in operation. The IETF both solicits and proposes changes to the Internet to accommodate changing needs. The IETF home page is www.ietf.org.

The foundation of the Internet rules are contained in RFCs, or Requests for Comment. Appendix A contains references to many of the RFCs. These are protocol descriptions, ideas, and other comments from individuals interested in the Internet, and in a real sense this is part of what places TCP/IP in the public domain. The full text of all RFCs in existence is located on the web at www.ietf.org/rfc.html. Individual RFCs have a state and status assigned to them. The RFC states and status are self-explanatory.

RFC states include:

- Standard
- Draft
- Proposal
- Experimental

RFC status includes:

- Required
- Recommended
- Elective
- Limited use
- Not recommended

Packets

Computers, and computing devices, are networked by physically linking the devices together in such a manner that they can transfer information using electrical signals from one to another. Some of the computing devices may act as repositories of large amounts of information and also act to connect other computers together into a network. These special computers are called *servers*. Computers that use server services, such as file management and electronic mail service, are called *clients*. Some networks require servers and some do not, depending upon the topology, or structure, of the network.

The active agents residing within computing hosts that produce and consume messages are called processes. Various levels of communications protocols in the networks, the gateways, and the hosts work together to support a data communications system that provides bidirectional data flow on logical connections established between process ports on computing hosts.

A common feature of networks is the transfer of large files from one host to another. In the rich, graphical world of computing today, files can easily be 1 Mbyte or larger. It is not convenient, or economical, to transfer such files from one computer to another as one massive file. Such a Herculean effort would certainly fail due to the vagaries of computer communications. Rather, transferring files, or any other type of data, is a much more manageable task if the job is divided into smaller pieces, or tasks. When the data is divided into smaller portions the resultant data pieces are called *data segments*. Routing and flow control information is then added to data segments to form *datagrams*. The local network may take the datagrams, now called a *packet*, and add additional routing information if the datagram is destined to traverse another network. The additional routing information, addresses, flow control, etc., to the original data segment is called *overhead*.

Overhead	Data
(ATM=53 bytes)	(128/512 bytes)

Figure 2-12 A packet

What is a packet? A group of data bits attached to a group of overhead bits. The data bits are typically either 128 bytes or 512 bytes in length, but can be much larger. Overhead bits contain addressing, flow control, and other packet management information. Networks that package data into "packets" in this manner are called packet-switched networks. The packet contains all the information necessary for the data segment to get from source to destination anywhere in the world.

The original ARPANET was, and still is, a packet-switched network. What is a packet-switched network? A network that provides for transmission of packets from node to node using the packet addressing information included in the packet header to route the packet to the next node. Packets continue on down the network in this manner until they finally reach their destination. Yes, in the olden days packets got lost. Now, with intelligent routing, fewer packets get lost.

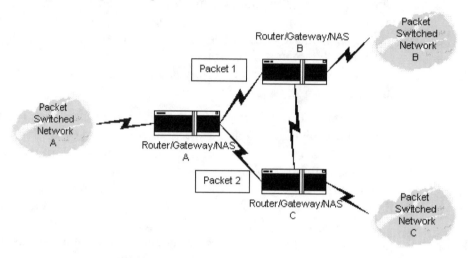

Figure 2-13 Packet-switched network

Packet Gateways/Switches

A model of internet communications includes the Internet Protocol (IP) module and its associated TCP module functioning as the interface between higher level processes, i.e., applications, and the physical local network, i.e., the physical hardware interconnecting the gateways, or network access servers (NAS). The TCP segments data while the IP packages the segments into internet datagrams. The datagrams are then routed to a destination Internet Protocol module or to an intermediate router or switch which may be a gateway to another network. If the datagram does not go directly from the source IP to the destination IP, but must pass through two or more network routers, it is repackaged into a packet. These "packet switches" are capable of performing additional operations on the datagram, including further fragmentation, to pass the datagram through the packet switch. A good example of the datagram manipulation by packet switches is the fragmentation of datagrams to accommodate the packet switch's smaller throughput buffer.

At each gateway, which may be a router or a switch, the Internet Protocol datagram is stripped of its local packet. The gateway examines the datagram and determines the optimum route of the packet through the adjoining network. The datagram is then repackaged with the new network's packet and sent on to either the next gateway or the destination if the destination resides in the current network.

Each gateway is capable of segmenting the datagram into smaller fragments of the original datagram. This may be necessary because the routers in the new network may not be able to accommodate the larger datagram size. Further fragmentation may occur at downstream gateways. The destination Internet Protocol is responsible for reassembling the fragmented datagrams into the original IP datagram before passing it on to the TCP module.

Why Do I Need a Network?

As pointed out at the beginning of this chapter, networks exist to share information. You need a network to gain access to information on computers other than the computer you are physically near to help you do your job, or to educate or entertain yourself.

Even with gigabyte size hard drives, a single computer cannot store all the information available to the general public. Information is created in a distributed fashion across the nation and the world.

If you ask ten people this question, you will probably get ten different answers. Some consensus exists, however. Ask this question of financial people or managers in corporations and they may respond by saying it will help them maximize technical resources within their company. Networking can do this if properly implemented. Ask a documentation or training department the same question and the response may be entirely different. A typical response from such a department might be something like, "It would enable all workers in the department to exchange files, have electronic mail, and have remote logon access to hosts not located on their desks."

There are many reasons for having a network. Commonalities exist among most networks, but differences also exist. Additionally, the reasons for building networks have changed over time. In the earliest days of networking, when networks were confined to workgroups or departments, the primary driving factor for building networks was sharing expensive computer resources. When a 5 MB hard disk cost $6,000 and the least expensive printer on the market that could be called "letter quality" cost

$3,500, sharing disk space and print services was the most important driving force in many organizations. However, with $99 gigabyte hard disks and $199 inkjet printers that make the old typewriter-technology letter quality jobs look prehistoric, the driving forces behind networking are no longer simply the basic sharing of peripherals. Today, the driving forces behind the implementation of networks certainly include the provision of basic file and print services, but the sharing of information itself has become the primary force. Several of the common reasons for installing a network are the following:

- Remote logon
  This service permits a user on his/her host to log on "remotely" to a host in a different location.

- File transfer
  This service permits network users to exchange files. It saves time and can eliminate duplication of resources. And, most of all, it is convenient for users.

- File services
  Different from file transfer, file service allows disk space that physically exists on another computer on the network to function identically to local disk space, either through the assignment of drive letters or named volumes, whichever is appropriate for the operating system of the user's computer.

- Electronic mail
  This service allows all users on the network to exchange mail electronically.

- Shared printers
  Print services allow multiple users to share a printer. Shared printers are typically either faster than inexpensive desktop printers or have special capabilities, such as extremely fine resolution, large paper size, or the ability to print in color.

- Information services
  Information services take many forms: the World Wide Web, Gopher, Usenet News, and Lotus Notes. Each of these information resources has its own system for presentation and navigation—but all are characterized by having a piece of client software on the user's computer (i.e., web browser, Newsreader, Notes client) that interacts with a corresponding piece of server software on the network to allow the user to interact with the information resource.

▶ Electronic commerce
The Internet provides every individual the opportunity to sell any product and be competitive with established businesses. And the Internet is fast becoming every shopaholic's dream, an electronic mail order mall. Original equipment manufacturers (OEMs) and value-added resellers can place orders for materials directly with vendor companies, reducing paperwork and man-hours, and speeding the ordering and delivery process.

The needs of the user and the type of network implemented determine what is available. A particular advantage networks offer is that some networks support different vendor equipment, thus providing interoperability between unlike equipment. Making computer systems from different manufacturers running different operating systems communicate with each other is often reason enough to install a network.

The Backbone is Connected to the ...

The term "backbone" can be most confusing, especially if the speaker or writer does not communicate precisely the intended meaning. The term backbone is used frequently in conversations about networking and the meaning is usually fuzzy. It means different things depending upon the context and point trying to be made. For example, the backbone could be used in reference to the topology of a network. If such is the case, the meaning conveyed is the physical connections, primarily the common point of connection, for devices attached to the network. See Figure 2-14.

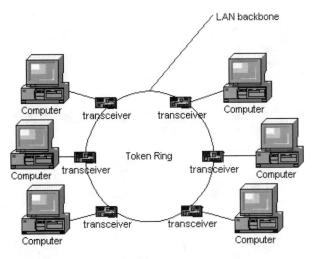

Figure 2-14 Topology backbone

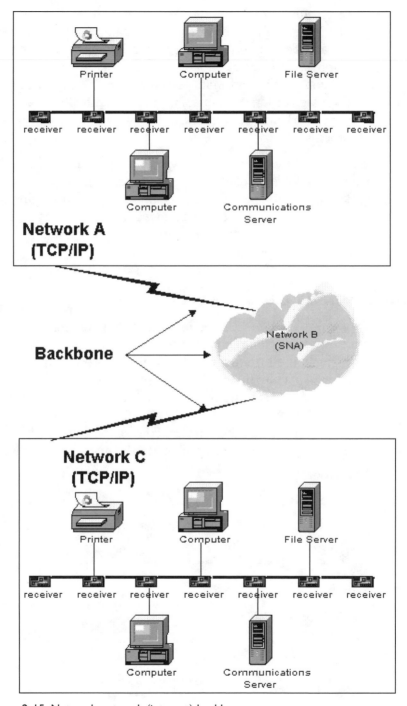

Figure 2-15 Network-network (intranet) backbone

Backbone is also used to refer to a network protocol. When this is the case, a larger concept is usually conveyed. An example of this could be someone using the term to refer to routing from network A to network C <u>through</u> an unlike network, say network B. An example of this is Figure 2-15. In this instance, the network backbone is network B. Included as part of the backbone is the interconnecting transmission media between network B and network A and the interconnecting transmission media between network B and network C.

Figure 2-16 depicts the Internet, or at least four Internet servers, as connected through the public switched telephone network (PSTN) via routers called gateways. To get a clearer picture of the real Internet, all you need do is add more Internet servers, more Local Access Transport Areas (LATAs), and more Interexchange Carriers.

In the figure, the Internet backbone is either easy to discern or difficult (isn't that peachy keen?), depending upon the perspective one takes. Either it is all backbone, or pieces of it are. Actually most, but not all, of it is backbone. It is perhaps most convenient to describe what is not network backbone. In this case, it is the Internet servers, their associated routers, and the subscribers. Everything else is backbone.

Now you should be getting the idea that network backbone really refers to the transport medium that a device, either an individual computer or individual network comprised of two or more computers, uses to pass data from itself to whatever destination (computer or network) is intended.

As networks proliferated during the first part of the 1990s, the backbone of a network system was typically implemented as a series of network connections between routers. In the later '90s, advances in switch technology challenged some of the fundamental assumptions associated with the traditional construction of networks, especially in the context of a building or campus network. When a traditional router-based network system is drawn on paper, it is typically possible to identify the primary communications links that constitute the backbone of the network. If these core routers and communications links are replaced with a high-capacity switch, the network backbone moves from a series of wires interconnecting routers into the backplane of a switch. When a switch is used to replace a system of interconnected routers, the resulting network is typically referred to as having a collapsed backbone. Such a collapsed backbone can often provide improved network throughput, as switches are typically faster than the routers they replace.

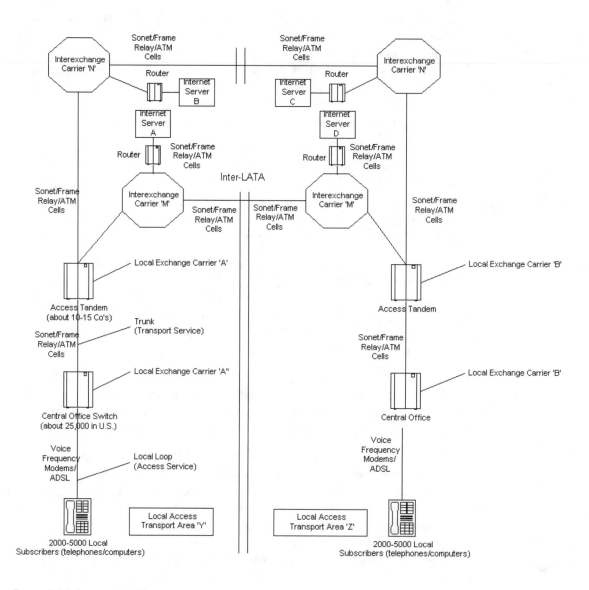

Figure 2-16 Internet backbone

Figure 2-17 depicts a network of national proportions. Such a network might be used by a Fortune 500 company, say a telecommunications company, or the government. Each connection to the network is called a *node*. The figure shows all nodes in each location as a single black dot. In reality there may be thousands of nodes connected to the network at each location. One important point to remember about networks is every node connected to a network, either internetwork or intranetwork, represents the demarcation, usually just called the demarc, between the network and the local equipment, commonly called customer premises equipment (CPE). The physical demarcation may be a jack panel, a router, or a high-speed switch. Regardless of the physical configuration of the demarcation, it is clear that one side of the network is local in scope, the CPE side which is usually privately owned, and the other side is metropolitan, regional, national, or international in scope and is usually owned by a data transport, i.e., telephone, company. At the demarc, the upstream/downstream data is usually fed into a larger/smaller data pipe.

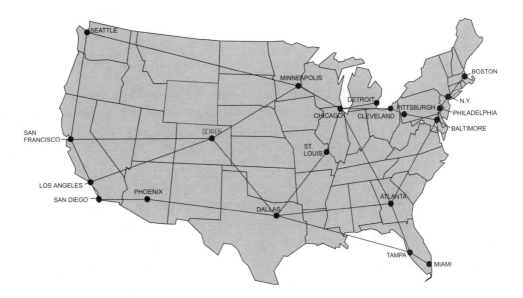

Figure 2-17 A network of national proportions

As one digs through the voluminous networking literature, the term "domain" usually pops up frequently. Perhaps the most convenient way to define a domain is to explain what a domain is in terms of network service providers (anyone connected to the Internet is familiar with that term) and network service subscribers (most of us). Network service providers are domains that share their resources with other domains. Network service subscribers are domains that utilize in some way the resources of network service providers. Any particular domain may be both a provider and a subscriber. So, we have described domain as anyone connected to a network, because everyone is either a network provider or a network subscriber.

Summary

Networks can be a valued addition to a corporation or a small company. The type of network chosen will dictate features and functions available for users, programmers, and others accessing the network. When choosing a network, keep the network capabilities and the organizations in full view.

Networks are comprised of protocols. Network protocols themselves are rules defining how things will be done, such as remote logons, file transfers (which is what browsing on the Internet is all about), and electronic mail, for example.

The protocol chosen for a network should be based upon the one that best meets users' needs. Consideration for interoperability among different vendor equipment should be taken into account also. Other issues may need evaluation, and each site should be able to define its own needs.

The physical layout of a network will vary. The site will determine this to some degree. But many protocols dictate which physical arrangement must be used with network implementations. In any case, economics always plays a major role in which network topology is used.

The difference between the physical layout of a network and the logical implementation can be confusing, but it is nevertheless important. The term backbone should be understood in light of how vendors use it to explain their equipment. A variety of meanings are currently associated with the term, and as a result confusion abounds.

Getting acclimated to computer networks is half the battle. The remainder of the battle is the constant challenge to remain current, understanding the technology used and changes to existing equipment. The pace of change in network technology continues to escalate with technologies such as ATM and Gigabit Ethernet now on the market.

Now more than ever companies are harnessing the power in networks to leverage company resources. The explosion of the World Wide Web has demonstrated the worldwide scalability of open information systems based on the TCP/IP protocol. In its wake, organizations around the world are looking at ways of applying TCP/IP-based technologies to their internal as well as their external networks. TCP/IP is enabling communications technologies that just a few short years ago were the stuff dreams were made of. And VPNs are just one of those TCP/IP-enabled technologies that is finding a very useful home in networking.

Chapter 3 Network Protocols

Questions answered in this chapter:

/// What is a networking protocol?

/// What are some networking protocols?

/// What is the relationship between VPNs and network protocols?

Introduction

What is a protocol? Diplomats use something called protocols in the exercise of diplomacy. Diplomatic protocols are the established ceremonial forms and courtesies used by diplomats. In the world of diplomats, deviations in the established diplomatic protocol are considered serious breaches of convention and can lead to unfortunate consequences, perhaps even wars. Similarly, communications protocols define acceptable queries and responses between users of a particular network type. The objective, of course, is to provide for the orderly and predictable behavior of hardware and software used in the network. Breaches of protocol conventions in the world of communications generally result in the inability to communicate.

While governing bodies have established communications protocols to be machine independent, setting down rules and guidelines for the general cases without regard to the specific platforms performing the communication tasks, protocols, in a sense, are very environment oriented. Designers must consider the specific equipment and their peculiarities, or uniqueness, used in assembling network components. A DOS-based machine will not behave identically to a UNIX-based machine in a network unless such behavior differences are accounted for in the design of the network, which includes intermediate software programs to convert the bit streams from one type of machine's representation of the data to another type of machine's representation. That is, the binary representation of a carriage return/line feed on one type of machine may not be the same on another type of machine. Currently, the most common method of accounting for machine dependencies in network communications is to purchase third-party software and hardware.

Protocols are concerned with every aspect of communications, from equipment physical interfaces, data formats, and communication speeds to high-level software interfaces. The objective is to provide a communications service to users that is reliable. Communications protocols are rules that attempt to define specific events, which are intended to control, in some acceptable and understandable manner relative to the objective to be accomplished, the devices that are involved in a communications network. The events of interest and the sequence or manner in which they occur define the protocol. There are numerous communications protocols existent today. Some such protocols are IEEE 488, RS-232, and IEEE 803. Various governing bodies including ISO, ITU-T, ATM Forum, and the ADSL Forum define communications protocols.

Why does the world need communications protocols? Variety. Someone said variety is the spice of life. I do not know the context of the statement, but I can certainly see how it may be applicable in some settings and totally inappropriate in others. Variety is certainly the norm in communications. There are many different ways to transport information from end to end and there are many different ways of encoding information for transport. For any two similar transport or encoding systems to work, a defined set of rules must specify all the particulars of any importance. Two similar transport or encoding systems will provide gibberish, i.e., garbage, results unless all the rules are followed within any specified tolerances. Just as humans need varied behavioral protocols to define acceptable behavior in varied social settings so that human actions may be interpreted with a certain degree of accuracy, so do communication systems need protocols to define acceptable behavior, that all communications between end users of a similar system will be understandable.

What if a rebel, with or without a cause, decides to flaunt convention and attempt to communicate outside the established protocol? A communication outside the established protocol may go unrecognized or result in a message to the sender, and perhaps to the intended recipient, that an unacceptable or unrecognizable communiqué was attempted. Totally unexpected results may occur, or in poorly designed systems, equipment may crash.

OSI Networking Protocol Model

What is a network protocol and which network protocol is needed? To decide this expansive question, a point of reference is needed. A good reference point is a model of what parts should exist in networks. A standards-making body called the International Organization for Standardization has what it calls the Open Systems Interconnection (OSI) model.

This OSI model defines elements that should exist in any network. The OSI model used here will be a reference point to explain basic aspects about network protocols. The OSI model consists of seven layers. To better understand this, picture a cake with seven layers and envision the cake cut in half; the seven layers would be identifiable. The OSI model is similar to the seven-layered cake cut in half. OSI network layers have names and perform specific functions. This model, including the layers and their names, is identified in Figure 3-1.

Before we examine what each layer does, consider this: Envision a network consisting of computers, software, cables, and everything that goes into making a network. Most networks can be divided into layers. Network layers can be explained in accordance with their function. Usually, there is not a one-to-one correspondence when attempting to explain different networks by layers. Some protocols, like VPN, predate the OSI model. In other cases, vendors developing protocols have found that there are advantages in terms of speed, memory, or another efficiency that made it to their advantage to not strictly adhere to the OSI model. Many network protocols do not appear like the OSI model.

A protocol template to use for modeling communication systems is beneficial that we might more easily visualize the underlying concepts. ITU-T (formerly CCITT) developed the Open Systems Interconnection (OSI) model that serves the purpose of a protocol template very well. The OSI model represents a stack of seven layers that can be considered as gradations from simpler to more complex functionality as one goes up the stack. This does not mean that one layer is simpler than another. In fact, each layer in its own right is a complex interworking of rules, hardware, software, and human endeavor.

The OSI model, especially above the physical layer, is really a hierarchical software model that provides for coherent communications between groups of software procedures and/or programs. Each layer can be represented by a software program that communicates only with the layer above and below it. Typically, each layer is comprised of software routines that are called by the next higher or lower layer, when appropriate. The software routines are written for specific communication applications. The interface between higher and lower layer routines is performed by procedure calls known as application programming interface (API) calls.

The first three layers—the physical layer, the data link layer, and the network layer—are closely linked together. Kind of a "you can't have one without the other" sort of thing. The three layers comprise the minimum structure required to establish and maintain communications between two entities (nodes). These three layers, in a sense, pass from node to node in the transmission path and contain, besides the data, source and destination addresses and error-detection information necessary to ensure error-free routing to the correct destination. The control and routing information is called Operations Administration and Management (OAM) data and is added to the user data stream in quantities called headers and trailers. Each layer adds its own headers and trailers to the data "packet." A complete package of data, headers, and trailers that is ready for transmission is called a datagram.

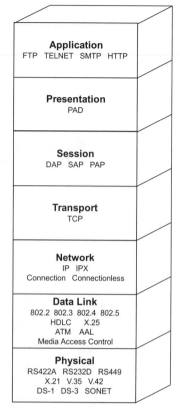

Figure 3-1 Open Systems Interconnection (OSI) model

The control and routing information is interpreted by switches, routers, gateways, and bridges along the transmission path. The control information and data are bound together until received by the destination, where the control information and data are separated. Generally, the first three layers represented by the OSI model comprise the fundamental ISDN/BISDN software package running on a host processor responsible for the physical switching duties, with the user providing the application-

specific software package, comprising the remaining OSI layers, that typically runs on a remote host computer.

Table 3-1 OSI model layer functionality

Layer	Functionality
7	application (mail relays)
6	presentation (data representation)
5	session (remote procedure calls)
4	transport/end-to-end (IP hosts)
3	network/internetwork (IP gateways)
2	data link/subnetwork (bridges)
1	physical (repeaters)

Table 3-1 shows the functionality of each layer of the OSI model. The table
is not all-inclusive. There is much networking functionality that is not covered in this table. It is intended as a representation only of what types of
software modules one will find at each layer.

A layer synopsis from top to bottom follows:

Application

This layer provides services software applications require. For example,
it provides services necessary for a file transfer program to operate. It is
called the application layer because it works with or is a provider of
services to applications (in certain network protocols).

Presentation

This layer determines data syntax. In short, whether data is ASCII or
EBCDIC is determined here. This layer performs encoding values that
represent data types being transferred.

Session

This layer is considered the user's interface into the network. However,
the user is not aware of it. This layer is where logical connections are
made with applications. The session layer has addressable end points
that relate to programs or a user.

Transport

On the sending node in a network the transport layer takes data from
the session layer and puts a header and trailer around the data itself.
Some transport protocols ensure the data arrives correctly at the destination; this type of protocol is connection oriented. Conversely,
connectionless-oriented protocols do not ensure this. On the receiving

node the transport layer removes the header and trailer and passes the data to the session layer.

Network

This layer routes data from one location to another (source to destination). The network protocol in use determines how this layer works. In the case of VPN, this is Internet Protocol (IP).

Data Link

The main goal of the data link layer is to provide reliable data transfer across a physical link. This layer puts data into frames, transmits these frames sequentially, and ensures they have been received in order by the target host.

Physical

This layer is an interface between the medium and the device. This layer transmits bits (ones and zeros). Specifically, it transmits voltage or light pulses.

Different network protocols can be evaluated with the OSI model serving as a baseline. OSI itself is a network protocol, but the focus here is VPN. Once, it was thought that everyone might switch to the OSI network protocol. Various parts of the federal government issued mandates for future compliance. State governments mandated state agencies to plan for a conversion to OSI. However, very few organizations actually built an OSI network. Sensing a lack of a sizable market, network vendors developed hardware and software to build the kind of networks that their customers would purchase today. The OSI protocol may be the protocol of the future that ends up as a historical footnote.

The OSI model, however, provides an excellent framework for discussion of how various parts of other protocols work. The OSI model will be used later in the book to explore further aspects of VPN.

Data Flow Through a Network

In a network, data flows from the sending node from top to bottom (with respect to layers in the network). This means that as data passes down the network protocol stack, headers and trailers are added to the data at each layer. Likewise, in a network the receiving node's data flows from bottom to top (with respect to the network layers). These headers and trailers are removed by layer as the data moves up the protocol stack.

In some cases the sending node is a terminal user and the receiving entity is an application program. In other cases, both sending and receiving entities can be application programs.

These headers and trailers wrapped around the data include information particular to the needs of a specific layer. For example, the network layer header includes routing information. Consider Figure 3-1, which depicts the OSI model and how headers are added to data as it passes down the OSI protocol stack.

Why Do I Need a Protocol?

Connecting computers, printers, disk drives, terminal servers, communication servers, and other devices requires some form of a network. For a network to function, rules and regulations must be followed. In the technical community, these rules and regulations are called *protocols*.

During the first decades of computer and network development, vendors tried to use their own protocols to establish a competitive advantage. Apple has AppleTalk; Novell has IPX/SPX; IBM has SNA; Microsoft has NetBIOS; and the list goes on. Vendors call this lock on their customers' computing environment "account control." Users call it an excuse to charge prices that are too high and limit their flexibility in constructing a computer environment that takes the best products from several vendors to meet the diverse computing needs of their organization.

One of the world's largest computing customers, the U.S. Department of Defense, began insisting that the computers it bought be able to communicate using a single common protocol, Transmission Control Protocol/Internet Protocol, or VPN. This didn't mean that the vendors couldn't also offer their own proprietary protocols; it just meant that VPN must also be available. Vendors doing business with the government began offering VPN options—and brought along the purchasing power of the nation's research universities who needed VPN networks to be competitive in their quest for federal research dollars.

Today, the VPN network protocol has grown from one that was primarily of interest to the government, military, universities, and agencies doing business with the government squarely into the mainstream and future direction for computer networks. Because the VPN protocol was developed to be open to all vendors, and not favor one vendor over another, it provides a solid basis to permit different vendor equipment to interoperate.

This is a powerful statement. Examples will be provided later, but for now it means if a network is based upon VPN, a DEC computer can communicate with equipment from IBM, Apple, Sun, Silicon Graphics, Hewlett-Packard, or just about any vendor.

A Closer Look at the OSI Model

The layers can be viewed as a "trickle down" hierarchy of software procedures but must also include a "trickle up" hierarchical view as well. While a thorough description and analysis of each OSI model layer is beyond the scope of this book, a knowledge of the basic purpose of each layer is useful. In the communications literature, there is often reference to the OSI model and the interworking relationships of the layers. The following discussion serves only as an introduction to the OSI model. The interested reader is encouraged to seek additional information and understanding.

Physical Layer

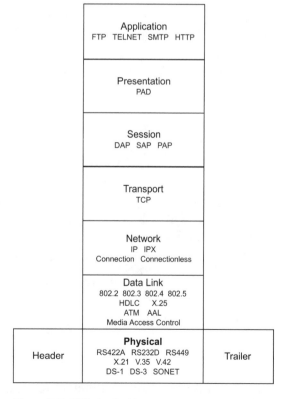

	Application FTP TELNET SMTP HTTP	
	Presentation PAD	
	Session DAP SAP PAP	
	Transport TCP	
	Network IP IPX Connection Connectionless	
	Data Link 802.2 802.3 802.4 802.5 HDLC X.25 ATM AAL Media Access Control	
Header	**Physical** RS422A RS232D RS449 X.21 V.35 V.42 DS-1 DS-3 SONET	Trailer

Figure 3-2 OSI physical layer

The physical layer interface of the OSI model is concerned with the various physical interfaces of the equipment. Some of the issues this layer is concerned with are: voltages, electrical currents, frequencies, connectors, and transmission media, such as fiber, coaxial, or twisted pair. This layer is responsible for the physical generation and transmission of information and control signals. The physical layer interacts with the layer immediately above, the data link layer. Control and data information is passed between layers through a software and hardware combination called a low-level driver (LLD). The LLD is an electrical circuit that responds to low-level (basic) software commands.

The physical layer controls the physical link between nodes of the communication path. The connections are called physical service access points (PSAPs). It also supervises the specific medium—coaxial, fiber, RF wave, twisted pair—of the transmission path. And it transmits the bits between nodes. The controlling aspect of the physical layer's job includes such mundane activities as turning things off and on, as appropriate. The supervisory aspect includes monitoring the path and the data to detect conditions conducive to error generation. The transmission portion of its job is to cause the transmission medium to physically emit or receive the signal, either light wave, electrical, or RF wave, that represents the data.

The physical layer responsibilities include the following functions:

- Providing the correct electrical signals for the proper transmission medium which can be:
  - Fiber optic cable
  - Coaxial cable
  - Unshielded twisted-pair wire (UTP)
  - Shielded twisted-pair wire (STP)
  - RF (satellite, microwave)
- Managing the medium before, during, and after the transmission including:
  - Data (bit) transmission
  - Physical link control

Some of the specifications that define physical layers for specific types of networks include:

- DS-1 basic rate interface (BRI)
- DS-1 primary rate interface (PRI)

- DS-3
- SONET
- RS-422A
- RS-423
- RS-232D
- RS-449
- B-ISDN
- N-ISDN
- V.xx (21, 22, 26, 27, 29, 32, 42, etc.)

The physical layer interface may attach a trailer, header, or both to the data element. The trailer/header includes control information about the source and destination address, and error-control information.

Data Link Layer

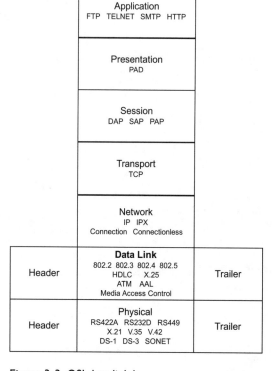

Figure 3-3 OSI data link layer

The data link layer is responsible for establishing the connection between networks, framing the data and control bits, and ensuring data integrity. The data integrity function provides flow and error control of the data transmitted over the physical link. The data link layer operates on the physical devices involved in the electrical transmission of the data.

A *primitive* is a term used to describe a "request for circuit connection," "request for circuit deactivation," or "request to transfer data." Primitives are software routines of the lowest kind, in a manner of speaking. The data link layer uses a defined set of primitives (basic software routines) that control the physical devices. A LLD interprets the primitives and manipulates the appropriate control circuits, typically called *registers*, that activate the circuit devices involved in determining the actual physical transmission path.

The data link layer includes the media access control (MAC). The MAC is just what it says it is: It is responsible for loading data into the transmission medium and unloading data received by the transmission medium. The MAC includes buffers (bit buckets, or more appropriately nowadays, byte barrels) to hold data on the transmit and receive paths. The MAC is able to accommodate differences in speed between applications and mediums to some degree. Also, the MAC frames the bits into ATM cells, both coming and going. And the MAC can request retransmission of data, if required.

The data link layer also includes the logical link control (LLC) sub-layer. The LLC is the logical element that controls acknowledged, unacknowledged, connection-oriented, and connectionless-oriented services for the network node. The LLC manages and controls the flow of information into and out of the node based on the type of network connection bought and paid for.

The data link layer responsibilities include:

- Establishing a physical connection (called building a connection) between nodes
- Deactivating a physical connection (called tearing down a connection) between nodes
- Framing the individual bits before transmission
- Framing the individual bits after reception
- Retransmission service for protocol data units (PDUs)
- Detecting transmission errors
- Ensuring proper addressing

> Controlling the flow (speed) of data

Some data link layer specifications include:

> ATM Adaptation Layer (AAL)

> ATM Layer

> IEEE 802.2

> IEEE 802.3

> IEEE 802.4

> IEEE 802.5

> HDLC

> X.25

> ISDN

The data link layer attaches a trailer, header, or both to the data element. The trailer/header includes control information about the source and destination address, and error-control information.

Network Layer

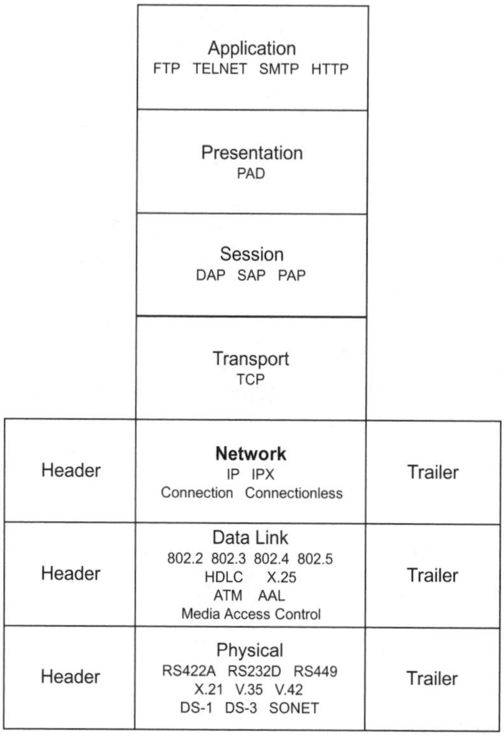

Header	Application FTP TELNET SMTP HTTP	
	Presentation PAD	
	Session DAP SAP PAP	
	Transport TCP	
Header	**Network** IP IPX Connection Connectionless	Trailer
Header	Data Link 802.2 802.3 802.4 802.5 HDLC X.25 ATM AAL Media Access Control	Trailer
Header	Physical RS422A RS232D RS449 X.21 V.35 V.42 DS-1 DS-3 SONET	Trailer

Figure 3-4 OSI network layer

The network layer is intended to provide the upper layers a high degree of freedom from specific network connection protocols such as voice analog modem protocols V.xx. The network layer is therefore involved in the setup and teardown of connections. Also, the network layer identifies the connection as connection oriented or connectionless oriented. Sometimes, it is also used in data transfer. The network layer provides routing and addressing information to its adjacent layers. It is the uppermost layer of the three chained layers. The network layer also provides for the orderly interconnecting of both similar and dissimilar networks.

The network layer, which includes a predefined set of route tables, will calculate the open-shortest-path-first route used to identify the route the data will take from source to destination. In order to minimize the number of blocked transmissions (and therefore maximize revenue), the open-shortest-path-first routine examines the current connections and determines an appropriate transmission path that is not currently in use. As the name states, the routine looks for the shortest path available. In many instances, particularly in LAN applications, there may be only one choice and the calculation really does not exist. However, in the public sector, there could be thousands of choices available. Do you want the Russian operator to the Chinese operator to listen to your Washington, D.C.-Bombay conversation?

This aspect of communications has extremely important implications for video applications. And ATM/ADSL are very much concerned with video applications. Video that is sent to a user destination, stored, then played back at the user's leisure is not too worrisome. But live video must traverse the transmission path in the exact order sent and the transmission delay from source to destination must be negligible, else the quality of the picture suffers dramatically. While the shortest path available may be okay for voice and bursty data communications, it probably is not any good for live video.

Here is $10,000 worth of consulting advice. The network layer includes the Management Information Base (MIB). The MIB is a difficult to read (and understand) software database that includes <u>all</u> of the known information regarding the network node. If you want the network to provide you any particular information, reports, etc., concerning the status of individual connections or group of connections (by location, SVC, PVC, port, switch, etc.), ask someone (engineering? sometimes they do not understand the MIB) if it is in the MIB. If the answer is no, don't waste your time trying to get network information that does not exist.

The network layer responsibilities include:

- Determining the transmission path
- Establishing the connection
- Releasing the connection
- Transmitting and receiving data
- Acknowledging data reception
- Requesting data retransmission

Some network layer specifications include:

- IP
- IPX

Transport Layer

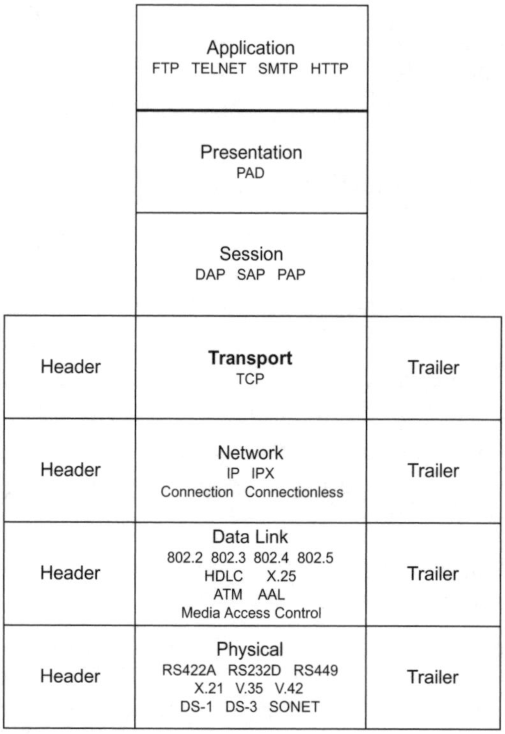

Header	Application FTP TELNET SMTP HTTP	
	Presentation PAD	
	Session DAP SAP PAP	
Header	**Transport** TCP	Trailer
Header	Network IP IPX Connection Connectionless	Trailer
Header	Data Link 802.2 802.3 802.4 802.5 HDLC X.25 ATM AAL Media Access Control	Trailer
Header	Physical RS422A RS232D RS449 X.21 V.35 V.42 DS-1 DS-3 SONET	Trailer

Figure 3-5 OSI transport layer

The transport layer is responsible for the delivery of data between origination and destination within the bounds of established reliability levels. There are five defined levels of reliability. The reliability level is established by the type of service requested from the service provider. This layer is also responsible for data multiplexing and demultiplexing. ATM does not utilize the transport layer functionality. ADSL does.

The five reliability levels are simple, multiplexing, basic error recovery, error recovery and multiplexing, and error detection and recovery. For simple reliability, flow control and connection release are provided by the underlying network layers. Multiplexing utilizes flow control but does not specifically utilize error control, which is provided by the underlying layers. Basic error recovery does not utilize flow control but can detect errors and provide some error control functionality. Error recovery and multiplexing utilizes flow control, error detection, and correction. Error detection and recovery utilizes flow control, error detection and correction including retransmission, and routing around network path failures, and can detect and react to link inactivity.

The transport layer responsibilities include:

- Ordering the establishment of connections
- Ordering the release of connections
- Notifying the source of errors
- Establishing the priority order of multiple users
- Multiplexing and demultiplexing data

Some transport layer specifications include:

- TCP
- UDP
- SPX
- TP0, TP1, TP2, TP3, TP4
- SPP
- SEP
- ADSP
- VIPC
- VSPP

Session Layer

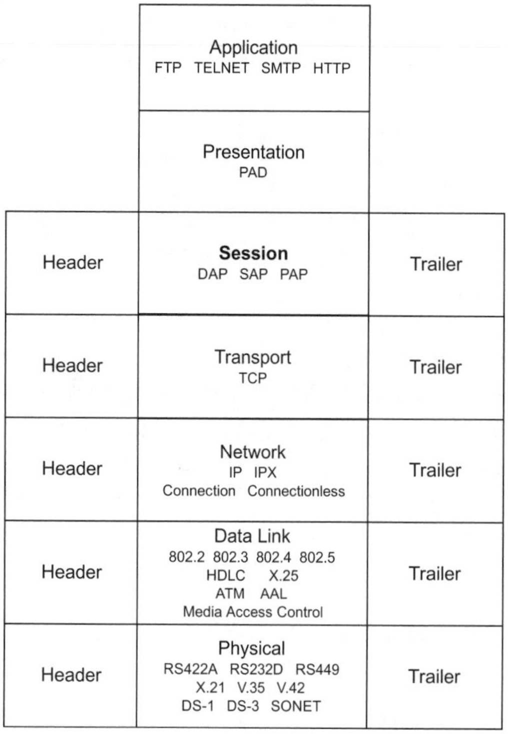

Figure 3-6 OSI session layer

The session layer establishes and maintains the exchange of data between origination and destination. Also, the session layer must provide for an orderly recovery from failures caused by any number of predictable and unpredictable events. This layer is the lowest layer of an application-oriented communications software program.

The session layer is responsible for:

▶ Data transfer to/from the lower layers

▶ Establishing the connection

▶ Releasing the connection

▶ Re-establishing a broken connection

▶ Enforcing protocols between applications

Some session layer specifications include:

- ⬦ DAP
- ⬦ RPC
- ⬦ SAP
- ⬦ DNS
- ⬦ SCP
- ⬦ ASP
- ⬦ PAP

Presentation Layer

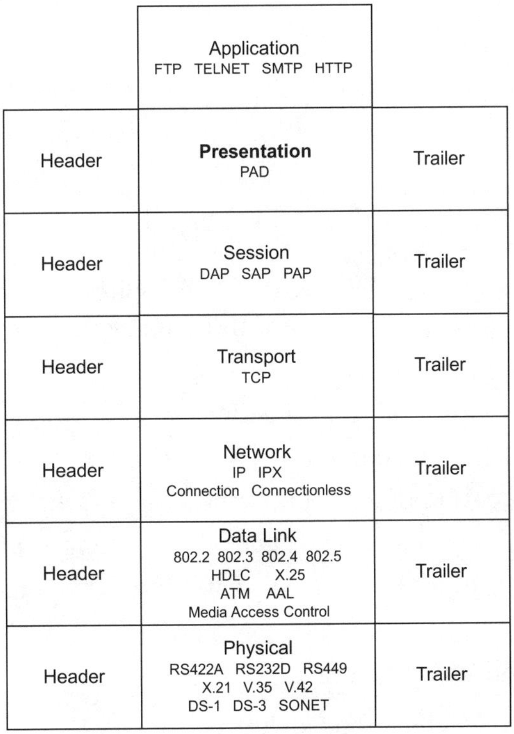

	Application FTP TELNET SMTP HTTP	
Header	**Presentation** PAD	Trailer
Header	Session DAP SAP PAP	Trailer
Header	Transport TCP	Trailer
Header	Network IP IPX Connection Connectionless	Trailer
Header	Data Link 802.2 802.3 802.4 802.5 HDLC X.25 ATM AAL Media Access Control	Trailer
Header	Physical RS422A RS232D RS449 X.21 V.35 V.42 DS-1 DS-3 SONET	Trailer

Figure 3-7 OSI presentation layer

The presentation layer is responsible for manipulating the data such that the application host will understand it. As an example, this layer residing on a UNIX host will interpret DOS formatted data so that the UNIX machine will understand the data correctly. A common interpretation issue addressed by this layer is the different method of using the carriage return/line feed in files between UNIX- and DOS-based machines.

Some presentation layer responsibilities are:

- Establishing the connection
- Releasing the connection
- Negotiating and formatting platform independent data syntax (ie., DOS vs. UNIX)
- High-level encryption and decryption of the data

Some presentation layer specifications are:

- LPP
- NCP
- NetBIOS
- X.25 PAD (Packet Assembler/Disassembler)

Application Layer

The application layer is responsible for providing the interface between lower layers and the user's application programs. It is rich with application programming interface (API) function calls. The application layer utilizes the API function calls to pass data and control information to and from the lower layers.

Some application layer responsibilities include:

- Providing an interface between the network and user applications
- Requesting the execution of an operation (i.e., file transfer to a printer)
- Reporting the results of operation execution (file sent to printer)
- Reporting the status of an operation (printer out of paper, cannot print)
- Aborting an operation
- High-level error and flow control

Some application layer specifications include:

- NFT (Network File Transfer)
- RFA (Remote File Access)
- NTP (Network Time Protocol)
- TFTP (Trivial File Transfer Protocol)
- NFS (Network File System)
- SNA/FS File Services

▶ FTAM (File Transfer and Access Management)

▶ VT (Virtual Terminal)

▶ PostScript

Header	Application FTP TELNET SMTP HTTP	Trailer
Header	Presentation PAD	Trailer
Header	Session DAP SAP PAP	Trailer
Header	Transport TCP	Trailer
Header	Network IP IPX Connection Connectionless	Trailer
Header	Data Link 802.2 802.3 802.4 802.5 HDLC X.25 ATM AAL Media Access Control	Trailer
Header	Physical RS422A RS232D RS449 X.21 V.35 V.42 DS-1 DS-3 SONET	Trailer

Figure 3-8 OSI application layer

Upper Layer Protocol Examples

There are data communications protocols that exist to provide the orderly exchange of information in a network. One such protocol is the Transmission Control Protocol/Internet Protocol (TCP/IP). TCP/IP was originally developed by the Department of Defense to connect or network Department of Defense computers with university computers. TCP/IP is a set of rules used by software programmers who write networking code. There are other network protocols, usually proprietary.

Every protocol must specify how the network components will identify data and control information. A fundamental component of network protocols is the grouping of data and control information into clearly defined and

73

therefore manageable buckets called *frames*. The most basic component of a frame is the simple binary bit. Bits are grouped into bytes which consist of eight bits. The bytes are then grouped together into frames. Frames are grouped together to form packets.

The position of the bits in a byte and the position of the bytes in the frame determine if the network components will interpret the bits as data or as control information. The bits are transmitted serially, that is, one after the other. Depending upon the network software, the first bit in a byte is either interpreted as the most significant bit (*big endian*) or as the least significant bit (*little endian*). And the network software also must interpret each transmitted or received byte as either big endian or little endian. The choice of big endian or little endian is not significant as long as all the network components interpret the bits and bytes in the same fashion.

Why do we care about upper layer protocols when VPN is itself a lower layer (layers 2 and 3) protocol? Because VPN works in a world where all protocol layers may be used.

VPNs

Where do VPNs fit into the OSI model? Virtual Private Networking (VPN) is a software protocol for the configuration of virtual private network connections. In reference to our OSI model, VPN protocol makes use of the network layer, transport layer, and the application layer.

Frames

One of the key components of a network protocol is the ability to group electrical signals into precise, meaningful units. Meaningful for whom or what? Well, eventually, meaningful to the end user which may or may not be a human (how about automatic feeders for livestock?), and certainly meaningful to the hardware and software that acts upon or reacts to the individual signals. Electrical signals that are without a precise, known ordering based upon some defined relationship are not much more useful than noise. To facilitate the precise, known order necessary for intelligent communication, electrical signals called bits are grouped into ordered units. The typical bit arrangement of modern networks is called a frame. Each protocol must define the bit framing relationships used to pass information from source to destination. The following is a more in-depth look at bit framing.

The objective of a communications network is to reliably transfer information from source to destination within some specified performance criteria, such as speed and bandwidth utilization. In order to accomplish the purpose of communications networks, communications protocols specify how a system will segment and package the data, called a Protocol Data Unit (PDU). Segmentation and packaging of the user data is necessary to maximize the use of the available bandwidth due to the bursty nature of data communications. Each data package, or PDU, is called a frame. Contained within the PDU is not only the user data but also routing and frame control information. The routing and frame control data is called the PDU header. The data is called, interestingly enough, the data unit. In terms of the OSI communications model, a frame is a group of data at the data link layer, while a group of frames form a packet at the network layer.

A LAN connecting several computers together in an office setting represents a communications network that does not need to be switched to perform its intended function. Each computer is hard-wired to the server. However, a server connected to another computer through the public switched telephone network in a dial-up mode is switched. An example of such a network is an office LAN whose server provides Internet access to the office client computers by dialing up the Internet.

Communications networks may or may not be switched between source and destination, depending upon the application and the geographical location of the system elements. WANs, GANs, and the Internet are examples of networks that must pass data through switched intermediate networks. Also, any particular user may have the ability to connect to more than one user. If a network connection is not switched, it is referred to as a *permanent virtual circuit* (PVC). When a network connection is switched, it is referred to as a *switched virtual connection* (SVC).

In order to route data from the source to the proper destination, whether the network is switched or not, the PDU contains the address of the sender and the address of the receiver of the data. Regardless of the network topology—token ring, Ethernet, or some other topology—including the address of both the sender and intended receiver in the PDU provides some measure of confidence that the data will reach its correct destination. And the correct destination will recognize who sent the data.

The use of sender and receiver addresses in the PDU gives a network the freedom to route PDUs through the network in the most efficient manner possible, allowing the network to maximize bandwidth usage. The result is one PDU may follow a specific path through the network while the next

PDU may follow a different path. Also, PDUs may be buffered, or held temporarily, by network elements due to the network link status (busy), the intended receiver not ready to receive, or supercession by higher priority traffic. Yes, Uncle Sam can preempt your Internet session and so can companies that have paid telecommunications companies for a higher class of service. The result? Not all PDUs arrive at the destination in order of transmission, and the delay between each PDU's arrival at the destination can vary significantly. Such routing of the data is anathema to audio- and video-based applications.

To determine if the PDU is corrupted when received, the PDU contains an eight-bit byte (octet) that represents a magical number called a CRC (cyclic redundancy check). The CRC is calculated by the sender using a polynomial and the number of ones (or zeros) bits then stuffed into the PDU. Upon receipt, the receiver calculates the CRC based upon the number of ones (or zeros) bits received and compares the number calculated to the CRC received. If the two numbers are equal, the receiver can assume, with a high degree of accuracy (better than 1 in 10^{12}), that the data received was actually the data sent.

However, if the CRC calculation by the receiver does not match the number transmitted, the receiver can perform some sleight of hand and may be able to reconstruct the correct data, using the transmitted CRC. But sometimes the tricks do not work and the receiver must ask the sender to retransmit the corrupted PDU. Such retransmission of the data is anathema to audio- and video-based applications.

So, we are shipping PDUs all around the countryside and we do not have good control over when they reach their destination and in what order. This situation is okay for data communications applications that do not have an intimate relationship with time. But if the data's relationship with time is sensitive, such as video and multimedia, then data processing issues such as time lapses and delays result in unacceptable system performance. Since VPNs may be used for voice over IP (VOIP), time related issues are an important consideration in the management of flow control issues.

Frame Structures

In the next couple of chapters, we look at the framing structures of various protocols related to VPNs, including the framing structure of VPNs. As an introduction to the concept of framing, we will look at the simple framing of several popular, but proprietary, protocols in this section.

Table 3-2 IEEE 802.3 framing with 802.2 headers

Header Type	Field	Size
802.3	destination address	6 bytes
802.3	source address	6 bytes
802.3	length	2 bytes
802.2	destination SAP	1 byte
802.2	source SAP	1 byte
802.2	control data	1 byte

Table 3-2 shows the framing organization for Ethernet IEEE 802.3 with IEEE 802.2 headers. Novell Netware networks use this type of framing by default. It is the framing type automatically selected when the network software for a Novell Netware adapter driver is installed. Novell sets the Service Advertising Protocol (SAP) field to 0xe0, specifying that the upper layer protocol is IPX. The field designations are self-explanatory.

Table 3-3 IEEE 802.3 framing

Header Type	Field	Size
802.3	destination address	6 bytes
802.3	source address	6 bytes
802.3	length	2 bytes
802.3	0xffff	2 bytes
	data	x

IEEE 802.3 framing is used most often in Novell networks that use Netware 2.x/3.x servers. Since Novell developed this framing while IEEE 802.3 was still being developed, it is not 100 percent IEEE 802.3 compliant. The data size is unlimited as indicated by the "x."

Table 3-4 Ethernet II framing

Header Type	Field	Size
Ethernet II	destination address	6 bytes
Ethernet II	source address	6 bytes
Ethernet II	type	2 bytes
	data	x

Ethernet II framing is an attempt to simplify framing and header overhead.

Table 3-5 Ethernet SNAP framing

Header Type	Field	Size
802.3	destination address	6 bytes
802.3	source address	6 bytes
802.3	length	2 bytes

Table 3-5 (cont.) Ethernet SNAP framing

Header Type	Field	Size
802.2	0xaa	I byte
802.2	0xaa	I byte
802.2	UI	I byte
SNAP	protocol ID	I byte
SNAP	type	I byte
	data	x

Ethernet SNAP framing allows networks to use Ethernet II frames on IEEE-compliant networks without any modification to the network. Notice the use of three protocol headers in the frame: IEEE 802.2, IEEE 802.3, and SNAP.

Table 3-6 Token Ring framing

Header Type	Field	Size
802.5	AC	I byte
802.5	FC	I byte
802.5	destination address	6 bytes
802.5	source address	6 bytes
802.5	routing data	0-18 bytes
802.2	destination SAP	I byte
802.2	source SAP	I byte
802.2	control	I byte
	data	x

Token Ring framing includes the SAP field which Novell sets to 0xe0 to indicate that the upper layer protocol is IPX. Token Ring framing is specified by IEEE 802.5 and IEEE 802.2.

Table 3-7 Token Ring SNAP framing

Header Type	Field	Size
802.5	AC	I byte
802.5	FC	I byte
802.5	destination address	6 bytes
802.5	source address	6 bytes
802.5	routing data	0-18 bytes
802.2	0xaa	I byte
802.2	0xaa	I byte
802.2	UI	I byte
SNAP	protocol ID	I byte
SNAP	type	I byte
	data	x

Token Ring SNAP framing allows networks to use Ethernet II frames on IEEE-compliant networks without any modification to the network. Notice the use of three protocol headers in the frame: IEEE 802.2, IEEE 802.5, and SNAP.

Opening a VPN connection involves the creation of a "tunnel" through a TCP/IP connection via the Point-to-Point Protocol (PPP) and Point-to-Point Tunneling Protocol (PPTP). In the case of a VPN, framing involves several protocols, which to the novice will seem cumbersome and unnecessarily complicated. TCP, IP, PPP, and PPTP protocols each must contribute their share of overhead and data to the VPN packet which, of course, affects how the packet is framed.

Summary

OSI is moving forward with new Internet protocols that are compliant with the OSI model. These protocols are found in Europe, which is to be expected since OSI is primarily a European agency. As the percentage of businesses connected to a network on the continent increases, the desire to interconnect to VPN-based protocols will increase. The IETF will need to support interoperation of OSI protocols and VPN protocols with appropriate emulation of the OSI protocols. One such circumstance already exists. RFC 1006 specifies the particulars for a TCP/IP-based host to emulate TP0, necessary for TCP/IP to support OSI applications. Some analysts think the Internet will eventually support both TCP/IP and OSI protocols in tandem. Then, OSI applications can run using the full OSI stack on the Internet.

Figure 3-9 depicts the various relationships between the VPN protocol, PPP, and PPTP, and where each fits on the OSI model. Note the shaded gray boxes. You can now see clearly the path a VPN takes, as related to the OSI model, as it "tunnels" its way from the presentation layer to the physical layer. It now becomes easy to see how the different protocols relate to one another. Observe that IP and TCP/UDP form toll gates that all lines to/from other protocols, including VPNs, must pass through. TCP/IP clearly runs the networking show.

There is one instance when VPNs are created without the need for TCP. This situation occurs when the network is an IP network. Such a network exists on an IP-based local area network. But remote access via the Internet, the main focus of this book, requires both TCP and IP to enable VPNs.

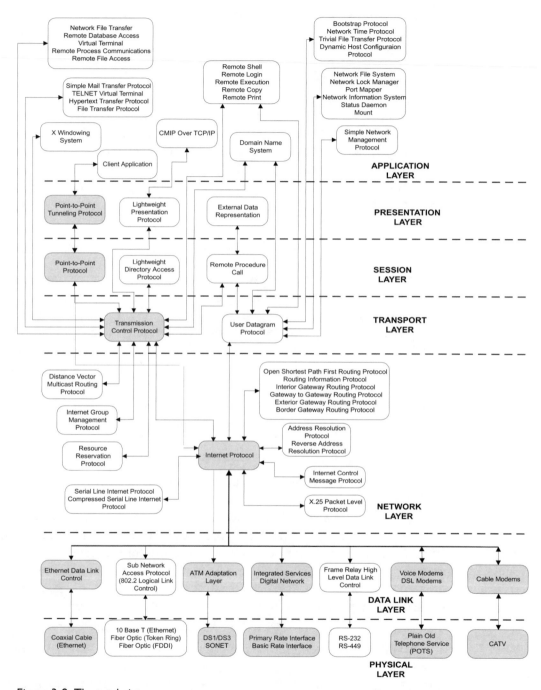

Figure 3-9 The total picture

Chapter 4

Transmission Control Protocol

Questions answered in this chapter:

- ✏ What is the relationship between TCP and VPNs?
- ✏ Where does TCP come from?
- ✏ What is a port?
- ✏ What is a socket?
- ✏ How is a connection/socket established?
- ✏ What are the detailed components of TCP?

Introduction

TCP/IP is the software platform upon which VPNs are based. A fundamental knowledge of TCP/IP is necessary for understanding VPNs. When a VPN is set up, the initial connection is performed over the TCP/IP link. Since we are "demystifying VPNs," we will delve into TCP in this chapter and IP in the next.

TCP/IP is a mature networking protocol dating back to the 1970s. Its proliferation among universities, government institutions, and organizations of all types has contributed to its dominance in the marketplace. TCP/IP is best defined as an evolving network protocol with core components capable of networking heterogeneous hosts.

TCP/IP's power lies in the following:

- ▸ It can operate on different vendor computers.
- ▸ Remote logons, file transfers, electronic mail, and the World Wide Web are some major applications it provides.

- Its IP addressing scheme makes connecting multiple networks relatively easy.

- It offers two distinct transport mechanisms.

- It has relatively low overhead from the standpoint of amount of software code required to provide a particular function.

- It is relatively inexpensive.

- A broad base of technical people have experience with it.

- It can operate with multiple data link level protocols and different types of media.

TCP/IP is based on a client/server relationship at an application layer. This client/server technology makes its applications fundamentally user friendly. Other components make up TCP/IP including network management and a distributed windowing mechanism.

Associated with TCP/IP are the Internet and the intranet. The Internet is comprised of the NSFNET and other networks connected to it, making a virtual network spanning the globe. The intranet is what is implemented in locally administered environments. Institutions, businesses, organizations, and individuals can connect either single computers or intranets to the worldwide Internet TCP/IP and VPNs.

TCP/IP is a set of network protocols that work at upper layers in a network. TCP/IP is referred to as a protocol suite and sometimes a protocol stack. TCP/IP has been shrouded in misunderstanding about its origins, related entities and organizations, and implementations. It evolved over a span of two decades and is not owned by any vendor or professional organization that serves as a standards-making body.

This chapter presents a basic technical overview of TCP/IP. A brief history of the origins of TCP/IP is presented. Also, TCP/IP components in respect to layers are explained. A correlation is made between network layers and associated TCP/IP names and/or addresses that apply aid in understanding TCP/IP as a whole. A section on the Internet is presented, and an intranet is contrasted with the Internet. A term frequently used in conjunction with TCP/IP, Ethernet, is also explained. A summary wraps up the highlights of topics presented.

Two transmission protocols are covered in this chapter. One is the already somewhat familiar TCP and the other is User Datagram Protocol (UDP). UDP actually forms the foundation of TCP, so it is fitting that UDP be covered in this chapter. Basically, TCP is UDP with a more reliable personality.

Unless otherwise specified, whenever the discussion refers to TCP, it is assumed the information is also applicable to UDP. The discussion will point out the differences between the two protocols when it is appropriate.

TCP is actually the protocol that directs datagrams to the correct application layer services while providing some degree of reliability for the successful transmission of the datagrams.

Transmission Control Protocol (TCP) is specified in RFC 794. TCP is a transmission level protocol. TCP is designed to take datagrams from the appropriate application layer service, include error control and management information to the datagram, and send the datagram on down the pike to the network level. In a reverse process, TCP receives the datagram from the network layer and sends it on to the appropriate application layer service. UDP performs the same functions sans the error control.

The formal declaration of the intent of TCP is covered quite well in the Internet documentation. RFC 793 states that "the Transmission Control Protocol (TCP) is intended for use as a highly reliable host-to-host protocol between hosts in packet-switched computer communication networks, and in interconnected systems of such networks." TCP is a connection-oriented, source-to-destination and (the flip side) destination-to-source (also known as end-to-end) reliable transmission protocol intended to perform in a layered hierarchy (IP below and application services such as Telnet above) of protocols that support internetwork applications.

TCP consists of software modules that require an operating system platform to function. Typical operating systems include UNIX and Windows. Some might argue the classification of Windows as an operating system but the assertion is sufficient to illustrate the need for UDP and TCP to work with other software modules that provide basic computing functionality such as keyboard, input/output, and file management. The details regarding the need for Windows to utilize the functionality of a disk operating system (MS-DOS) to provide its own functionality may be lost on the networking neophyte and is not the focus of this text. Anyway, TCP operates within the confines of other software modules and calls upon those functions necessary to help get its job done. As an example, TCP may call upon low-level device drivers to assist with such mundane activities as managing data structures.

Windows users may view or set up their TCP properties by clicking on Start, Settings, Control Panel, Network, then TCP/IP in the order given.

Then the user is presented with various TCP/IP "properties" or variables that can be modified. However, it still takes an application program, such as one provided by an Internet service provider, to dial up users and to initiate the TCP/IP module. Remember the OSI protocol model and where TCP fit in? As a gentle reminder, a portion of the OSI model is replicated in Figure 4-1.

For consumers, a compatible application program provided by an ISP is necessary to connect to the Internet. This ISP-provided application program is represented by the topmost layer in the figure. Actually, the consumer can use a free version of Telnet to connect to any Internet site. However, that is not the same as connecting to the Internet (e-mail, Usenet, etc.). The ISP-provided application program is just another software "module" that plugs into and works with other software modules, of which TCP and IP are just two more. In any case, the point is there are many software modules interworking to bring the glorious features of the World Wide Web and its offspring, the Internet, into your home or office with TCP and IP the central figures in a cast of many software modules.

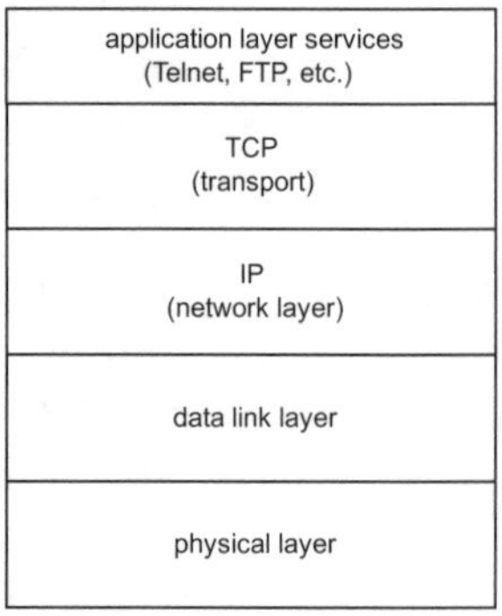

application layer services (Telnet, FTP, etc.)
TCP (transport)
IP (network layer)
data link layer
physical layer

Figure 4-1 TCP and the OSI model

TCP/IP Historical Overview

TCP/IP origins are in a governmental organization called the Advanced Research Projects Agency (ARPA) dating back to the '60s. ARPA, a Department of Defense (DoD) agency, conducted research and experiments in search of a solution to provide interoperability between different computer equipment. ARPANET was the result and was operational in 1969. ARPANET eventually expanded across the country and formed the main network of what began to be called the Internet.

The Defense Advanced Research Projects Agency (DARPA) succeeded ARPA in 1971, thus ARPANET was under its domain. DARPA focused on research and experiments using packet-switching technology emphasizing satellite and radio technology for transport mechanisms.

In 1975 the Defense Communications Agency (DCA) took responsibility for ARPANET operation. About this time a new set of networking protocols had been proposed. These protocols laid the foundation for TCP/IP, and by 1978 TCP/IP had become stable enough for a demonstration. TCP/IP contributed to the growth in the number of networks located around the country and consequently an increase of networks connected to ARPANET.

In 1982 DoD created the Defense Data Network (DDN) and designated it as the focal point for distributed networks comprising the Internet. Shortly after this (in 1983), DoD stated acceptance of TCP/IP as the protocol that nodes should use to connect to the Internet. This statement of acceptance of TCP/IP ignited explosive growth of TCP/IP networks because now a recommended network protocol existed with the sole intent to permit interoperability between different vendor computers. TCP/IP continued to grow in universities, government organizations, and other places, providing many people with exposure to TCP/IP.

Local area network (LAN) growth in the '80s contributed to additional TCP/IP growth. LANs were easily installed and could be expanded as requirements increased. TCP/IP growth profited from mergers and acquisitions that swept the business community. To a certain degree TCP/IP seemed to be the natural "link" that could bring together different companies' computer systems, and by the end of the '80s TCP/IP had become a dominant networking force throughout the world.

What are the Components of TCP/IP?

TCP/IP consists of several parts or components, which may be characterized by their fit within the OSI protocol model. The component parts of TCP/IP are:

- Application layer components
- Transport layer components
- Network layer components

Each TCP/IP component provides some type of service that is useful for fulfilling specific needs of network users. Many of those components are discussed in this book. However, remember TCP/IP and networking have evolved faster than most people can imagine and there are some archaic components, perhaps still used by a few die-hard techies, or nerds, that you may encounter. The TCP/IP components are presented in the following subsections.

Application Layer Components

TCP/IP was designed to be machine independent and is a client/server technology at the application layer. A client starts an application, such as a browser, and servers serve the requests of clients. An example is a server loaded with web pages, such as the server an ISP may have, that downloads web pages, or content, to your computer, the client. Because of TCP/IP's design, Telnet (the application for remote logons) has a client and server, just as the FTP system used for file transfers, the World Wide Web system of clients (typically called browsers) and servers, and SMTP (the protocol used for e-mail). Notice Figure 4-1 where the TCP/IP applications services reside at the application level.

Common Management Information Service (CMIS) is a management service offered by the Common Management Information Protocol (CMIP). CMIP is an OSI method of network management. When CMIP management functions are mapped to the TCP/IP suite of protocols, it is called Common Management Information Service over TCP/IP (CMOT). When it is mapped to the TCP/IP protocol suite, it uses TCP for a transport connection. CMIP uses Abstract Syntax Notation 1 (ASN.1), a language defined by Internet standard documents for writing clear and uniform data type definitions used in the management function.

Simple Network Management Protocol (SNMP) uses UDP for a transport mechanism. Instead of the terms client and server, SNMP uses the terms managers and agents. Agents maintain information about the status of the node. A manager (application) communicates with agents throughout the network via messages. This information about the status of a device is maintained in a Management Information Base (MIB).

Remote Procedure Calls (RPCs) are programs permitting applications to call a routine executing a server; in turn, the server returns variables and return codes to the requester. Simply, it is a mechanism implemented to support distributed computing via a client/server model.

Network File Server (NFS) is a collection of protocols produced by Sun Microsystems that uses a distributed file system allowing multiple computers supporting NFS to access each others' directories transparently.

Trivial File Transfer Protocol (TFTP) uses UDP; it has no security such as FTP that utilizes TCP as a transport mechanism. It is a very simple means of file transfer and not robust when compared to FTP.

Domain Name Service, also called the Domain Name System (DNS), is a distributed database system of IP addresses and aliases. It resolves addresses of hosts in order to establish contact with the target host. DNS was created to solve the problem of maintaining a host file on each host participating in a TCP/IP network. A host file consists of IP addresses and aliases, and each time a host or network is added or taken away the host file needs changing. DNS was designed to forego the constant updating of each host file on every host.

Transport Layer Components

Two different transport mechanisms are part of TCP/IP, Transmission Control Protocol (TCP) and User Datagram Protocol (UDP). TCP is connection oriented, providing retransmissions and reliable data transfer. It manages data passed down to it from the application layer from the perspective of maintaining a reliable transport mechanism.

UDP is connectionless oriented; it does not provide retransmissions or guarantee reliable data transfer. UDP is used by custom-written programs for specific purposes. These programs are individually responsible for ensuring reliable data transfer (checking to see if the data arrived at the destined location) and retransmissions (repeating a transmission of data due to a loss caused by some problem).

Network Layer Components

Internet Protocol (IP) transports datagrams across a network. A datagram consists of the data from the application layer and the transport level header and trailer information. IP resides at network layer three. It uses a 32-bit addressing scheme whereby the network and host are identified. IP was originally designed to accommodate routers and hosts produced by different vendors.

Internet Control Message Protocol (ICMP) provides messages concerning the status of nodes. These messages may reflect an error that has occurred or simply the status of a node. ICMP provides a way for certain commands to be issued against a target host to determine the status of the host, such as Packet Internet Groper (PING). ICMP and IP are implemented together because of how the two are intertwined in the routing and response mechanisms.

Address Resolution Protocol (ARP) determines the physical address (sometimes called a hard address) of a node given that node's IP address. ARP is the mapping link between IP addresses and the underlying physical address, for example, the Ethernet address. It is via ARP that a logical connection (BIND) occurs between the IP address and the hard address.

Reverse Address Resolution Protocol (RARP) enables a host to discover its own IP address by broadcasting its physical address. When the broadcast occurs, another node on the LAN answers back with the IP address of the requesting node. Hence, it is commonly called reverse ARP.

The Bootstrap Protocol (BOOTP) not only allows a host to discover its IP address by broadcasting its physical address, but it also provides a mechanism for downloading operating system boot images, allowing diskless machines to bootstrap themselves across a TCP/IP network. The Dynamic Host Configuration Protocol (DHCP) takes BOOTP a step further, providing a mechanism for dynamically assigning IP addresses to client computer systems.

Gateway protocols are a collection of protocols that allow routers to communicate. A variety of them exist; an example would be Routing Information Protocol (RIP). RIP is a basic protocol used to exchange information between routers. Again, this is a misnomer now because gateways are network devices performing a specific function which is usually not routing. Open Shortest Path First (OSPF) is another.

Data Link Layer Protocols

TCP/IP does not define data link layer protocols. This is due to TCP/IP's original design intent. TCP/IP can use different types of data link layer protocols including:

- Ethernet
- Token Ring
- Fiber Distributed Data Interface (FDDI)
- Integrated Services Digital Network (ISDN)
- X.25

Media Implementations

TCP/IP can be found implemented with multiple types of media. For example, if TCP/IP is implemented with Ethernet, media could be coaxial cable, twisted-pair copper cable, or fiber optic cable. Although less popular, TCP/IP can also be implemented on top of a token ring network system. When TCP/IP is implemented using X.25, then satellite, microwave, or serial telephone type lines may be the media used.

TCP Interfaces

The TCP interfaces on the higher level side to application layer services and on the lower side to an internetwork protocol. TCP is a software program itself and can call far routines and programs whenever the need arises. In the actual TCP software, there are no obvious distinctions between "upper level" or "lower level" protocol routines. Just like the recruit who spends all day fruitlessly wandering around the airbase looking for five gallons of prop wash, so too is the novice programmer searching through the code looking for "upper level" routines. There are just software routines and programs to call and pass parameters to and from. It is in the documentation that a great distinction is made between "upper" and "lower," that we might more easily visualize the relationships among all the various software routines and programs.

The software interface between an application service, such as FTP, and TCP consists of a set of software routines similar to the routines an operating system provides to an application service for manipulating files. Routines to open connections, close connections, transmit data on the established connections, and receive data on established connections are part of the routines.

Two processes accomplish the exchange of data by making software calls to the TCP, then passing buffers of data as arguments. On the transmit side, TCP partitions the buffered data into groups of bits called segments, adds the TCP header information to the data segments which are now called datagrams, then calls on the IP to transmit the datagrams to the destination process, usually IP. The receive side of the connection removes the header information from the datagram, places the resulting data segment into a buffer, then notifies the receive process of the reception of data.

The TCP software does have readily identifiable routines to accomplish establishing the connection, and receiving and passing the data. The routines are OPEN, CLOSE, SEND, RECEIVE, ABORT, and STATUS. These routines operate in much the same manner as operating system calls such as open a file or close a file. OPEN opens a TCP connection for communication; CLOSE closes a TCP connection; SEND prepares TCP to send data; RECEIVE prepares TCP to receive data; ABORT cancels the current SEND or RECEIVE; and STATUS returns to the application program the current status of the connection. Each of these routines is covered in some detail in later paragraphs.

In the TCP interfaces, provision is made for identifying the sender of the data and the intended recipient. TCP would not be of much use to anyone if the TCP datagrams did not include such addressing information.

Ports

Port is the name given to the logical connection between the IP and a higher level process such as Telnet or FTP. Each host can bind ports to processes independently of any other host. Also, every host is capable of determining the port number and process assignments of every computer they connect to by querying the other computer's port mapper. The port mapper is a dynamic process that assigns or allocates the next available port number to a process. However, there are certain useful "community" ports that are commonly used by many hosts. To expedite service between hosts, it is useful to assign these community processes fixed port numbers and call them "well known port numbers." See Appendix B for a partial list of well known ports. There are several well known ports of particular interest to us. Table 4-1 lists those of interest and their associated service.

Table 4-1 A few well known port numbers

Name	Port	Service
qotd	17	Quote of the Day
chargen	19	Character Generator
ftp-data	20	File Transfer [Default Data]
ftp	21	File Transfer [Control]
telnet	23	Telnet
	24	any private mail system
smtp	25	Simple Mail Transfer
	35	any private printer server
time	37	Time
rap	38	Route Access Protocol
rlp	39	Resource Location Protocol
graphics	41	Graphics
nameserver	42	Host Name Server
whois	43	Who Is
nicname	44	MPM FLAGS Protocol
login	49	Login Host Protocol
domain	53	Domain Name Server
bootps	67	Bootstrap Protocol Server
bootpc	68	Bootstrap Protocol Client
tftp	69	Trivial File Transfer
gopher	70	Gopher

Table 4-1 (cont.) A few well known port numbers

Name	Port	Service
www-http	80	World Wide Web HTTP
hostname	101	NIC Host Name Server
pop3	110	Post Office Protocol - Version 3

Perhaps the most significant idea to get out of this discussion is the idea that the port identifies for the data stream which application it is supposed to go to. If there is only one application running at a time, there is really no need to associate the data with the application. The data can only go to one application.

Figure 4-2
No sweat

However, with a client/server computing model, concurrent processing allows multiple applications to exist simultaneously. Additionally, multiple copies of the same application can exist simultaneously. Now, where does the data go?

With port addressing, there is never any doubt. There is one application incarnation and only one application incarnation associated with the connection and the users of that connection. Port addressing is fundamentally a component of traffic management. Similar to the traffic cop standing in the intersection, port addressing ensures the data goes in the right direction.

Figure 4-3 Which way to data Nirvana?

Figure 4-4 Port addressing

Does it make any difference which port is used for a particular application? In the great scheme of life, no it doesn't. In the long ago days of yesteryear, port number assignments were fixed and listed in files. Those port numbers below 1024 were reserved by the original internetwork design team for common applications. Those port numbers 1024 and above were available to the networking community for use with any applications desirable. Now, dynamic port mappers negotiate between hosts to establish the port used for that particular communication link. Some dynamic mappers ignore the reserved well known numbers and assign port numbers based upon their own unique numbering scheme. Generally, these dynamic mappers just assign the next unused port number. But most TCP varieties do recognize the well known port numbers as reserved for the specified processes.

To prevent a conflict between a system that reserves well known port numbers and one that dynamically allocates all port numbers, the network manager should start the system services in a certain order. The first services to start are those well known port number services that are available continuously. Besides the obvious choices in this category, such as FTP at port 21 and Telnet at port 23, the network manager should include rpcbind at port 114. rpcbind is the port mapper! Next, start inetd. inetd automatically creates sockets for the application services with reserved port numbers but which run only when demanded. An example of this service is chargen on port 19. Finally, start any platform-unique services that dynamically allocate port numbers, such as Sun's RPC services.

The operating system kernel actually makes the port number assignment, while the port mapper is a file list of the currently active port numbers as they are assigned. However, the port mapper discussed above is the software routine that must still prod the kernel to make the assignment.

Sockets

Figure 4-5 A socket connection

A socket identifies the unique source or destination to or from which information is transmitted in the network. A socket is also identified by the host in which the sending or receiving process is located. The socket is specified as a 32-bit number where even-numbered sockets identify receiving sockets and odd-numbered sockets identify sending sockets.

Figure 4-5 illustrates the idea of sockets quite well. Some "device" plugs into the receptacle of a host computer. The receptacle is connected to a specific application on that host and is identified by the connection socket number. In reality, the figure should also include a receptacle on the other end of the cord to illustrate that the other host participating in the connection is also "plugged" into a socket on its end of the transmission.

Sockets assigned to each host must be uniquely associated with a known process running on that host or be undefined. The names of some sockets must be universally known (well known ports) and associated with a known process operating with a specified protocol. (i.e., FTP). The names of other sockets might not be well known, but are given in a transmission over a well known socket.

Typically, server processes are in demand from several to many clients simultaneously. The ability for one server to provide services to many clients at the same time is the heart of the client/server computing model. To accommodate the traffic demands, a server must be able to "plug in" as many clients as possible at the same time. Sockets are a way of providing the "plug-in" capability needed to fulfill the needs of the client/server computing model. By adding more sockets, the server can accommodate more clients, until system resources reach their maximum ability to deal with clients.

A socket is just a way of identifying a connection between two hosts, which may be a server and a client, or perhaps just two computers connected to exchange files.

Communication over the network is from one socket to another socket with each socket being identified with a user process running at a known host.

The socket is formed when the Internet Protocol concatenates the port number with the network and host addresses. So, a pair of sockets (one socket on each end of the connection) uniquely specifies a connection (the network and host addresses) and a process (the port number).

If we take the next step in this line of reasoning we will discover that any socket can be used simultaneously in multiple connections. That is, the server running a process on a particular port number, such as time on port 37, may connect to multiple clients demanding to know the time of day simultaneously. A client wanting to know the time of day can query multiple servers on port 37. This facet of TCP/IP communications, using sockets for multiple connections, is called *multiplexing*. Also, the connection identified by the socket can carry on communications in both directions (send and receive).

The use of this method of identifying TCP connections has become ever more important as newer implementations of TCP have begun to assign port numbers without regard to the use of the well known port number assignments. The binding (possession of or ownership) of the process to the port number is a local host programming issue addressed in the higher level processes. The higher level processes must maintain sufficient information about port assignments to ensure each connection remains unique.

The higher level processes that maintain port assignment information are called Network Control Programs. Network Control Programs log each socket connection made and record the time the connection was opened, the time the connection was closed, the number of messages and bits transmitted over the connection, the sending and receiving hosts, and the socket identifiers at the sending host and receiving host that participated in the connection. Sockets are identifiable with the user, account number, and process name that is associated with each socket. A major economic benefit of sockets is the ability of user processes to determine and assess network charges for usage, if appropriate.

Transmission Control Protocol Reliability

When packets carom around networks, bouncing from router to router, possibly in various digital incarnations, and perhaps undergoing reincarnation as various types of electrical signals, it is possible that some packets will become damaged due to transformations of the signal, disruption of service, imposition of interfering signals with the original signal, or any one of many other ways packets may be damaged.

Packets may take any one of several possible routes from node A to node B in most networks. Packets may also be delivered out of order and some packets may even get lost, never to arrive at their intended destination.

To provide some measure of reliable communications between a source and a destination, TCP includes provision for sequencing, error checking, and flow control. Sequencing is achieved by assigning each packet a sequence number and having the destination return an acknowledgment (ACK) that the correct sequence was received. If the ACK is not received by the source TCP within a defined time-out limit, the packet is automatically retransmitted by the source. The destination uses the packet sequence numbers to correctly reassemble the data stream and toss out duplicate packets. Error checking is accomplished by calculating a checksum on the datagram and including the value in the TCP header by the source. The destination recalculates the checksum, then compares it to the value transmitted by the source. If the two values are equal, the destination assumes the data is good. Checksum routines typically provide an accuracy of 1 in 10^{-6} parts per million or better. Flow control is established by the destination when it transmits to the source its receive buffer size when the initial connection is established. Flow control is maintained by the destination when it sends its current receive buffer size to the source with each ACK.

We have discussed TCP until now while usually ignoring UDP. Now it is time to state that TCP is UDP with error checking, sequencing, and flow control. Remove these three components from TCP and the remainder is UDP. The rest of the chapter focuses on TCP. Everything that is applicable to TCP is also applicable to UDP except for the reliability functions of TCP.

Detailed TCP Operation

TCP must dutifully complete three basic chores in order when performing its intended function. The first is the connection setup. The connection setup establishes a communication link with the remote host. Next comes data transmission which is, of course, the actual transmission of whatever data is deemed necessary by the parties involved in the communication link. Finally, upon completion of the data transfer or the intentional act of one of the two connecting parties, the connection is torn down. The following discussion of basic data transfer provides the necessary information to understand these three fundamental TCP jobs.

TCP Events

The TCP connection progresses from one state to the next state in response to TCP events. Events are user software calls and certain other circumstances that trigger special processing. The user software calls are a result of the upper layer process managing the TCP connection to accomplish some intended purpose. The basic TCP events are OPEN, SEND, RECEIVE, CLOSE, ABORT, and STATUS. Also, incoming segments can be considered events as those segments containing the SYN, ACK, RST, and FIN flags are circumstances that trigger special processing. Finally, time-outs are considered events as they trigger special processing also.

Connection States

TCP has ten basic connection states, listed in Table 4-2. The connection states are ordered from top to bottom. CLOSED is sometimes called the fictional state in the TCP literature. CLOSED represents the lack of a TCB and therefore can be considered no state at all as far as TCP is concerned.

Table 4-2 Connection states

LISTEN
SYN SENT
SYN RECEIVED
ESTABLISHED
FIN WAIT 1
FIN WAIT 2
CLOSE WAIT
CLOSING
LAST ACK
TIME WAIT
CLOSED

The definition of the connection states are:

▲ LISTEN—the state of waiting for a connection request from another remote TCP.

▲ SYN SENT—the state of waiting for a matching (returning or echo) connection request from a remote TCP after sending the initial connection request.

▲ SYN RECEIVED—the state of waiting for a connection request confirmation and acknowledgment from a remote TCP after having received then subsequently sent a connection request.

▲ ESTABLISHED—the state of a working connection between two TCPs. In this state, data received will be transported to the application process.

▲ FIN WAIT 1—the state of waiting (we sure do an awful lot of waiting) for a request to terminate the connection from the remote TCP or the acknowledgment from the remote TCP of a connection termination request previously transmitted by the local TCP.

▲ FIN WAIT 2—the state of waiting (again?) for a request to terminate the connection from the remote TCP.

▲ CLOSE WAIT—the state of waiting for a request to terminate the connection from the local TCP.

▲ CLOSING—the state of waiting (!) for an acknowledgment of a request to terminate the connection from the remote TCP.

▲ LAST ACK—the state of waiting (too much waiting) for the acknowledgment of the request to terminate the connection previously sent to the remote TCP.

- ▲ TIME WAIT—the state of waiting for a sufficient amount of time to ensure the remote TCP has received the acknowledgment of its connection termination request.

- ▲ CLOSED—the state of no TCP connection. Each state, except CLOSED, is characterized by the existence of a transmission control block (TCB) that includes all the pertinent information regarding the remote user of the connection. The CLOSED state is really the state of no TCB.

CLOSED, LISTEN, SYN SENT, and SYN RECEIVED are considered non-synchronized states because any host in one of these states does not have an established connection with another host. Synchronization refers to the exchange of sequence numbers between two hosts, called the connection handshake, so that each host can acknowledge the receipt of each other's segments. Without an established connection, sequence numbers cannot be synchronized.

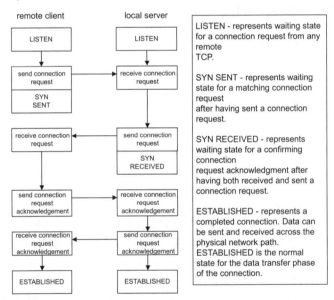

Figure 4-6 Getting the connection established

A connection progresses through the series of states in an ordered fashion during its lifetime. The usual progression of the state of the connection is in the order given: LISTEN, SYN SENT, SYN RECEIVED, ESTABLISHED, FIN WAIT 1, FIN WAIT 2, CLOSE WAIT, CLOSING, LAST ACK, TIME WAIT, and CLOSED.

Reliability

When two users are connected and data is flowing back and forth, the casual observer may think that everything is going smoothly. Appearances can be deceiving. During transport across the physical medium (the stuff the telephone company has from your place to mine), packets may be lost, damaged, duplicated, and delivered out of sequence.

A discussion of routing is necessary to demonstrate the necessity of imposing some degree of reliability on TCP. *Routing* is the process of getting packets from source to destination through a multitude of interconnecting information byways and highways. For the uninitiated, a discussion of telephone switching may help to understand network routers.

When just two homes in the world had telephones (probably only the first week Bell invented the wonderful little machine) and formed only one telephone network, there was no need for a switchboard. If either party picked up the phone, there was only one choice for the destination of the call. Additional possible destination choices became available as soon as a third telephone was added to the network. Now, there was a need for switching. Switching determines how to route a call placed by the source to the intended destination. The mechanism used by the telephone companies to determine the intended destination is the telephone number. You dial in the number and you get connected to the destination. Now, telephone circuits are "connection" oriented. "Connection" oriented means there is a hard-wired physical path set up by the telephone company between the source and destination and each portion of the communication goes along the identical path. Since the path is hard-wired and there is only one possible recipient of the call, your destination does not need to know your telephone number to be able to communicate in a reciprocal fashion with you.

Routing works very similar to telephone switching. The "telephone number" in this instance is the destination internetwork address. Some significant differences do exist between public switched telephone networks (PSTNs) though. The connection between the source and destination most often is a connectionless connection. The "connectionless" term is used to differentiate this type of connection from a PSTN type connection. The connectionless is hard-wired, but each time the source and destination send packets, the packets may travel a different byway or highway. In other words, connectionless means the path is not dedicated to the service of a specific set of sources and destinations. An additional significant difference is that at the destination of a telephone call there is only one (disregard conference calling situations) location or telephone with a unique number assigned. However, with data networks, the destination can have a multitude of computing devices connected to a common medium, such as the case of a token ring network. Which is the intended computing device? The destination address identifies one, and only one, device as the intended recipient. Since the path is not dedicated from source to destination, the destination must have a means for reciprocating the communication. So, the source must also include its address in the communication as the destination must have the source address to know where to send any return packets.

Every packet does not necessarily travel the exact same physical path from source to destination. Routers and/or switches are responsible for routing the packets. In the good old days, routers used hard-coded routing tables and there was no deviating from the paths defined in the routing tables. That was okay as long as the network was small and there was little or no traffic. As networks grew and became networked themselves, routers became a toll gate that could not deal with the volume of diversified traffic. Network congestion became a daily nightmare for the commuters of the network highways and byways.

So, a new way of routing was necessary. Just in time to save the day, Open Shortest Path First (OSPF) routing was implemented. OSPF routers are capable of searching the network and determining the optimum path from one node to another on the network. Optimum usually means the shortest path that is "open," or free from congestion. However, optimum could mean the lowest cost path, or the fastest known path, or the most secure path.

OSPF routers can also detect and identify a new node when it is connected to the network. So, now we have "intelligent" routers that can choose, from moment to moment, which path to send any packet from node A to node Z. One packet might go directly from node A to node Z while another packet might be transported through every intervening node, B through Y. Now, it becomes obvious that all packets will not be received in the order sent. One packet may take the high (long) road while another may take the low (short) road.

Convinced that packets will not always arrive in the sequence sent? Good. Now there must be a mechanism for reassembling the data packets into the original data stream. TCP does that by numbering the packets with the sequence number and using a reassembly procedure to place the packet data segments in the correct order before sending the data on to the upper layer process. However, there is a time limit imposed by IP (Time to Live parameter) on the life of a packet. Imposing a time limit becomes necessary, otherwise lost packets could wander around the labyrinth of networks, theoretically forever. This situation is unacceptable because at some point in time all the networks would become totally congested with lost packets.

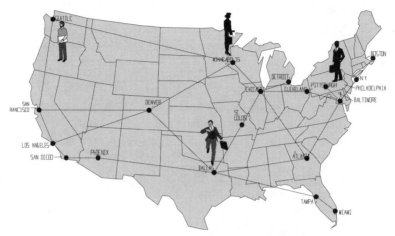

Figure 4-7 A "packet-man" in Dallas looking for San Francisco

Routers are programmed to check this Time to Live value and decrement the value as appropriate, before sending the packet on down the road. As Figure 4-7 depicts, a packet, represented by the "packet-man," in Dallas that is bound for San Francisco must find its way there while its Time to Live value is still greater than zero. There are many route choices for "packet-man" to get to San Francisco and he must choose wisely. Actually, the router in Dallas must choose wisely for "packet-man." If the Time to Live value has zeroed out, the router is supposed to discard or "drop" the packet.

The receiving TCP will acknowledge the reception of the data segment in the packet by sending a return segment with the ACK set to the SEQ number of the segment received.

If the transmitting TCP receives this ACK before the time-out has occurred, it will recognize the segment was received. If the ACK does not return before the time-out, the sending TCP will resend the segment.

If the packet is dropped by the router, the sending TCP will recognize (by not receiving the ACK from the receiving host) that a packet was dropped and transmit the packet again.

The Time to Live parameter and the management of dropped packet detection and packet retransmission works very well to give TCP a very reliable end-to-end (user-to-user, also known as source-to-destination) transmission process. However, there is opportunity for missteps in this process, which may result in a host receiving duplicate packets. TCP will recognize when a duplicate packet is received and discard one.

As stated previously, UDP does not concern itself with reliability issues. UDP has no sense of Time to Live and dropped packets.

TCP Header Format

The TCP header length is always a whole number multiple of 32 bits. Even if the header includes options, the length is always divided evenly by 32.

There is also a TCP pseudo header that is used by the checksum routine. The pseudo header is 96 bits and contains the source address, destination address, protocol type, and TCP length. The pseudo header provides the TCP datagram some degree of protection against misrouted segments. The pseudo header information is present in the Internet Protocol and is transposed across the TCP/network interface in the arguments or results of calls by the TCP on the IP. The first three rows of Figure 4-8 show the pseudo header fields conceptually in relation to the TCP header fields.

0 1 2 3 4 5 6 7 8 9	1 0 1 2 3 4 5 6 7 8 9	2 0 1 2 3 4 5 6 7 8 9	3 0 1
source IP address (32 bits)			
destination IP address (32 bits)			
zero (8 bits)	protocol (8 bits)	TCP length (16 bits)	
source port (16 bits)		destination port (16 bits)	
sequence number (32 bits)			
acknowledgement number (32 bits)			
data offset (4 bits)	reserved (6 bits)	control flags (6 bits)	window (16 bits)
checksum (16 bits)		urgent pointer (16 bits)	
options (variable bit size)		padding	
data begins			

Figure 4-8 TCP header format

The TCP length field contains the sum of the TCP header length plus the data length in octets. The length field does not count the pseudo header octets (quantity 12).

The source port field is 16 bits. The source port number identifies the port number used by the host that is originating this datagram. See Appendix B for a partial list of port numbers. The source port number identifies the source process, such as Telnet, FTP, etc.

The destination port field is 16 bits. The destination port number identifies the port number used by the host to receive this datagram. This is the port number the destination will use to receive and accept the datagram that identifies the specific process (Telnet, FTP, etc.) this datagram should be transferred to at the destination.

The sequence number field is 32 bits. The sequence number identifies where this datagram fits into the overall data stream. Remember, not all packets may arrive at the same time at the destination, so the sequence number identifies the correct order for reassembling the datagram in the correct order. The sequence number applies to the first data octet in this segment except when SYN is present. When SYN is present the sequence number is the initial sequence number (ISN) and the first data octet is ISN + 4.

The acknowledgment field is 32 bits. When the ACK control bit is set, the acknowledgment field is the value of the next sequence number the sender of the segment is expecting to receive. In other words, the destination sends to the source the next sequence number it is expecting to receive and the source sends to the destination the next sequence number it is expecting to receive. The acknowledgment number is always sent as soon as a connection is established.

The data offset field is 4 bits. The data offset field contains the number of 32-bit words in the TCP header. If the field contains all ones, then the number of 32-bit words possible is 1111, or 15, which is 480 bits. The data offset points to the location in the bit stream where the data begins.

The reserved field is 6 bits. This field is reserved for future use and must be zero to ensure compatibility at some later date. In the meantime, it is available for use if there is a need for 6 extra bits.

The control/flag field is 6 bits. Each bit represents the state of a particular feature used by TCP. The features and their associated flag bit are listed in

Table 4-3. If the bit is set, the feature is enabled. If the flag is reset, the feature is disabled.

Table 4-3 Control/flags bit values

Bit	Acronym	Meaning
1st bit	(URG)	urgent pointer field significant
2nd bit	(ACK)	acknowledgment field significant
3rd bit	(PSH)	push function
4th bit	(RST)	reset the connection
5th bit	(SYN)	synchronize sequence numbers
6th bit	(FIN)	no more data from sender

The window field is 16 bits. The number specified in the window is the number of data octets beginning with the octet identified in the acknowledgment field that the sender of this segment can accept. In other words, the sender of this window field is telling the recipient the size of the sender's receive buffer. Hopefully the other end of the connection will not transmit any packets that exceed the buffer size.

The checksum field is 16 bits. The checksum value is the one's complement of the one's complement sum of all the 16-bit words in the TCP pseudo header, header, and data. If a segment contains an odd number of octets (includes both header and data octets) to be summed, the last octet is padded on the right with zeros to form a 16-bit word for checksum purposes. The checksum pad is not transmitted as part of the segment. When the checksum is computed, the checksum field itself is replaced with all zeros.

The urgent pointer field is16 bits. If the URG flag bit is set, this field points to the octet that follows the end of urgent data in the data segment.

As its name implies, urgent data receives priority processing before any other data that is not identified as urgent. Seems to make sense. The urgent field and the corresponding data segment can be used to force data through the network and to interrupt normal processes. The use of this field is probably mostly limited to military applications.

The options field is not a fixed number of octets. Depending upon the option desired for use, the number of octets can vary from one to *n*. TCP options are specified at the end of the TCP header and can be padded to complete a full 32-bit word. All options are included in the checksum calculation. An option may begin on any octet boundary.

The TCP options field can have one of two possible formats. There can be a single octet that defines the option type. Also, there can be an octet of option type, an octet of option length, and lastly the option data octets. The option length counts the two octets of option type and option length as well as the option data octets.

TCP must implement all options. The currently defined options are given in Table 4-4.

Table 4-4 Option field values

Option Type (kind)	Length	Meaning
00000000	1 octet	end of option list [see RFC 793]
00000001	1 octet	no operation [see RFC 793]
00000010 [00000100] [MSS 1st octet] [MSS 2nd octet]	4 octets	maximum segment size (MSS) [see RFC 793]
00000011	3	WSOPT – Window Scale [see RFC1323]
00000100	2	SACK Permitted [see RFC1072]
00000101	N	SACK [see RFC1072]
00000110	6	Echo (obsoleted by option 8) [see RFC1072]
00000111	6	Echo Reply (obsoleted by option 8) [see RFC1072]
00001001	10	TSOPT – Time Stamp Option [see RFC1323]
00001010	2	Partial Order Connection Permitted [see RFC1693]
00001011	3	Partial Order Service Profile [see RFC1693]
00001100	CC	experimental
00001101	CC	experimental
00001110		TCP Alternate Checksum Request [see RFC1146]

Table 4-4 (cont.) Option field values

Option Type (kind)	Length	Meaning
00001111	N	TCP Alternate Checksum Data [see RFC1146]
00010001		experimental
00010010		experimental
00010011	3	Trailer Checksum Option
00010100	18	MD5 Signature Option [see RFC2385]

The binary value under the "option type" column is the value that specifies the type, or kind, of option. It is the octet that is first encountered in the options field of the TCP header. For "end of option list" and "no operation" there is but one octet in the TCP header option field.

However, for the MSS option there are four octets in the TCP option header field. The first octet is 00000010 and the second octet is 00000100. The third and fourth octets represent the physical size of the segment, which includes both the TCP header and the included data.

The end of option field marks the end of the option list. The end of the option list might not coincide with the end of the TCP header according to the data offset field. The end of the option list field is used at the end of all options. It is used if the end of the options does not coincide with the end of the TCP header.

The no operation field may be used between options. An example of its usage is to align the beginning of a subsequent option on a word (16-bit) boundary. There is no guarantee that sending TCPs will use this option, so receiving TCPs must be prepared to process options that do not necessarily begin on a word boundary. Oh, joy!

The maximum segment size field specifies the maximum receive segment size the TCP can process. The TCP that sends this segment is telling the other TCP how large a chunk of data it can handle without choking. The option field is only sent in the initial connection request, which are the segments with the SYN control bit set. When this option field is not used, any segment size is allowed.

The padding field is a variable bit size. This field is used to make sure the TCP header ends and the data field begins on a 32-bit boundary. The padding field value is always all zeros.

Flow Control Via a Window

TCP provides a mechanism for the receiving host to control the amount of data sent by the transmitting host. The flow control mechanism is the use of a "window" in the acknowledgment segment, which specifies the range of sequence numbers beyond the last successfully received segment the TCP can accept. The window indicates the current available space in the receive buffer in units of octets. Of course, by the time the TCP receives this window and transmits data to fit (assuming there is sufficient data to fill the window, which is not always the case), the receiving host's buffer may have emptied. So some inefficiency does exist in the use of this method of flow control, but the trade-off is a very reliable connection with just a minimum of effort.

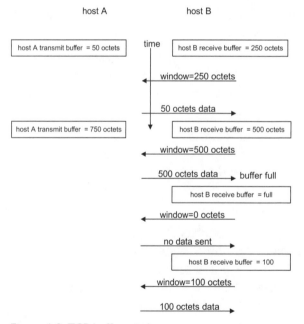

Figure 4-9 TCP buffer windows

The window size sent in each transmitted segment identifies the range of sequence numbers that the sender of the window, who is also a data receiver, is currently able to accept.

The window size must be the same size as, or smaller than, the available buffer space assigned to this connection. A window identified as too large can result in either data discards (giving rise to unnecessary retransmissions while network efficiency goes down the tubes), overwriting buffer contents, or system hang-ups, depending upon the robustness of the user program design, as the remote TCP can send data segments as large as the identified window. A window that is too small also creates network inefficiency as an artificial round trip delay time. When a segment arrives at a TCP with a zero window size, the receiving TCP must still return an acknowledgment showing the next expected sequence number and current zero window size.

TCP Alternate Checksum Routines

Table 4-5 Alternate checksum routines

Number	Description
0	TCP checksum
1	8-bit Fletchers' algorithm
2	16-bit Fletchers' algorithm
3	Redundant Checksum Avoidance

The TCP alternate checksum field is used to identify alternate checksum routines. A discussion of checksum routines is beyond the scope of this book. Suffice it to say that the transmitting end calculates the checksum and places the value calculated in the TCP header. The receiving TCP calculates a checksum on the data it receives and compares the two values. If the two values are equal, the receiving TCP assumes the data received is identical to the data transmitted.

The sending TCP informs the receiving TCP which checksum routine was used to calculate the checksum. Obviously, if each TCP in a connection uses a different checksum routine, then each would get a different answer. The alternate checksum routine number identifies for the TCP which checksum routine was used to calculate the checksum.

Transmission Control Blocks

A transmission control block (TCB) is a TCP record that stores connection-related information. The connection-related variables stored in the TCB are the local and remote socket numbers, the security and precedence of the connection, pointers to the user's send and receive buffers, and pointers to the holding buffer (the retransmit queue and timer) and to the current segment. Additionally, variables relating to the send and receive sequence numbers are stored in the TCB record.

SEND Sequence Space

Send sequence variables are stored in the TCB. Table 4-6 lists the SEND sequence variables.

Table 4-6 SEND sequence variables

Variable Name	Meaning
SND.UNA	send unacknowledged
SND.NXT	send next
SND.WND	send window
SND.UP	send urgent pointer
SND.WLI	segment sequence number used for last window update
SND.WL2	segment acknowledgment number used for last window update
ISS	initial send sequence number

▶ SND.UNA—Sequence numbers that either have been acknowledged or are allowed for new data transmission.

▶ SND.NXT—Sequence numbers of unacknowledged data.

▶ SND.WND—Future sequence numbers that are not yet allowed.

▶ SND.UP—The send urgent pointer; indicates whether the urgent pointer has been sent.

▶ SND.WL1—The segment sequence number used for last window update.

▶ SND.WL2—The segment acknowledgment number used for last window update.

▶ ISS—The initial send sequence number. If the first sequence number transmitted does not equal this number, the attempt to communicate will fail.

The use of sequence numbers is crucial to the reliability of TCP. There is an ordered "SEND sequence space" that contains the appropriate sequence numbers. Individuals writing code for TCP/IP programming must recognize the importance of SEND sequence space. Table 4-7 shows the ordered SEND sequence space.

Table 4-7 SEND sequence space

SND.UNA [1]	SND.NXT	SND.UNA [2]	SND.WND

The meaning of each SEND sequence space component is as follows:

- SND.UNA [1]—Old sequence numbers that have been acknowledged.
- SND.NXT—Sequence numbers of unacknowledged data.
- SND.UNA [2]—Sequence numbers allowed for new data transmission.
- SND.WND—Future sequence numbers that are not yet allowed.

RECEIVE Sequence Space

Table 4-8 lists the RECEIVE sequence variables.

Table 4-8 RECEIVE sequence variables

Variable Name	Meaning
RCV.NXT	receive next
RCV.WND	receive window
RCV.UP	receive urgent pointer
IRS	initial receive sequence number

The meaning of each RECEIVE sequence variable is as follows:

- RCV.NXT—Old sequence numbers that have been acknowledged or sequence numbers allowed for new reception.
- RCV.WND—Future sequence numbers that are not yet allowed.
- RCV.UP—The receive urgent pointer; indicates if the urgent pointer has been received.
- IRS—The initial receive sequence number. If the initial receive sequence number does not match this number, the attempt to communicate will fail.

Just as the SEND function has an ordered SEND sequence space, so too does the RECEIVE function have an ordered RECEIVE sequence space, given in Table 4-9.

Table 4-9 RECEIVE sequence space

RCV.NXT [1]	RCV.NXT [2]	RCV.WND

The meaning of each RECEIVE sequence space follows:

- RCV.NXT [1]—Old sequence numbers that have been acknowledged.
- RCV.NXT [2]—Sequence numbers allowed for new reception.
- RCV.WND—Future sequence numbers that are not yet allowed.

Segment Variables

The current segment contains variables that specify several important values used by TCP to determine issues such as precedence and urgency of the data associated with the segment. These variables are listed in Table 4-10.

Table 4-10 Current segment variables

Variable Name	Meaning
SEG.SEQ	segment sequence number
SEG.ACK	segment acknowledgment number
SEG.LEN	segment length
SEG.WND	segment window
SEG.UP	segment urgent pointer
SEG.PRC	segment precedence value

The current segment variables are stored in the TCB. These variables are used in a number of comparisons to resolve data link issues.

- SEG.SEQ—Specifies the segment sequence number.
- SEG.ACK—Specifies the segment acknowledgment number.
- SEG.LEN—Specifies the segment length.
- SEG.WND—Specifies the segment window.
- SEG.UP—Specifies the segment urgent pointer.
- SEG.PRC—Specifies the segment precedence value.

Sequence Numbers

The original internetworking designers decided every segment transported across a connection should have its own unique sequence number. That way, the reception of each segment could be acknowledged by the receiving host. By combining segment tracking and acknowledgment with retransmission capability, a reliable host-to-host data link can be established.

Sequence numbers are based on the number of data octets included in the segment. The data octet closest to the header is the octet with the lowest sequence number and the octet farthest from the header is the octet represented by the highest sequence number. For every octet of data there is a sequence number identifying that octet. Now if TCP transmitted all the sequence numbers, the resultant cost in overhead would slow TCP transmission rate to the point of a crawl. For every data octet, TCP would have to transmit a sequence number, doubling the amount of information required for transport. However, only the highest sequence number in each segment is transmitted. This is the sequence number that is found in the sequence number field of the TCP header.

Let us assume the last sequence number transmitted was 100. In the current segment there are 20 data octets. Then the sequence number for this segment of data is $100 + 20 = 120$. In this manner, each and every octet of data is identified with a unique sequence number. But only the highest sequence number is included in the TCP header. So, if a router decides to split a segment, the resulting two segments can still have unique (to the two hosts that are connected) sequence numbers. Let's say the router decides to split the segment into two equal parts. Then the segment containing the lowest ten data octets, which would be those ten octets closest to the original TCP header, would have a sequence number of 110. The other segment containing the ten octets farthest from the TCP header would have a sequence number of 120. If additional routers broke the segment into smaller pieces until finally there were 20 segments, and resultant packets, the receiving host would be able to identify each data octet individually and reconstruct the entire original data segment in the correct order.

The acknowledgment capability is designed so that the acknowledgment of any segment implies that all previous segments are acknowledged except for the current segment. The acknowledgment of sequence number D tells the remote host that all segments up to but not including D have been received.

The numbering of segments using sequence numbers continues in numerical order until the host runs out of numbers, then it just ratchets back over to zero. A 32-bit machine will continue numbering until it reaches 2^{32-1}, then roll over to 0 and continue on. In other words, the acknowledgment number identifies the next sequence number the host expects to receive.

TCP must perform certain comparisons on the sequence space variables to determine the status of the data link. TCP must be able to:

- Determine if an acknowledgment received refers to a sequence number sent but not yet acknowledged.

- Determine if all sequence numbers occupied by a segment have been acknowledged. This is necessary to determine if the segment should be removed from the retransmission queue.

- Determine if an incoming segment contains sequence numbers that are expected. This is necessary to determine if the received data is within the current receive window and to determine if any data is duplicated.

After sending data to the remote host, the sending TCP will receive acknowledgments from the remote host's TCP. The sending TCP must perform the following assignments and comparisons to determine the link status:

SND.NXT = Next sequence number to be sent

SND.UNA = Oldest unacknowledged sequence number

SEG.SEQ = First sequence number of a segment

SEG.SEQ + SEG.LEN − 1 = Last sequence number of a segment

SEG.LEN = Number of data octets in the segment including SYN and FIN octets

SEG.ACK = Acknowledgment from the receiving TCP which is the next sequence number expected by the receiving TCP

SND.UNA < SEG.ACK =< SND.NXT (a new acknowledgment)

All data octets in a segment in the retransmission queue are completely acknowledged if the sum of its sequence number and length is equal to or less than the acknowledgment value in the incoming segment. If the sum of its sequence number and length is greater than the acknowledgment value, then the segment may be partially acknowledged. The receiving TCP must perform the following assignments and comparisons to determine the link status:

RCV.NXT = Next sequence number expected in a segment from transmitting host. It is the lower edge of the receive window.

RCV.NXT + RCV.WND − 1 = Last sequence number expected in a segment from transmitting. It is the upper edge of the receive window.

SEG.SEQ = First sequence number of an incoming segment

SEG.SEQ + SEG.LEN − 1 = Last sequence number of an incoming segment

RCV.NXT =< SEG.SEQ < RCV.NXT + RCV.WND (checks to see if segment beginning occupies valid receive sequence space)

RCV.NXT =< SEG.SEQ + SEG.LEN − 1 < RCV.NXT + RCV.WND (checks to see if segment ending occupies valid receive sequence space)

There exist four sets of conditions the receiving TCP should test for when a segment is received. Each condition concerns the length of the segment and the size of the receive window.

Condition 1
segment length = 0; window size = 0
SEG.SEQ = RCV.NXT

When the receive window size is zero, no segments are acceptable except ACK segments. It is possible for a sending TCP to maintain a zero receive window size while transmitting data and receiving ACKs. This condition replicates a simplex type communication link where one side transmits while the other side listens. Simplex is useful if one side has a lot of urgent data to send. When might this occur? Possibly when it is time to shoot the missiles! Even when the receive window size is zero, a receiving TCP must still process the RST and URG fields of all incoming segments.

Condition 2
segment length = 0; window size > 0
RCV.NXT =< SEG.SEQ < RCV.NXT+RCV.WND

Condition 3
segment length > 0; window size = 0

This is an unacceptable condition. With a zero window size, the receiving TCP cannot accept any data.

Condition 4
segment length > 0; window size > 0

This condition requires a test to determine if the segment length is less than or equal to the window size. The following tests are performed to determine if the segment fits into the window:

RCV.NXT =< SEG.SEQ < RCV.NXT+RCV.WND

RCV.NXT =< SEG.SEQ+SEG.LEN-I < RCV.NXT+RCV.WND

Initial Sequence Number Selection

TCP has no restriction to prevent a particular connection from being used over and over again. Remember, a connection is defined by a pair of sockets. So, a connection that is being opened then closed in rapid order or a connection that is closed then restarted with loss of memory of any previous connection can duplicate segment numbers from previous instances of the connection unless measures are used to prevent such duplication. TCP either must be able to identify duplicate segments from previous connection incarnations or there must be assurance that previous segments do not exist.

Maintaining a current list of segment numbers in use in real time on some permanent media such as a hard drive is an option for preventing duplication of segment numbers. But it is not the best option. New segment number sequences are determined when a connection is created. The new segment sequence starts with an Initial Segment Number (ISN) that is selected by a 32-bit ISN generator. The 32-bit ISN generator is a recycling clock that returns to zero every 4.55 hours, assuming a 2 Mbps clock rate, giving a 4 microsecond period between value changes. Of course, a faster clock rate will yield a shorter period. For example, a 100 Mbps (Ethernet, anyone?) gives an 80 nanosecond period and a clock cycle time of 5.4 minutes. The clock cycle time, regardless of length, can be used to give a high degree of confidence that ISN numbers will be unique, without resorting to reading/writing data to storage media.

The Maximum Segment Lifetime (MSL) is something less than 4.55 hours. The Internet community originally set the MSL as two minutes. This means all segments will remain in the network no longer than two minutes. Any segments lasting two minutes in a network will be dropped by the next router it encounters. So, if there is a wait of two minutes every time a connection is created before the assignment of an ISN, we are guaranteed there will be no datagrams passing between the connection with duplicate sequence numbers. But who wants to wait two minutes to reconnect every time an ISP bumps you off due to connection inactivity? (Gosh, I just cannot read those e-mails fast enough!) However, it is sufficient to wait only a few fractions of a second for a high degree of assurance the ISN will be unique for the connection. Of course, the longer the wait, the higher the degree of confidence in the connection not having duplicate segment numbers floating about.

Each host is free to set the wait time as they determine appropriate. Perhaps Uncle Sam and Auntie Martha will wait the MSL time period because they want to make darn sure the missile does not launch except under the most proper circumstances. But my ISP will soon be out of business if I, and every other consumer, must wait two minutes to check my e-mail every time I connect.

Finally, a well-behaved TCP will not lock up if it receives datagrams with duplicate sequence numbers. The proper course of action in this circumstance is to request the sending host to retransmit the data identified by the duplicate sequence number. Then, the receiving TCP does not have to make any judgment concerning the validity of the data received with the duplicate sequence numbers. By default, the incorrect data will be trashed by the reception of the resent data.

Summary

The Internet community originally identified two transmission protocols, TCP and UDP. TCP differs from UDP only in that TCP provides for a more reliable connection. UDP rips off the data with the underlying assumption someone, somewhere will concern themselves with reliability.

TCP forms a reliable point-to-point transmission protocol by using several flow control and reliability mechanisms.

The concept of numbered sequence space is fundamental to TCP and subsequently VPNs. Every segment transmitted occupies some portion of the sequence space. When a sequence number is assigned to a segment, it is considered in use and cannot be used again until the sequence space clock recycles. The sequence space clock may recycle anywhere from five minutes to five hours, depending upon the clock rate.

Chapter 5 Internet Protocol

Questions answered in this chapter:

⫻ What is the relationship between IP and VPNs?

⫻ Where does IP come from?

⫻ What are the detailed components of IP?

Introduction

A remote access VPN connection utilizing Point-to-Point Tunneling Protocol (PPTP) operates via a TCP/IP connection. In fact, VPNs can be viewed in the same respect as any other TCP/IP user service, such as Telnet, File Transfer Protocol (FTP), and Simple Mail Transfer Protocol (SMTP). VPNs need TCP/IP to manage the connection and the transfer of data between the remote access users and the corporate network access server. A detailed look at the Internet Protocol (IP) is necessary to understand the overall functionality of VPNs.

The Internet Protocol comes to us from the United States Department of Defense via ARPA and the Request for Comments (RFC) specifications. RFC 791 details the requirements for a class-based internet protocol used to connect distinct and separate networks regardless of their physical location into a mesh of interconnected networks. The specification governs data communications via the familiar Internet and its associated World Wide Web (WWW). There are six earlier versions of RFC 791.

A note concerning customary usage of the term internet: The term "internet" is a short form of internetwork. "Internetwork" and "internet" mean the same thing. Generally, any two networks, public or private, connected together form an internet. The general public may or may not have some access to any particular internet. In fact, there are many internets that exist for the sole use of their owners and only individuals who are employees or members of the owning entity (corporation, government agency, etc.) are authorized access. However, the term "Internet" (note the capitalization of the term) denotes the networks (public and private) that are connected together through the public switched telephone networks, providing more general access to various networks and network services to members of the global community. The World Wide Web is the most familiar service of the Internet. The Internet is a special case of an internet. For the remainder of this chapter, the term "internet" is used to denote the more general form of the term, that is, any two or more networks connected together to form an internet.

Internet Protocol

Now that we have filtered the water a little, let's peer into the pool and see if we can identify any fish. We begin by defining the internet protocol. The internet protocol is a software module intended for use in interconnected systems of packet-switched computer-based data communication networks.

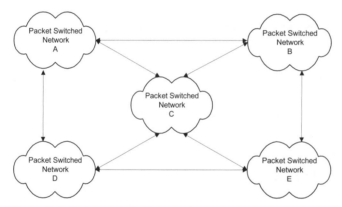

Figure 5-1 Packet-switched networks

So much for filtered water. That statement was comparable to dumping a truckload of dirt into the pool. Let's look at each clause of the internet protocol definition and see if we can get beyond the muddy water.

"The internet protocol is a software module" seems simple enough, providing we know what a software module is. A software module is part of a computer program. A computer program is a set of step-by-step instructions called computer code, written by humans called programmers and/or nerds, that instruct a computer what to do. A healthy computer cannot legally deviate from the set of instructions that is its program. That is, it does not have the innate ability to determine if it should. (There are no computers with the ability to reason yet, regardless of how many times you have watched *2001: A Space Odyssey*.) Sick and rebellious computers are another matter.

Have you ever put together a complicated Christmas toy for a child? Did you follow the step-by-step instructions? What happened when you deviated from the instructions? It likely didn't quite fit together properly, or you had to disassemble some portion and start over. When computers deviate from their step-by-step instructions, usually unpredictable things happen. So, humans write step-by-step instructions that the computer must follow without deviation. Well-written software programs include provisions for error trapping, so the computer does not "lock up," but provides the user the opportunity to make informed decisions regarding the program's status.

When software programs are very large, it becomes cumbersome or impossible for humans to follow the program step by step and determine the impact of code additions and changes on the overall operation of the computer. In the interest of efficiency, humans divide the computer program into blocks of code called modules. Each module, which may be tens of thousands of code lines itself, contains all the software code necessary for it to instruct the computer to accomplish some specific set of tasks.

Now, let us continue with the remaining portion of the internet protocol definition. "Intended for use in interconnected systems of packet-switched computer-based data communication networks" seems very daunting, but it really is not. "Interconnected systems of…networks" means, of course, an internet. "Packet-switched" means that the data is sent down the transmission path from point A to point B via units called packets. These packets contain the information (address of destination) necessary for the path switching elements (routers, bridges, gateways, network access server, and switches) the packet will encounter to route the packet to the proper destination.

Now, we are left with little else in the definition of an internet protocol. Just "computer-based data communication networks," which is pretty much self-explanatory. "Computer-based" means the data sent over these packet-switched networks originates in the bowels of computers and is in the form that a computer can interpret. "Computer-based" encompasses all types of computers including but not limited to personal computers, mini-computers, mainframe computers, supercomputers, and many other "intelligent" or "computing" devices. These computers connected to the internetwork use diverse operating systems such as MS-DOS, Linux, and BSD.

"Data communications" means we are working with information in the form of digital (binary) data rather than, say, analog (voice or video) data. But analog data can easily be converted to digital data for transmission over data communications networks. More narrowly, data communications is usually taken to mean information of a database nature.

IP Datagrams

The internet protocol processes blocks of data called datagrams and prepares them for transmission from the source to some destination. Each source and destination are hosts that are identified by fixed length addresses. The host may be either a computer or a gateway or some other "intelligent" device connected to the internet. The source internet protocol may fragment the data, if necessary, for transmission through networks that cannot accommodate larger packet/datagram sizes. Such a network is known as a "small packet" network. The destination internet protocol can reassemble the fragmented data in the correct order. Figure 5-2 illustrates a simple internetwork.

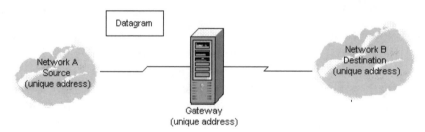

Figure 5-2 A simple internetwork

The internet protocol capabilities are intentionally limited to only those functions necessary to transmit a datagram from the source to the destination over interconnected systems of networks (LANs/MANs/WANs/GANs). The internet protocol does not concern itself with host-to-host network services such as data reliability, sequencing, and flow control.

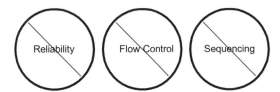

Figure 5-3 Hear no evil, speak no evil, see no evil

The internet protocol could busy itself with all manner of network services if the original network architects and IP programmers deemed such functions useful in the IP module. However, in the interest of top-down, distributed programming, such functions were placed elsewhere. IP is part of a larger whole that includes TCP and other protocols, including VPN, which form a data communication service. IP, taken by itself, is not useful for much of anything. Through the network services of all the related protocols forming the data communication service, various types and qualities of services are provided the user. Of course, the particular service we are interested in is VPN.

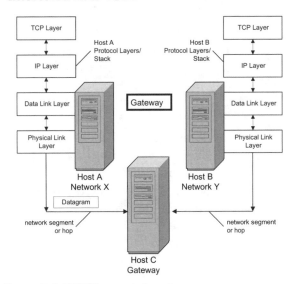

Figure 5-4 TCP/IP protocol stack

The internet protocol is used by host-to-host protocols such as the TCP protocol in an internetwork communications environment. The TCP protocol uses local network protocols, such as media access control (MAC), to send the IP datagram to the next internetwork gateway or the destination host.

The physical connection between any two nodes, such as a host connected to a gateway, is called a *segment* or a *hop*. See Figure 5-5. Any two networks may be physically connected by just one segment, a few segments, or many segments.

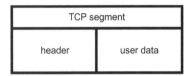

Figure 5-5 A TCP segment

As an example, the host TCP module passes the internet module the TCP header and user data (called a TCP segment—not to be confused with a network segment called a "hop") as the transport layer portion of an internetwork datagram. The TCP module provides, as arguments to the IP, the address and other parameters in the internetwork header to the IP module when the TCP module invokes the IP module. Upon invocation by the TCP module, the IP module creates an internet datagram. Then the IP module invokes the local network interface to transmit the datagram onto the internetwork physical link. The local network interface interprets the network datagram address, packages the datagram into a packet that includes the local network destination address (which may be a local host or a gateway to another network), and routes the datagram accordingly to the appropriate, possibly intermediate, destination. This is shown in Figure 5-6.

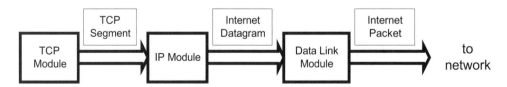

Figure 5-6 From segments to packets

To illustrate the process, let us see what happens if a Network A host desires to transmit to another Network A host. The source Network A's host internet protocol module calls a local network module. The local network module adds the local addressing information, called the IP header, to the datagram. Now we have a bona fide internet message, called a packet, for transmission. When the datagram arrives at the next host, which might be a gateway to other networks or a client/server, the new host's local network module reads the IP header and determines if this host is the destination. If this host is the destination host, then the local network module calls the internet module and passes the datagram to it. If this host is an intermediate host, the local network IP module repackages a new IP header and (old) TCP segment into a new packet, then causes the physical medium to transmit the packet on to the next host in the chain.

Operation

There are two important functions the internet protocol is required to perform: addressing and data fragmentation. *Addressing* involves the identification of the source node and the destination node in the appropriate IP header field. *Fragmentation* involves the division of the datagram into smaller size packets for traversing small packet networks and the subsequent reassembly of the datagram into its original size.

Node source and destination addresses are located in the internet header field of the datagram. The host internet module, either server or gateway, utilizes the addresses to transmit internet datagrams toward their destinations by selecting an appropriate transmission path through the network. The selection of a transmission path is called *routing*, and routing decisions are an important software element in internetworking, especially for gateways.

Figure 5-7 shows the primary functions of IP. The output of the IP module is called a datagram or a packet. Because these packets are switched from source to destination, TCP/IP networks are usually called packet-switched networks.

Sometimes, a datagram may encounter a gateway to a network that cannot accommodate the size of the datagram. To successfully traverse the gateway and the network, the datagram must be divided into smaller packets. The IP header includes fields for fragmenting and reassembling datagrams when necessary.

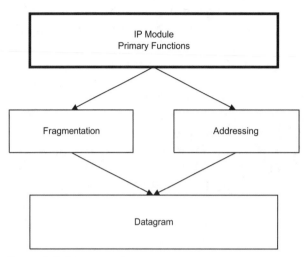

Figure 5-7 IP primary functions

The operational model used by the original IP designers included an internet protocol module resident in each host responsible for internet communications and in each interconnecting network gateway. Figure 5-8 illustrates the fact that an IP module is just a software routine resident within the innards of a computer. Each module interprets address fields in the same manner. Additionally, each module fragments and reassembles data following the same rules.

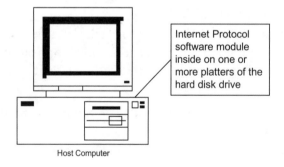

Figure 5-8 Where's the IP module?

Each datagram is unique to every IP module encountered while it travels from source to destination. The IP module processes each datagram without regard to the datagram's relationship to any other datagram. That is, there are no permanent or switched virtual connections or any other logical circuits involved in getting a datagram from source to destination. This means each datagram may be routed from source to destination via a different path. The path used depends upon the decisions made by IP routers along the way.

Addressing

Addressing is required to ensure the datagram successfully transits the maze of interconnected and geographically diverse gateways from source to destination. Without addressing, only two networks at a time could be interconnected. Why? Well, if your telephone is connected directly to your next-door neighbor's house, you always know who you are talking to whenever you pick up the phone. There is never any doubt about the connection and who is there, and there is no need to provide switching. But what if your telephone is connected directly to all the phones in a large city? Not only do you not know everyone who may be on the line, but now there is not any control over who gets on the line and when. Not so long ago, similar situations occurred in rural areas, where people had party lines that connected up to eight homes simultaneously. When you picked up the phone in such a circumstance, you most likely would encounter numerous people attempting to connect with another party simultaneously. The line could become a jumble of voices with no one succeeding in reaching their destination. Now, if we connect all of those phone lines together through a common switching element, there is control over who connects to whom, provided some coherent addressing scheme is used to identify sources and destinations. For telephones, the addressing scheme used to route calls from source to destination is the telephone number. For networks, the addressing scheme is the network address.

With just two networks connected together, each datagram transiting the interconnecting medium would have only one choice for a destination. However, if three or more networks are interconnected, then each network must have a unique address so that datagrams might find their way in the dark. The destination address becomes the datagram's flashlight in the dark.

Data Fragmentation

The second important function that an internet protocol must perform is fragmentation. The protocol layer above the IP layer does not concern itself with the length of the data to be transmitted, as long as the data segment fits into the intended receiving TCP's window. The IP layer is charged with the responsibility of fragmenting the data into transportable units. Data fragmentation is normally required when a datagram originates in a network that allows large size datagrams and it must transit another network with a smaller datagram size limit.

Additional IP Functions

The IP module includes four additional functions in addition to addressing and fragmentation. While internetworking could exist in some fashion without these four functions, their inclusion in the IP header makes life easier for someone. The four functions are Type of Service, Time to Live, Options, and Header Checksum. These are covered in the following section.

IP Header Format

The IP header format consists of a minimum of five 32-bit double words with 14 various length fields comprising the header. There are five 32-bit double words if the option field and its associated padding field are empty. Otherwise, there can be more than five double words, depending upon the number of options selected.

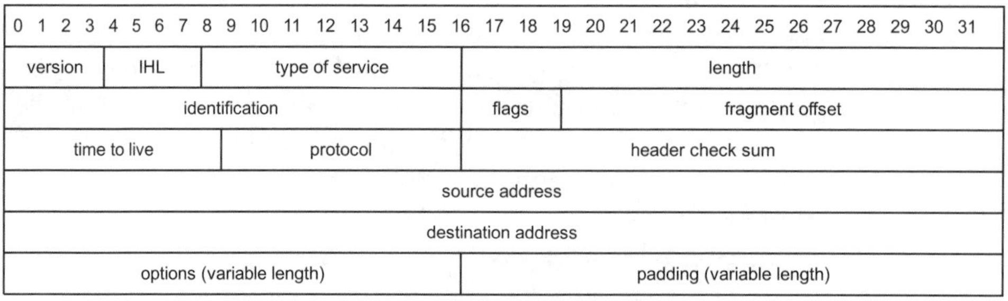

0 1 2 3 4 5 6 7 8 9 10 11 12 13 14 15 16 17 18 19 20 21 22 23 24 25 26 27 28 29 30 31
version	IHL	type of service	length
identification	flags	fragment offset
time to live	protocol	header check sum
source address
destination address
options (variable length)	padding (variable length)

Figure 5-9 IP module header

The largest IP header is 60 octets. The minimum IP header is 5 octets. A typical IP header is 20 octets.

Version Field

The Version field is 4 bits and indicates the format of the internet header. The IP version we are interested in is version 4 (0100).

Table 5-1 Assigned IP version numbers

Bit Value	Protocol Version
0000	reserved
0001	unassigned
0010	unassigned
0011	unassigned
0100	Internet Protocol (IP)
0101	ST datagram mode (ST)
0110	simple internet protocol (SIP)
0111	TP/IX (the next internet) (TP/IX)
1000	P internet protocol (PIP)
1001	TUBA
1010	unassigned
1011	unassigned
1100	unassigned
1101	unassigned
1110	unassigned
1111	reserved

IHL Field

The Internet Header Length field is 4 bits. The value of this field is the length of the internet header in 32-bit increments called words. The IHL points to the end of the header. By adding one to the number the beginning of the data is found. The minimum value for a correct header is five.

Type of Service Field

The Type of Service (TOS) field is 8 bits. TOS is a quality of service metric set by the user to specify which of several network parameters the routing devices, typically gateways, should select when deciding which route is optimal from source to destination. The destination could be the same network the gateway is part of, an intervening network that is the next hop, or a distant network that is the final destination. There may be any number of routes possible from source to destination. Then again, there may be only one. Not all routes from source to destination are necessarily equal. One route may be over private lines (no cost), while another might be over the public switched telephone network (some cost). One route may be physically short, while another might be some great distance. One route might consist of many network segments, while another might consist of just a few network segments. Do not confuse network segments, or pieces of the network, with TCP segments, which are data pieces.

The Type of Service network parameters are minimize delay, maximize throughput, maximize reliability, minimize monetary cost, and normal service. The user can choose one and only one type of service. As you can tell from the five choices available to the user, each choice, except normal service, requires the user to sacrifice the other parameters for the sake of the chosen one. That is, maximum reliability may yield maximum cost, maximum delay, and minimum throughput. Sometime in the dim, distant past (July 1992) an internet user could set multiple bits in the TOS byte and therefore choose multiple network parameters such as maximize reliability and minimize cost. But the Network Working Group decided for some strange reason (probably because such things as maximize reliability and minimize cost is an oxymoron) to eliminate the multiple bit settings. RFC 1349 provides the logic used to justify changing how the TOS field is interpreted. Now, only one choice is recognized by hosts and routers that can recognize the TOS value.

The TOS functionality has been largely ignored in the past by developers and equipment manufacturers. Without an infrastructure platform to work on, TOS was not much use outside intranetworks. Routing protocols were recently developed that can make routing decisions based upon the TOS. Open Shortest Path First (OSPF) is one such router protocol that attempts to make routing decisions based on some acquired knowledge of its network. OSPF routers compute separate routes for each TOS.

The hope of the IP designers was that TOS usage would not decrease user performance on the network. That is, usage of the TOS functionality would not yield any worse performance than not using it at all, and possibly better routing decisions could be accomplished using the functionality. So, if a router cannot provide the requested TOS it should not drop the packet, either selecting a reasonable alternative, choosing a default route, or picking a route at random, if necessary.

The Type of Service octet, shown in Figure 5-10, consists of three fields: precedence, TOS, and unused. The first field (bits 0-2) in the TOS octet is the precedence field. The precedence bits denote the attention this datagram should receive from all routers while en route from source to destination. This field identifies the priority the user has established for this datagram.

0	1	2	3	4	5	6	7
Precedence				TOS			not used

Figure 5-10 New Precedence/TOS octet

The TOS field (bits 3-6) identifies for routers the criteria the router should use when making routing decisions for this datagram. The TOS criteria are delay, cost, reliability, and throughput.

The last field (bit 7) is not currently used in normal network operations. It is normally set to zero. The usage of this bit is confined to internet experimentation.

Precedence Field

The precedence field of the TOS octet consists of three bits. As previously explained, the three bits comprise a binary integer value. Each value has a unique meaning. Table 5-2 lists the meaning of each precedence value. The default value is 000 (routine) and should be used most often.

Table 5-2 Precedence values

Bits	Meaning
000	routine
001	priority
010	immediate
011	flash
100	flash override
101	CRITIC/ECP
110	internetwork control
111	network control

The precedence values are more or less self explanatory. As the numerical value of the precedence value increases from 000, so does the import of the datagram. The datagram with the highest precedence is 111. There are all kinds of scenarios that make use of precedence from the military wanting its data to pass before any others, to businesses that demand priority for their traffic. There is much room for abuse here and the network manager who sends all of his traffic "routine" can probably be assured his data sits and waits at the gateways. Policing the use of the precedence functionality by limiting how many datagrams per minute/hour/day/week/month a user can send at any particular precedence level will become a necessity before too many moons pass.

TOS Field

The four bits of the TOS field represent binary integer values, rather than individual bits that are set or reset to indicate a particular TOS parameter.

Table 5-3 TOS values

Value	Meaning
0000	normal service
0001	minimize cost
0010	maximize reliability
0011	not used
0100	maximize throughput
0101	not used
0110	not used
0111	not used
1000	minimize delay
1001	not used
1010	not used
1011	not used
1100	not used
1101	not used
1110	not used
1111	not used

Table 5-3 lists the TOS values and their intended meaning. The TOS value of 0000 is the default TOS value and should be used unless there is compelling reason to use another value. The unused values are legal TOS values and may be assigned a particular meaning in the future.

"Minimize" and "maximize" in the TOS meanings are not concrete terms but are relative to the ability of any individual router to make decisions concerning the appropriate path based upon the TOS value. Routers most often do not have full and complete knowledge of the interconnecting networks. Additionally, routers do not have real-time knowledge of the status of the networks known to the router. So, while the TOS values have a meaning, the meaning is relative only with respect to the current knowledge the router has of the known networks. Minimize cost means the router, at the moment it makes its routing decision, will attempt to route the packet along the route it has knowledge of that is of minimum cost. In fact, the route might not be the lowest cost route available at all. Routers attempt to choose paths based upon their often imperfect knowledge of the paths available to them.

There are no laws governing when and for what purpose each TOS value is used. However, there are some rules of thumb concerning the assignment of TOS values that should provide the network manager with a little better network performance. Applications that deal with network management including diagnostics should use the maximize reliability TOS value. Obviously, the network will not function as smooth if the management of it is problematic. Applications that ship around huge amounts of data should choose a maximize throughput TOS unless cost is of significant concern. If cost is the primary consideration, then, of course, minimize cost should be the TOS selected. If the application involves direct human participation, such as a text echo mode, the TOS value of interest is minimize delay.

Table 5-4 TOS values for specific protocols

Protocol	TOS Value	Meaning
BOOTP	0000	default
DNS UDP Query	1000	minimize delay
DNS TCP Query	0000	default
EGP	0000	default
FTP Control	1000	minimize delay
FTP Data	0100	maximize throughput
ICMP Errors	0000	default
ICMP Requests	0000	default
ICMP Responses	0000	default
NNTP	0001	minimize monetary cost
SMTP Command	1000	minimize delay
SMTP Data	0100	maximize throughput
SNMP	0010	maximize reliability
TELNET	1000	minimize delay
TFTP	1000	minimize delay
Zone Transfer	0100	maximize throughput
Any IGP	0010	maximize reliability

RFC 791 recommends the TOS values for the services identified in Table 5-4. The bottom line is each network manager must set the values to get the best performance out of the network. Most likely, the settings will require some trial and error if the network is to perform at its optimum efficiency.

The Old Way

RFC 791 changed the definition of the TOS octet. Figure 5-11 shows the values and meanings of the old TOS octet.

Value	0	1	2	3	4	5	6	7
0		precedence		normal delay	normal throughput	normal reliability	reserved (always low)	
1				low delay	high throughput	normal reliability		

Figure 5-11 The old TOS octet

Previous to RFC 791, each individual bit of the TOS octet could assume a unique value and meaning. RFC changed the interpretation of the octet to discrete binary integer values with a defined meaning for each value. Before, a user could test the TOS octet by determining if a bit was set or reset for a specified meaning. Now, the user must interpret each group of bits (precedence or TOS fields) as numerical values. While the interpretation of each bit as a unique meaning is history, the information is provided here because routers installed in networks prior to the issuance of RFC 791 will use the old interpretation of the precedence and TOS fields.

Choosing the TOS

The user process requests the transport protocol (TCP in this case) to utilize a specific TOS. Neither TCP nor IP require both ends of the connection to use the same TOS value. A transport protocol might be designed to discover the sending IP's TOS value and utilize the same value in its TOS field. Or a protocol might be designed to change TOS values as appropriate while the socket is still hot (connected). A user process that transmits large amounts of data periodically interrupted by small housekeeping packets might go for a maximize throughput with the bulk data packets and minimize delay for the housekeeping packets. Of course, switching TOS values in this manner will most likely invalidate the round trip time estimates used to determine the Time to Live value.

The Assigned Numbers document (RFC 2000) lists the TOS values that are used by a number of common applications. For any other applications, user processes are responsible for choosing the desired TOS values for any traffic originated by the user process. The designer of the user application should assign suitable values based upon the network design criteria reflecting application, system, and business objectives. A desired application feature is the ability to override the default TOS and assign any other TOS as the need may arise. Network traffic diagnostic programs especially must have the ability to assign TOS values on the fly (while the socket is connected) to be able to perform appropriate diagnostic functions. If the ability to change the TOS value while the socket is connected is not a feature of the application, then only the default TOS should be used by the application.

Length Field

The Length field is 16 bits. It is the total length of the datagram, measured in octets (8-bit increments), including the IP header and the TCP header and data. This field provides for datagrams to be up to 65,535 octets long. Aspiring network managers will not make use of the maximum total length! Imagine the blockage of the internetwork intestines if network managers made use of the maximum length! A practical length that yields good efficiency is something in the neighborhood of 1,200 octets of data for bulk data transfers. The network manager can use a little trial and error adjusting the Length field to fine tune the network's performance. The IP RFC recommends all hosts be prepared to receive 576 (512 data octets and 64 header octets) octets, which implies the preferred transmit size is 576 octets.

Identification Field

The Identification bit field is 16 bits. Identification is a value assigned by the sending IP to assist in assembling the fragments of a datagram. Each fragment that contains the same Identification field value will be reassembled in the correct order.

Flags Field

The Flags bit field, shown in Figure 5-12, is three bits and identifies the control flags status.

value	0	1	2
0	reserved	may fragment	last fragment
1	not allowed	cannot fragment	more fragments

Figure 5-12 Flags bit field

Bit zero is reserved for future use.

Bit 1 is used to identify when fragmentation of data is allowed. Fragmentation may be necessary to pass through a gateway and travel through the next hop. However, fragmentation is not always a good thing. In real-time audio and video applications, fragmentation most likely will destroy the timing relationship of the original signal, resulting in incoherent audio and distorted video.

Bit 2 is used to identify the last fragment if the original datagram was fragmented anywhere along the road to its destination. The flag determines when an IP should cease looking for more fragments of the original datagram and start reassembling the pieces into the original.

Fragment Offset Field

The Fragment Offset bit field is 13 bits. The Fragment Offset indicates where in the original datagram this fragment belongs. The Fragment Offset is measured in units of 8 octets (64 bits). If the datagram is not fragmented, the Fragment Offset is always equal to zero. Also, the first fragment always has a Fragment Offset equal to zero.

Time to Live Field

The Time to Live bit field is 8 bits. The Time to Live field specifies the maximum time the datagram is allowed to remain in transit in the internetwork. If the Time to Live value is zero, then the datagram must be destroyed. The IP header processing performed by every network router and gateway recalculates this value and modifies it as appropriate. However, if the value decreases to zero (or below), the router or gateway will immediately destroy the datagram. The Time to Live value represents time measured in units of seconds. There is a requirement imposed on routers and gateways to decrement this value by a minimum of one when the header is processed. What if the transit time from source to this gateway was only 250 milliseconds? It still must be decremented by one full second. So the value really represents a limitation that is loosely associated with time. If the datagram passes through 63 gateways (not conceivable just a year or two ago but very possible today) in less than 64 seconds the datagram will still be dropped by the 64th gateway, as it will zero out the value. So, the field really represents a limitation on the life of a datagram imposed by the combination of time and number of gateways the datagram is allowed to pass through. This limitation on the life of a datagram generates some interesting network analysis and design issues rendered pressing as networks continue to grow exponentially. The upper bound on the life of datagrams may become a stumbling block to TCP/IP usage.

Every network manager should be aware of the number of dropped packets occurring on the network links. The number of dropped packets is an excellent measurement of the real-time health of the network. The IP RFC currently recommends a default Time to Live of 64. The savvy network manager will use the faithful trial and error method to determine the optimum value for his network.

Protocol Field

The Protocol bit field is 8 bits. The Protocol field identifies the next level protocol (transport layer) used in the data segment portion of the IP datagram. The Protocol field can identify 256 ($2^8=256$) different protocols. There are not, however, 256 protocols used. Most of the values are unassigned, such as the block of values from 101 to 254. Table 5-5 is a partial listing of the protocol numbers.

Table 5-5 Assigned transport layer protocol numbers for IP header

Bit Value	Internetwork Protocol Acronym	Internetwork Transport Layer Protocol
0		Reserved
1	ICMP	Internet Control Message Protocol
2	IGMP	Internet Group Management Protocol
3	GGP	Gateway-to-Gateway Protocol
4	IP	IP in IP (encapsulation)
5	ST	Stream
6	TCP	Transmission Control Protocol
7	UCL	UCL
8	EGP	Exterior Gateway Protocol
9	IGP	any private interior gateway protocol
10	BBN-RCC-MON	BBN RCC Monitoring
11	NVP-II	Network Voice Protocol
12	PUP	PUP
13	ARGUS	ARGUS
14	EMCON	EMCON
15	XNET	Cross Net Debugger
16	CHAOS	Chaos
17	UDP	User Datagram Protocol

Header Checksum Field

The Header Checksum bit field is 16 bits. This checksum is calculated on the IP header only. Since some header fields change at each point that the internet header is processed, the header checksum is recomputed and verified at each processing point.

The IP RFC recommends the following algorithm be employed by all devices (hosts, routers, gateways, etc.) to calculate the header checksum:

"The checksum field is the 16-bit one's complement of the one's complement sum of all 16-bit words in the header. For purposes of computing the checksum, the value of the checksum field is zero.

"This is a simple to compute checksum and experimental evidence indicates it is adequate, but it is provisional and may be replaced by a CRC procedure, depending on further experience."

The following example demonstrates the header checksum calculation in action. The example, intended only to illustrate the process, is representative of the way the procedure works and does not actually use IP header values.

Table 5-6 shows the first 16-bit value to be complemented. To complement a bit, just take the inverse value. Replace ones with zeros and replace zeros with ones.

Table 5-6 The first value and its one's complement

Bit	0	1	2	3	4	5	6	7	8	9	10	11	12	13	14	15
First value	1	1	1	1	1	0	0	1	1	0	0	1	1	0	0	0
One's comp	0	0	0	0	0	1	1	0	0	1	1	0	0	1	1	1

Table 5-7 shows the second 16-bit value to be complemented and its one's complement.

Table 5-7 The second value and its one's complement

Bit	0	1	2	3	4	5	6	7	8	9	10	11	12	13	14	15
Second value	1	0	0	1	1	1	0	0	0	1	1	0	0	1	0	0
One's comp	0	1	1	0	0	0	1	1	1	0	0	1	1	0	1	1

Now, we add the one's complement of the two data values. The result is shown in Table 5-8.

Table 5-8 The sum of the one's complement

Bit	0	1	2	3	4	5	6	7	8	9	10	11	12	13	14	15
One's comp	0	0	0	0	0	1	1	0	0	1	1	0	0	1	1	1
One's comp	0	1	1	0	0	0	1	1	1	0	0	1	1	0	1	1
Add	0	1	1	0	1	0	1	0	0	0	0	0	0	0	1	0

The last step is to take the one's complement of the one's complement sum, which is calculated in Table 5-9.

Table 5-9 One's complement of the one's complement sum

Bit	0	1	2	3	4	5	6	7	8	9	10	11	12	13	14	15
Sum of one's	0	1	1	0	1	0	1	0	0	0	0	0	0	0	1	0
One's comp	1	0	0	1	0	1	0	1	1	1	1	1	1	1	0	1

See how easy it is? Even a Macintosh computer can do it!

Source Address Field

The Source Address bit field length is 32 bits. The source address identified the internet address of the data source.

Destination Address Field

The Destination Address bit field length is 32 bits. The destination address identifies the internet address of the intended destination of the data.

Options Field

The Options bit field is either one octet or four octets in length. It may or may not be present in a datagram. If the Options field is used it must be used by all hosts and gateways in the network. The transmission of options in any particular datagram may be optional itself. In some networks the transmission of options in every datagram may be mandatory. In military environments, the transmission of the security option may be mandatory. However, the implementation of options is not optional; if they are present, they must be utilized.

An option may be formatted in one of two ways—a single octet of option type or an option type octet, an option length octet, and two option data octets. For the latter case, the option length octet counts the option type octet and the option length octet as well as the option data octets.

The option type octet has three bit fields. Figure 5-13 shows the arrangement of these fields. Bit 0 is the Copy flag, bits 1-2 are the Option Class bits, and bits 3-7 are the Option Number bits.

bit	0	1	2	3	4	5	6	7
meaning	copy	option class				option number		

Figure 5-13 Options bit field

The Copy bit, also called the Copy flag, specifies if this option must be copied onto all fragments when the datagram is fragmented. Table 5-10 shows the possible states and the meaning of the Copy bit.

Table 5-10 Copy bit field

Bit Value	Meaning
0	do not copy
I	copy

The Option Class bit field states and meanings are shown in Table 5-11. The control class (00) is used by network management applications. The debug and measurement class (10) is used by diagnostic programs to troubleshoot and verify network status. Classes 1 and 3 are reserved for future use.

Table 5-11 Option Class bit field

Field Value	Decimal Value	Meaning
00	0	control
01	1	reserved
10	2	debug and measurement
11	3	reserved

The Option Number field describes the option carried in the IP header. See Table 5-12. Of particular interest are the LSR, SSR, RR, and TS options. The LSR option, option field = 3, requires all routing devices along the route to choose what it believes to be the optimum path to the destination. The SSR option, option field = 9, requires all routing devices along the route to route the packet to the next address specified in the packet. SSR may result in packets being dropped because the specified route is not achievable. RR requires each routing device to record its address in the packet. TS requires each routing device to include the time the packet transited the device in the packet. These options are useful if a user wishes to select a specific route from source to destination, to discover an unknown route, or to discover the transit times from source to destination. They are very valuable network management tools.

Table 5-12 Option Number field values

Copy Field no=0 yes=1	Option Class Field	Option Number Field	Decimal Option Number	Name
0	0	0	0	EOOL—End of Option List
0	0	1	1	NOP—No Operation
1	0	2	130	SEC—Security
1	0	3	131	LSR—Loose Source Route
0	2	4	68	TS—Time Stamp
1	0	5	133	E-SEC—Extended Security
1	0	6	134	CIPSO—Commercial Security
0	0	7	7	RR—Record Route
1	0	8	136	SID—Stream ID
1	0	9	137	SSR—Strict Source Route
0	0	10	10	ZSU—Experimental Measurement

Table 5-12 (cont.) Option Number field values

Copy Field no=0 yes=1	Option Class Field	Option Number Field	Decimal Option Number	Name
0	0	11	11	MTUP—MTU Probe
0	0	12	12	MTUR—MTU Reply
1	2	13	205	FINN—Experimental Flow Control
1	0	14	142	VISA—Experimental Access Control
0	0	15	15	ENCODE
1	0	16	144	IMITD—IMI Traffic Descriptor
1	0	17	145	EIP
0	2	18	82	TR—Traceroute
1	0	19	147	ADDEXT—Address Extension

End of Option List

End of Option List (EOOL) is a Class 0 option with no length value. It is only 1 octet long. End of Option List specifies this is the end of the option list. The end of the option list does not necessarily coincide with the end of the IP header as specified in the IP header length. The EOOL is used at the end of all options and is used only if the end of the options does not coincide with the end of the IP header. The EOOL may be copied, added, or deleted upon datagram fragmentation or for any other reason.

No Operation

No Operation (NOP) option is a Class 0 option with no length value. It is only 1 octet long and specifies this option does not perform any operation. The NOP may be used between options to align the beginning of a subsequent option on a 32-bit boundary. The NOP may be copied, added, or deleted upon datagram fragmentation or for any other reason.

Security

Security option is a Class 0 option with an 11-octet field length. The Security option identifies the Compartment, Closed User Group (transmission control code, or TCC), and Handling Restriction Code compatible with Department of Defense security requirements. The format for this option is shown in Figure 5-14.

8 bits	8 bits	16 bits	16 bits	16 bits	24 bits
10000010	00001011	security	compartment	handling restrictions	transmission control code

Figure 5-14 Security bit field

The Security subfield of the Security option, shown in Table 5-13, specifies one of 16 levels of security. Eight of these security levels are reserved for future use.

Table 5-13 Security subfield values

Bit Value	Meaning
0000000000000000	Unclassified
1111000100110101	Confidential
0111100010011010	EFTO
1011110001001101	MMMM
0101111000100110	PROG
1010111100010011	Restricted
1101011110001000	Secret
0110101111000101	Top Secret
0011010111100010	Reserved for future use
1001101011110001	Reserved for future use
0100110101111000	Reserved for future use
0010010010111101	Reserved for future use
0001001101011110	Reserved for future use
1000100110101111	Reserved for future use
1100010011010110	Reserved for future use
1110001001101011	Reserved for future use

The Compartment field is 16 bits. It is zero when the data is not compartmented. The values used for compartment data may be obtained from the Defense Intelligence Agency, Israeli intelligence agencies, or by hacking.

The Handling Restrictions field is 16 bits. The values for Handling Restrictions may be obtained from the Defense Intelligence Agency, Israeli intelligence agencies, or by hacking.

The Transmission Control Code (TCC) field is 24 bits. The TCC is used to segregate users with common interests into groups.

The values for TCC may be obtained from the Defense Intelligence Agency, Israeli intelligence agencies, or by hacking. The TCC cannot be copied upon datagram fragmentation. This option appears at most once in a datagram.

Loose Source and Record Route

Loose Source and Record Route Option (LSRR) is a Class 0 option with a variable length value. It is used to route the IP datagram based on information supplied by the source. Loose routing allows routers to decide the path the datagram should take through the network to reach the intended destination.

Table 5-14 LSRR bit field

1st octet	2nd octet	3rd octet	4th –6th octets
10000011	length	pointer	route info

The LSRR option provides a way for the source of an internet datagram to supply routing information to be used by the gateways in forwarding the datagram to the destination and to record information about the actual route taken.

The first octet of the LSRR option is the LSRR option type code. The second octet is the option length, which includes the option type code and the length octet, the pointer octet, and three octets of route information. The third octet is the pointer into the route information indicating the octet that begins the next source address to be processed. The pointer origin is the beginning of the LSRR, making 4 the smallest valid value for the pointer.

The procedure for recording the route consists of replacing the source route addresses with the recorded route addresses at the appropriate points along the route. Route information is composed of a series of IP addresses. Each internet address is 32 bits (4 octets). If the pointer is greater than the length, the source route is empty, the recorded route is full, and any additional routing is to be based on the destination address field. Here is how the IP records the route addresses along the way when the packet reaches the destination address: If the pointer value is not greater than the length value, the IP replaces the IP header destination address with the next address in the source route field. The source route address just moved to the IP destination address field is replaced by this destination's address and the pointer value is incremented by four.

The recorded route address is the IP module's own local internet address as known in the LAN/WAN environment into which the datagram is being transported. The LSSR option must be copied upon IP datagram fragmentation.

Strict Source and Record Route

Strict Source Record Route (SSRR) option is a Class 0 option with a variable length value. It is used to route the IP datagram based on information supplied by the source. Strict routing requires routers to follow the routing as specified in the datagram without deviation. The SSRR provides for the datagram to record the route taken. The structure the SSRR option is identical to the LSRR option structure. The process of recording the route taken is the same as described in the LSRR option.

Table 5-15 SSRR bit field

1st octet	2nd octet	3rd octet	4th –6th octets
10001001	length	pointer	route info

The LSRR option must be copied upon IP datagram fragmentation.

Record Route

Record Route (RR) option is a Class 0 option with a variable length value. The RR is used to trace and record the route an IP datagram takes from source to destination. The RR is identical to the LSRR and SSRR except no routing specifics are provided to guide the datagram through the network. The RR just records wherever the datagram goes.

Table 5-16 Route Record bit field

1st octet	2nd octet	3rd octet	4th –6th octets
00000111	length	pointer	route info

The source host must compose this option with a sufficiently large enough route address header area to hold all the anticipated addresses. The size of the option does not change due to adding addresses. The initial contents of the area reserved for the route addresses must be zero. When any IP module routes a datagram, the IP module tests for the presence of the record route option. If the RR option is present, the IP module inserts its own internet address into the header area reserved for recording route addresses. The address the IP module inserts is the address of the IP module in the LAN/WAN environment into which this datagram is routed. The IP module inserts the address into the reserved route address area beginning at the octet specified by the pointer. Then the IP module increments the pointer by four.

If the route address area is full (the pointer exceeds the length), the IP datagram is forwarded on to the next hop in the network without inserting the address of the current router. The IP module tests for a full address area by determining if the pointer exceeds the length. If the pointer value is less than the length value, the route address area is not yet full. If there is some room but not enough room for a full address to be inserted, the original datagram is considered to be in error and is discarded. In either case, an ICMP parameter problem message may be sent to the source host.

The Record Route bit field is copied on fragmentation into the first fragment only. The bit field appears at most only once in a datagram.

Stream Identifier

The Stream ID Option is a Class 0 option with a length of 8 bits. The Stream ID, shown in Table 5-17, is used to carry the stream identifier.

Table 5-17 Stream ID bit field

1st octet	2nd octet	3rd octet
10001000	00000010	Stream ID

The Stream ID option is specifically included in the IP datagram to accommodate the SATNET stream identifier. The Stream ID must be copied upon IP datagram fragmentation.

Internet Time-stamp

The Internet Time-stamp is a Class 2 option with a variable length field. When the Time-stamp option is used, the host generating the option must create a sufficiently large time-stamp data area to hold all of the expected time-stamps, since the time-stamp data area is fixed when it is created and does not get any larger when time-stamp additions are made. The user may have to do a little guesstimating to determine the right size for the specific connection of interest. When the time-stamp data area is created the originating host must set all time-stamp values to zero.

The Time-stamp bit field is right-justified, meaning the least significant bit is on the right. The 32-bit time-stamp value is measured in milliseconds since midnight Greenwich Meridian Time (GMT), also known as Universal Time (UT). Any time value can be used for the time-stamp if the time is not available in milliseconds or from GMT. If a time value other than GMT in milliseconds after midnight is used, the most significant bit (the high-order bit) of the time-stamp field is set to 1 to indicate the use of a non-standard time value.

When the time-stamp pointer exceeds the length value, the data area is full. If the data area is full, the datagram must be forwarded to the next router without inserting a time-stamp. In this case, the overflow count is incremented by one. If the available time-stamp area is more than zero octets but less than four, the datagram is considered corrupted and the router will discard it. The time-stamp option is not copied whenever the datagram is fragmented.

Table 5-18 Internet Time-stamp bit field

1st octet	2nd octet	3rd octet	4th octet	5th octet	6th octet
01000100	length	pointer	overflow (4 bits) flag (4 bits)	internet address	time-stamp

The internet address and time-stamp bit areas are shown, for simplicity, as single octet quantities. However, the originating host can increase the size of the two bit fields to any size necessary to include all addresses and time-stamps expected between source and destination. The two bit fields should always be the same size—if there is a time-stamp, there should be an address, and if there is an address, there should be a time-stamp.

The Time-stamp option length bit field value is the number of octets in the time-stamp option counting the type, length, pointer, and overflow/flag octets. The Time-stamp option length is a maximum of 40 octets.

The Time-stamp pointer is the number of octets from the beginning of the current Time-stamp option to the end of the last time-stamp octet plus one more. The Time-stamp pointer points to the beginning octet of the next Time-stamp option. The smallest valid value is 5 octets. The Time-stamp space is full when the Time-stamp pointer is greater than the length.

The Time-stamp overflow (4 bits) bit field represents the number of IP modules that cannot register time-stamps due to lack of space.

The Time-stamp flag (4 bits) values are defined as:

Table 5-19 Time-stamp flag bit field

Flag Value	Meaning
0	Time-stamps only are stored in consecutive 32-bit words
1	Each time-stamp is preceded with the internet address of the host registering the time-stamp
3	Internet address fields are prescribed and packet must follow prescribed route

If the Time-stamp flag value is 0, the time-stamp bit field contains only time-stamps. Time-stamps are stored in consecutive 32-bit words.

If the Time-stamp flag value is 1, then each time-stamp value is preceded by the IP address, in the fourth octet, of the module adding the time-stamp, in the fifth octet.

If the Time-Stamp flag value is 3, the IP address fields are prescribed in the fourth octet. An IP module will register its time-stamp if it matches its address with the next listed IP address (fourth octet) the pointer (third octet) is pointing to.

Padding Field

The IP header Padding field is a variable length bit field always set to zero. The Padding length is set to ensure the IP header ends on a 32-bit boundary.

Relation to Other Protocols

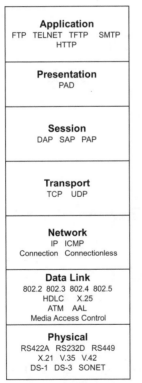

Figure 5-15 illustrates the place of the internet protocol in the networking protocol hierarchy.

Internet protocol interfaces on the higher level to a transport layer protocol. The transport layer protocol of interest to us is the TCP. On the lower side of the protocol hierarchy, IP interfaces to the data link layer. Data link layers are not covered in this book. Of course, the data link layers are intimately connected to a local network or WAN gateway.

Figure 5-15 Protocol relationships

Theory of Operation

The purpose of the Internet Protocol is to transport datagrams through an interconnected set of networks, whether they are LANs, MANs, WANs, or GANs. IP accomplishes the task by passing the IP datagrams, called packets when transiting the physical medium in between IP modules, from one IP module to another IP module until the destination is reached. The IP modules reside in local hosts and network gateways in the system of interconnected networks. The IP datagrams, now called packets, are routed from one IP module to another through individual and disparate networks based on the local interpretation of the destination Internet address. Addressing is therefore of critical importance to the success of the IP protocol. Addressing is covered in detail in the next section.

Now is a good time to illustrate the process of getting data from one application on a local host to another application running on a remote host. Obviously, if two applications are running on the same host, there is no need for TCP/IP to communicate the data from application to application. The theory of operation for transmitting a TCP data segment from one application program to another is illustrated in the following steps:

Step 1	The application program prepares the data to be transported.
Step 2	The application program calls the TCP module and passes the data and destination address.
Step 3	TCP prepares data segment.
Step 4	TCP prepares header.
Step 5	TCP attaches TCP header creating TCP segment.
Step 6	TCP calls IP and passes destination address and parameters.
Step 7	IP prepares header.
Step 8	IP attaches header to TCP segment, creating IP datagram.
Step 9	IP determines the local network address from destination address.
Step 10	IP calls data link layer, which is the local network interface.
Step 11	Local network interface creates a local network header.
Step 12	Local network interface attaches IP datagram to header, creating the network packet.
Step 13	Local network interface physically transmits packet onto network physical medium.

Step 14	Packet arrives at local network interface destination.
Step 15	Local network interface compares destination address to its address to verify it is intended destination.
Step 16	Local network interface removes local network header.
Step 17	Local network interface calls IP module and passes IP datagram to it.
Step 18	IP module receives datagram.
Step 19	IP checks to see if the destination address is this IP module.
Step 20	IP module decrements Time-to-Live value, discarding the datagram if less than zero, or continuing processing if the Time-to-Live is greater than zero.
Step 21	IP module calculates checksum and compares to IP header checksum.
Step 22	If calculated checksum is equal to header checksum, datagram continues processing.
Step 23	If calculated checksum does not equal header checksum, datagram is dropped.
Step 24	If this IP module is the final destination, IP module calls the transport layer protocol (TCP in our case) and passes the datagram to the TCP. Go to Step 26.
Step 25	Return to step 7.
Step 26	IP removes its header.
Step 27	IP calls the TCP module and passes the data segment.
Step 28	TCP module checks for such things as authorized access, valid sequence numbers, valid acknowledgment numbers, etc.
Step 29	If the data segment fails any TCP tests, it is dropped.
Step 30	TCP verifies all fragmented segments are available and reassembles the data into original segment. If any fragmented segments are missing, TCP sends the data fragments to a buffer to await the arrival of any additional fragments.
Step 31	If the data segment passes all TCP tests, TCP calls its application program and passes the data segment to it.

Addressing

Anyone with an Internet account is probably somewhat familiar with the use of Internet names and may be aware of the conventions used. To inform the rest of us, we will conduct a short discussion of the topic. Names are easier for humans to remember than long lists of lengthy numbers. How many names do you know and how many telephone numbers have you memorized? If you are like the majority of us, you may have hundreds, even thousands, of names memorized, but pitifully few telephone numbers, say maybe less than 25. Why? I don't know, other than to say it is easier for me to remember Jane Doe than it is to remember 888-591-7284 (Jane Doe's phone number).

The Internet consists of hundreds of thousands of hosts, each identified by an 11-digit number. Does anyone want to try to remember all the 11-digit numbers necessary to conduct their affairs over the Internet? Probably not. So, to make it easier for us humans to use the Internet, the Internet provides for the use of domain names. What is a domain name? Well, my e-mail address is mbusby@airmail.net. "airmail.net" is a domain name. "airmail.net" is a lot easier to remember than trying to remember "206.138.231.13." Names are used at the application/user interface to make it easier for us humans to understand who we are trying to conduct some type of discourse with.

While names are important in the machine/human interface, the machine/machine interface works much more efficiently when dealing with numbers. Numbers are the machines' native tongue. So, the Internet deals primarily with numbered addresses. The "206.138.231.13" portion of my e-mail address is the actual Internet address of my ISP provider. The "mbusby" portion of my address just identifies me to my ISP. The "airmail.net" is the name of my Internet ISP. To summarize, a name specifies who (or what) is sought, while an address specifies where the sought-after thing is located.

Now to get from source to destination, the packet must pass over a route. A route specifies how to get from one location to another. Routers are physical electronic devices connecting network elements that maintain routing tables. There are two basic types of routers. One type of (older) router requires a human to determine the routes through the networks and to build and maintain routing tables in files accessible by the router. A newer type of router can dynamically and on the fly determine the valid routes it is connected to by broadcasting messages onto the network seeking other connected routers, receiving responses, and building/maintaining routing tables. Whether the router tables are maintained automatically or by human hands, specific routes to all known points must be identified.

So, we have a diverse set of addressing tools to get data from one (local) application to another (remote) application. The tools are names, Internet addresses, local network addresses, and routes. User applications must map names to Internet addresses. The Domain Name Server (DNS) helps applications accomplish the name conversion activity. The IP module maps Internet addresses to local network addresses. Local network routers or network gateways map local network addresses to routes. Figure 5-16 illustrates the steps from name to route in the process.

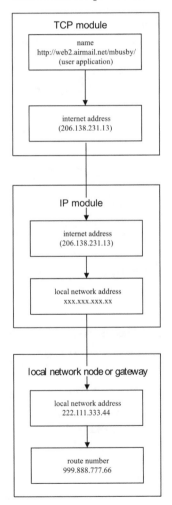

The Internet address bit field is fixed at 32 bits. An Internet address begins with a variable length network number, followed by a local address as shown in Figure 5-17.

Figure 5-16 IP address translation from name to route

address = 32 bits	
network number	local network address

Figure 5-17 Internet address bit field

There are two Internet addressing schemes in place today. One is a class-based scheme and the other is classless. The class-based scheme is the original Internet addressing scheme. Class-based addressing lumps all Internet addresses into one of five different classes, identified as Class A, B, C, D, and E. Classes A, B, and C addresses are used for unicast (single recipient) addresses. Class D addresses are used for multicast (multiple recipients) addresses. Class E addresses are reserved for future use.

The class-based method of assigning Internet addresses has three formats, as shown in Figure 5-18. For Class A format the left-most (high-order) bit is set to zero, the next 7 bits identify the network, and the last 24 bits identify the local address. In the Class B format, the two left-most bits are one and zero respectively, the next 14 bits identify the network, and the last 16 bits identify the local address. For the Class C format, the three left-most bits are one, one, and zero respectively, the next 21 bits identify the network and the last 8 bits identify the local address.

bit	0 1 2 3 4 5 6 7 8 9 1 1 1 1 1 1 1 1 1 1 2 2 2 2 2 2 2 2 2 2 3 3 0 1 2 3 4 5 6 7 8 9 0 1 2 3 4 5 6 7 8 9 0 1
class A	0	network address	local address
class B	1 0	network address	local address
class C	1 1 0	network address	local address
no class	1 1 1	classless addressing

Figure 5-18 Comparison of address classes

Some hosts may have several physical interfaces, usually identified by the number of network cards plugged into the host. Each physical interface will have at least one Internet address and could possibly have several.

The explosive growth of the Internet over the last five years has made obsolete some of the original TCP/IP design features. One such obsolete feature is class-based addressing. Due to the sheer volume of addresses in demand by users, 32-bit class-based addressing quickly became too restrictive. A means of addressing was needed that could work with the class-based addressing method and still allow for the assignment of any number of Internet addresses. The solution was a classless addressing scheme that allows the network portion of the address to be any length necessary. For now, the classless addressing scheme is undefined.

The following three reasons are given by the Internet community for the need for classless addressing. These reasons are quoted directly from RFC 1519.

1. Exhaustion of the class B network address space. One fundamental cause of this problem is the lack of a network class of a size that is appropriate for mid-sized organizations; class C, with a maximum of 254 host addresses, is too small, while class B, which allows up to 65,534 addresses, is too large for most organizations.

2. Growth of routing tables in Internet routers beyond the ability of current software, hardware, and people to effectively manage.

3. Eventual exhaustion of the 32-bit IP address space.

The class-based addressing scheme is still very much in use. At least eight companies producing networking products announced new IP-based "network tuners" in 1998. These "network tuners" can perform all the functions of a classic router and they can prioritize traffic based upon the network address class. So, while the old class-based addressing scheme will likely be around for another few years, the trend is to move away from classing the address.

As always, there are special cases that require special attention. Internet addressing is no exception. The following tables list the special network addressing cases.

Table 5-20 shows the address for "this host on this network." This address may only be used as a source address.

Table 5-20 "This host on this network"

Network Number	Host Number
0000000000000000	0000000000000000

Table 5-21 shows the address for the "specified host on this network." This address may only be used as a source address.

Table 5-21 "Specified host on this network"

Network Number	Host Number
0000000000000000	xxxxxxxxxxxxxxxx

Table 5-22 shows the address indicating limited broadcast. This address may only be used as a destination address, and a datagram with this address must never be forwarded outside the network of the source.

Table 5-22 Limited broadcast

Network Number	Host Number
IIIIIIIIIIIIIIII	IIIIIIIIIIIIIIII

Table 5-23 shows the address for a directed broadcast to the specified network, as identified by the network number. This address may only be used as a destination address.

Table 5-23 Directed broadcast to the specified network

Network Number	Host Number
xxxxxxxxxxxxxxxx	IIIIIIIIIIIIIIII

Table 5-24 shows the address for a directed broadcast to the specified subnet, as identified by the subnet number. This address may only be used as a destination address.

Table 5-24 Directed broadcast to the specified subnet

Network Number	Subnet Number	Host Number
xxxxxxxxxxxxxxxx	xxxxxxxx	IIIIIIII

Table 5-25 shows the address for a directed broadcast to all subnets of the specified network, as specified by the network number. This address may only be used as a destination address.

Table 5-25 Directed broadcast to all subnets

Network Number	Subnet Number	Host Number
xxxxxxxxxxxxxxxx	IIIIIIII	IIIIIIII

Table 5-26 shows the address for a host internal loopback address. This addressing mode is useful for testing and troubleshooting the host and should never be transported outside a host.

Table 5-26 Host internal loopback address

Network Number	Host Number
00000000IIIIIIII	xxxxxxxxxxxxxxxx

Fragmentation

IP datagram fragmentation is necessary when it originates in a local net that allows a large packet size and must traverse a local net that limits packets to a smaller size to reach its destination. The IP module acting as the gateway into the network requiring small size packets is responsible for fragmenting the datagram. However, the originating host can specify in the IP header whether or not to allow fragmentation. If the "don't fragment" flag is set (bit 2 of the IP header flags bit field) in an IP datagram and it encounters a gateway that requires a smaller size datagram, the gateway will drop the packet.

Fragmentation and reassembly that occurs outside of the internet protocol, such as the fragmentation and reassembly that may occur in a local net, or intranetwork, does not necessarily conform to any of the requirements for this internet protocol fragmentation and reassembly. The internet fragmentation and reassembly process must be able to fragment a datagram into any arbitrary number of datagrams, keeping in mind that certain minimum datagram sizes (1 octet of data minimum) are required. These datagram fragments must be capable of being reassembled when all the pieces arrive at the intended destination.

The destination IP module uses the fragment identification field to ensure that fragments of different datagrams are not mixed. The fragment offset field tells the destination IP module the position a fragment held in the original datagram. The fragment's position in the original datagram is determined by the offset and length values in the datagram containing the fragment. The IP module can determine whether or not any one fragmented datagram is the last one by testing the last fragment flag. If it is set, there are more fragments to come. This explanation assumes that all fragments travel through the internetwork along the exact same route and in order. Actually, since packets may take diverse routes through the internet to their intended destination, it is possible for the last fragment of a fragmented datagram to arrive at the destination before any other fragments. The "last fragment" flag just tells the IP module that the fragment carrying that flag goes on the end of the reconstructed datagram. The IP module identifies the original datagram fragments by the use of the identification, destination, source, and protocol fields of the IP header. The IP module can reconstruct the original datagram as soon as all the pieces are on hand (in the receive buffer), using the IP header fragment offset values.

Remember from the earlier fragmentation discussion that the Fragment Offset bit field is 13 bits, and the Fragment Offset indicates where in the original datagram this fragment belongs. If the datagram is not fragmented, the Fragment Offset is always equal to zero, and the first fragment always has a Fragment Offset equal to zero. With this information in hand, it is a reasonably simple matter to program a computer to keep track of fragments and where they belong in the original data bit stream.

The IP header Identification field is used to distinguish the fragments of different datagrams. The source IP module of a datagram sets the Identification field to a value that must be unique for the intended source-destination pair for the length of time the packet is a live packet in the internetwork.

Fragmentation of a large IP datagram by any IP module (for example, in a gateway) creates at least two new IP datagrams. Fragmentation cannot occur unless there are at least 9 octets of data, as the datagram is divided at 8-octet boundaries. So the first fragment must have any multiple of 8 octets of data for fragmentation to be enabled. Additional fragments must have at least 8 octets of data and must have integer multiples of 8 octets if they have more than 8, except for the last fragment which can have less than 8 octets of data. When a datagram is fragmented, the contents of the IP header fields are copied from the original datagram into each of the fragments.

When fragmentation occurs, the first set of data octets (any integer multiple of 8) from the original data bit field is inserted into the first new IP datagram, and the total length field is set to the length of this datagram. The "more fragments" flag is set to one to indicate at least one more datagram contains fragmented data. The Fragment Offset is set to the number of 8-octet groups of data in this fragment. Since there must be at least 8 octets of data in the first fragment, the Fragment Offset will always be at least one, if fragmentation occurred.

The next set of data octets from the original datagram is inserted into the second IP datagram and the total length field is set to the length of this second datagram. If this is the last of the data octets the "more fragments" flag is set to false; else it is set to true. The Fragment Offset field of the second IP datagram is set to the value of the fragment offset in the first fragment plus the number of octets in this datagram. And on and on and on... for however many fragments the data is divided into. The IP header fields that may be affected by fragmentation include: internet header length field, total length field, header checksum, options field, "more frag-ments" flag, and fragment offset.

The fragments of an IP datagram are assembled at the destination host by the IP module.

The IP module combines the IP datagrams having the same value for iden-tification, source, destination, and protocol header fields. The reassembly of the original datagram is accomplished by placing the data portion of each fragment in its correct position in the original datagram. The correct position is specified by the fragment offset in the fragment's IP header. The first fragment has a fragment offset of zero, and the last fragment has the "more fragments" flag set to false.

Gateways

Gateways, also called network access servers, are network routers that con-nect two or more networks together. Gateways utilize Internet Protocol to transport datagrams between networks, and also utilize the Gateway to Gateway Protocol (GGP) to coordinate routing and other internet control information. Gateways do not utilize higher level protocols above IP, so the GGP functions are added to the IP module.

Summary

IP is a software-based process for interfacing higher level protocols, such as PPTP, to the physical resources of a network-based system of intercon-nected computing devices for the purpose of transporting data from a source to a destination. IP is a robust software program that works very well for its intended purpose. IP has the ability to adapt to a changing pur-pose as the Internet blossoms, placing an ever-increasing burden on its ability to meet our evolving communications needs.

Chapter 6

Establishing and Closing the Connection

Questions answered in this chapter:

- How is a TCP connection established?

- What is the TCP handshake?

- How does the TCP transmit the data?

- How does the TCP receive the data?

- How does the TCP close the connection?

Introduction

Reliability (error checking) and flow control (sequencing) mechanisms need to know certain status information regarding each connection and its associated data stream. To meet this need, TCP must initialize and maintain the status information. The status information includes local host address, remote host address, and port number combined with the connection socket number, sequence number, and window size. This status information is maintained in the transmission control block (TCB) and is the actual "connection" between the two hosts. The remote host socket number and the local host socket number pair uniquely specify the connection between the two hosts.

Establishing the Connection or Socket

For any two processes to successfully communicate, the TCP of each host must establish the connection. The connection is established when each TCP initializes its TCB data structure containing the appropriate information concerning the connection. Connections are attempted, established, and torn down over a multitude of networks of varying distances using a variety of computing and transmission equipment. To ensure a reliable connection to an acceptable host, TCP uses a handshake mechanism to verify the connection request and to ensure the attempted connection is authorized. The handshake mechanism includes the use of sequence numbers that are time-based and the SYN (synchronize) control flag. TCP uses the handshake to garner information about the connection that is stored in the TCB. After completing the handshake, each TCP has a completed TCB structure.

A connection attempt occurs when one host transmits an active OPEN call to another host. When the datagram containing the SYN flag in the set condition is received by a host, it creates a TCB to record pertinent information about the connection. The receiving host then matches the local and remote sockets, thus initiating the connection. After the two hosts exchange sequence information and synchronize the sequence numbers, the connection is "established."

The Handshake

The method of establishing the TCP connection is usually called the *handshake*. It is known as a three-way handshake due to the number of times the two TCPs communicate during the handshake process. A three-way handshake is slightly more elaborate than a plain two-way handshake, but the three-way provides greater protection against the possibility of a false connection. While false connections may seem a rather mundane issue, it is a serious problem for servers connecting to hundreds or even thousands of users per day.

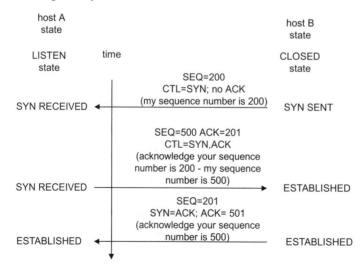

Figure 6-1 TCP connection setup—the handshake

Figure 6-1 illustrates the simple three-way handshake. The TCP of host B is in the CLOSED state. Upon prompting from the higher level process, it opens communication with TCP A, which is in the LISTEN state, by sending a segment with the CTL bit set to SYN (synchronize the sequence numbers). Host B is now in the SYN SENT state. Host A receives the request to connect (CTL=SYN) and immediately goes from the LISTEN state to the SYN RECEIVED state. Host A returns an acknowledgment of the request to connect segment received by setting the ACK value to the sequence number (201) received and by including its own sequence number (500) in the segment. When host B receives the return acknowledgment from host A, it immediately goes into the ESTABLISHED state and returns an acknowledgment (ACK=201) of host A's acknowledgment. As soon as host A receives host B's acknowledgment, host A changes to the ESTABLISHED state. Each host is aware of the other host's sequence numbering and can determine when a segment is received or not received, providing a fundamental cornerstone of the TCP reliability pyramid.

A note concerning the ESTABLISHED state. ESTABLISHED is the state where data communications may occur. When the connection is established, all valid segments must contain an acceptable acknowledgment of the reception of the previous data segment.

A send sequence number and a receive sequence number occupying the send sequence number space and the receive sequence number space, respectively, exist for every connection. The Initial Send Sequence number (ISS) is determined by the TCP initiating the connection. The Initial Receive Sequence number (IRS) is determined by the TCP receiving the connection request. Put another way, when you dial up your ISP, your computer generates the ISS while the ISP computer generates the IRS. For the connection request to succeed, the two TCPs must synchronize on the ISS and the IRS. (If only it were this easy in the dating game!)

This description of the way the connection is set up does not include such TCP features as windowing (flow control). Also, the above connection description assumes the connection will be completed without any problems such as might occur if one of the segments were lost in the maze of internets.

Post-handshake

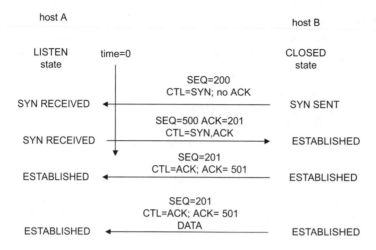

Figure 6-2 After the handshake

After the two TCPs have completed the handshake, they are ready to transport data across the network. Figure 6-2 shows the inclusion of the next segment after the handshake. This step shows the first data segment going from host B to host A. Notice that the sequence and acknowledgment numbers are the same as the last sequence and acknowledgments of the handshake. This is a crucial idea concerning TCP. The software is written so that each host knows the sequence number of the first data segment is the same as the sequence number of the last handshake acknowledgment segment. The duplicated sequence and acknowledgment numbers are necessary to prevent the TCP from going into an infinite loop acknowledging ACKs. For those who want to speed their TCP up, you can actually send data with the last acknowledgment of the handshake, since the connection/socket with the receiving TCP is established.

A common programming ploy dating from the 1960s is to send the text string "Hello World!" when initially checking a new computer program and/or data link. Don't ask: It's just one of those '60s things. In Figure 6-3, the transmission of the string "Hello World" from host B to Host A is illustrated. For instructional purposes only, we assume the string is divided into two text words that are transported sequentially. In reality, if echo character mode is on, each character is transported individually from host B to host A. If echo character mode is off, then perhaps all of the text string is transmitted at once, or maybe just a few characters. The number of characters transmitted in each packet depends upon the state of each host's receive and transmit buffers and is in the (good) hands of the TCP software.

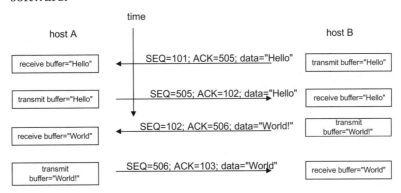

Figure 6-3 Data transmission

The figure does show host A echoing the data transmitted by host B. Data echoing may or may not occur, depending upon the desires of the users.

Reset

All manner of things can go wrong during the attempt to communicate over unreliable networks. Equipment can fail in any number of ways and places between a source and a destination. Acts of nature (mice eating wires/cables), acts of humans (uh-oh, shouldn't have pushed THAT button), and acts of God (lightning, hurricanes) work to give us communication links that can be very unreliable. Transporting data from point A to point B can be rife with uncertainty. TCP provides a means to cope with a lot of that uncertainty by using a Reset function designed to make sure two hosts are reading from the same page, same paragraph, and same sentence of the same book.

Every connection request should be prefaced with a request to Reset by the initiating TCP before the initiating TCP sends the request to connect. The purpose of the Reset request is to avoid confusion with old or duplicate connections. How could this occur? Well, if you are on the Internet and you get bounced off due to a physical medium failure somewhere in the network and you immediately attempt to reconnect, the server may still have an active TCB for your host and the particular service you are using. So, Reset clears the receiving host's TCB, allowing the sender to try again.

When a host receives a Reset, the receiving TCP returns to the LISTEN state if it is in the SYN SENT or SYN RECEIVED state. If the TCP is in ESTABLISHED, FIN WAIT 1, FIN WAIT 2, CLOSE WAIT, CLOSING, LAST ACK, or TIME WAIT state, the TCP aborts the connection (deletes the TCB) and informs its user process.

Reset should be used sparingly and only when it is clear from the state of the connection that it is necessary. Typically, a Reset should be returned to a remote host when a host receives a segment that does not fit in with the current state of the host.

Sending a Reset

Besides sending a Reset prior to requesting a connection, there are also times when a local TCP should return a Reset to a remote TCP. The following three situations always require a Reset to be returned to a remote TCP.

Situation 1

If the connection is CLOSED (does not exist—TCB is not present for the connection), the host sends a Reset in response to any incoming segment except another Reset. SYNs addressed to a nonexistent connection are rejected in this manner.

If the incoming segment has an ACK field, the Reset segment sequence number is taken from the ACK field of the segment. If the incoming segment does not have an ACK field, the Reset segment takes a sequence number of zero and the ACK field is set to the sum of the incoming segment sequence number and segment length. The local host keeps the connection in the CLOSED state.

Situation 2

If the connection is in LISTEN, SYN SENT, or SYN RECEIVED state and the incoming segment ACK field acknowledges a segment not yet transmitted, the local host issues a Reset.

The situation of one TCP sending a segment containing an acknowledgment of a segment never received is a critical situation. This situation occurs when two TCPs are no longer synchronized. Continued normal operation in this situation is impossible and the two TCPs must become synchronized again through the use of the Reset command.

The Reset takes its sequence number from the ACK field of the incoming segment with an incorrect ACK number. The connection remains in the same state it was in before the receipt of the incoming segment.

Situation 3

If the connection is in LISTEN, SYN SENT, or SYN RECEIVED state and the incoming segment has a security level, compartment, or precedence that does not match the security level, compartment, and precedence originally requested for the connection, a Reset is returned by the local host to the remote host. The connection reverts to the CLOSED state. The Reset segment sequence number is taken from the ACK field of the incoming segment.

Receiving a Reset

The receiving host of a Reset segment must first validate the Reset before changing state.

In every state except SYN SENT, a Reset segment is validated by checking its SEQ field. A Reset is valid if its sequence number is in the window of the receiving host. In the SYN SENT state, a Reset is received in response to an initial SYN that was sent. In this case, the Reset is valid if the ACK field acknowledges the SYN.

If the receiving TCP is in the LISTEN state, it ignores the Reset. If the receiving TCP is in the SYN RECEIVED state, the receiving TCP returns to the LISTEN state. If the receiving TCP is in any other state, the connection is aborted, the TCP advises the user process, and the TCP returns to the CLOSED state.

Data Transmission

After establishing a connection between two TCPs, data can be transported across that connection. Data transport, or communication, is accomplished by the two TCPs exchanging segments. When a TCP receives a data segment, it performs certain tests on the segment to determine its acceptability. Validating the segment as uncorrupted by its journey across the medium is the first order of business. The TCP will validate the segment by calculating and comparing the checksum. Checking the segment for a valid sequence number is the second important test. Next, the TCP must determine if the data segment will fit into its receive buffer window.

Afterwards, the TCP checks the acknowledgment number to determine if the other TCP received its last transmission.

The sending TCP tracks the next sequence number to use in the variable SND.NXT. The receiving TCP tracks the next sequence number to expect in the variable RCV.NXT.

The sending TCP tracks the oldest unacknowledged sequence number in the variable SND.UNA. If the connection becomes idle and all data sent has been acknowledged, the three variables, SND.NXT, RCV.NXT, and SND.UNA, will be equal. These variables are maintained in the TCB.

The sending TCP increments the TCB variable SND.NXT every time it sends a segment on down the road to the IP. When the receiving TCP accepts a segment it increments RCV.NXT and returns an acknowledgment segment to the sending TCP. The amount SND.NXT and RCV.NXT change is the number of data octets present in the segment.

When the original sending TCP receives the return acknowledgment, it increments its SND.UNA variable. The mathematical difference between SND.NXT and SND.UNA is a measure of the communication delay between the two TCPs.

An unacceptable segment is a segment received that contains a sequence number that is out of the receiving TCP's window or an acknowledgment number that is unacceptable. If a connection is in the ESTABLISHED, FIN WAIT 1, FIN WAIT 2, CLOSE WAIT, CLOSING, LAST ACK, or TIME WAIT state and an unacceptable segment is received, the receiving TCP returns to the other TCP a segment containing only an acknowledgment. The segment must also contain the current send sequence number and the correct acknowledgment number of the next sequence number expected. The connection does not change state.

Retransmission Timeout

Retransmission timeout is the time a TCP should wait to receive an acknowledgment before resending a segment.

Retransmission timeout can be determined in a variety of ways. Perhaps the simplest way is to measure the time to receive an acknowledgment of a segment during various times of the day. Network load is variable over a 24-hour period. The busiest period, if some portion of the network is connected to the public switched telephone network, is Monday morning from 5 a.m. to 11 a.m. Central Standard Time. If the network is privately switched, the busiest time must be determined. Even in this case, Monday morning is the most likely candidate, unless your company is a financial management company, in which case Friday evenings might be the peak traffic period.

After measuring the time to get an acknowledgment, the time-out variable could be set to the measured time plus some safety factor, say two times the amount measured. To ensure the TCP connection is efficient, the data flow should be monitored to determine if the timeout is too low or too high. A timeout too low results in sending packets again before the other TCP has had a chance to acknowledge the original segment, resulting in a loop condition where one TCP is repeatedly acknowledging the same segment over and over. Setting the timeout too high may result in the TCPs' retransmission buffers growing too large, possibly even overflowing, as each TCP waits, and waits, and waits.... So, there is a trade-off that the network manager must evaluate: buffer space versus loop conditions.

The original TCP specification, RFC 791, includes a calculation to determine the appropriate time-out value. It is included here, with several corrected typos, for the curious:

"Measure the elapsed time between sending a data octet with a particular sequence number and receiving an acknowledgment that covers that sequence number (segments sent do not have to match segments received). This measured elapsed time is the Round Trip Time (RTT). Next compute a Smoothed Round Trip Time (SRTT) as:

$$SRTT = (ALPHA * RTT) + ((1 - ALPHA) * RTT)$$

and based on this, compute the retransmission timeout (RTO) as:

$$RTO = min[UBOUND, max[LBOUND,(BETA*SRTT)]]$$

where UBOUND is an upper bound on the timeout (e.g., 1 minute), LBOUND is a lower bound on the timeout (e.g., 1 second), ALPHA is a smoothing factor (e.g., .8 to .9), and BETA is a delay variance factor (e.g., 1.3 to 2.0)."

After all of the above is accomplished, there is still no guarantee that the RTO is a valid RTO. So much depends upon the network characteristics that the above calculation is not really useful except for very stable, constant bit rate networks. While some such networks exist, most network traffic is very variable from moment to moment, hour to hour, and even day to day.

Seems a lot easier to just multiply the measured two-way transmit time, determined during a network traffic peak, by a good fudge factor and "let it be." Of course, the good fudge factor must be acquired through some trial and error and good networking management by observing what is happening on the network.

Precedence and Security

TCP includes a mechanism for providing a degree of transmission security. This mechanism is of use to the Department of Defense where the level of security classification is indicated by the value. Security and precedence are intended to allow only connections between ports operating with identical security values or with the higher of the two precedence levels of the two ports if the two ports have differing security levels.

TCP also includes a mechanism for providing transmission precedence. Ever wonder why your home connection to the Internet is suddenly disconnected? Perhaps a business customer with a higher precedence just dialed into your ISP and the ISP needs your connection to service the higher precedence connection. Have you checked with your ISP to determine if it uses precedence? Would you be surprised to learn that businesses get precedence over personal user accounts? You shouldn't be, since businesses usually pay a higher fee for their connection. Connection attempts that have mismatched security or precedence values will be rejected. If precedence and security level are not set by the user, the TCP supplies default values.

Is the use of precedence and security important? Decidedly so, regardless of any one person's perspective of the equation. Right now, as this book is written, the U.S. Army is undergoing field trials of a battlefield management system at the Army corps level that makes extensive use of TCP/IP and internetworking. This battlefield management system is supposed to work so well that corps level efficiency will result in a reduced force of several thousands of troops per division. Can you imagine sitting in your office and instead of plugging into your favorite Internet service provider you get plugged into the Army's battlefield management system and now YOU can direct the troops? Much better than your favorite simulated computer game. This is the real stuff! Let us assume you are not an avid war game hound. Security and precedence are still issues of grave national concern. We don't want the captain to get precedence over the general unless the captain has something really important to communicate.

Of great concern not only to the military but also to business is the unauthorized access to privileged information. For the military, privileged information might be the state of the battlefield and status of individual units. Any commander worth his rank would love to have that information about his opponent. Business is concerned about access to corporate data including financial information, trade secrets, strategic plans, etc.

To prevent unauthorized access to privileged information, internetwork users erect "firewalls." The typical firewall approach to safeguarding sensitive data is the use of passwords. Passwords may use any number of character-based text and/or numerical values to try to befuddle the hacker intent on crashing into the system. This approach to network security generally requires the user to frequently change passwords in the mistaken belief that frequent password changes will keep the system free from unwanted intrusions. Any hacker with the time and patience can overcome any password-based system.

Another solution for network and data security is encryption. Unsophisticated hackers sitting for long hours at a PC in their attic (or basement or bedroom) and typing in typical passwords (names of children, birthdays, etc.) can eventually overcome the password-based system and get into the target network but they cannot decipher encrypted data if the encryption process is sophisticated encryption algorithm. However, sophisticated hackers sitting in expensive foreign government offices can, and routinely do, hack into networks and acquire sensitive information and/or destroy data. Deciphering encrypted data is relatively easy for these types of operations. And they are numerous. The best solution to network security is to keep all sensitive information on computing devices that are not connected via any networking to the outside world. Then access control involves controlling the physical access to the computing devices, a much easier situation to manage.

Of course, for the security attributes of TCP to be implemented, the higher level processes must be able to manage the security attributes. Higher level processes should specify who gets to connect to the socket and when. Otherwise, anyone can connect. When security is implemented, TCP only performs the initial check to verify authorized access. This is just a basic go/no-go test. Additional passcodes, such as those used by the U.S. military, may be necessary to protect especially sensitive information.

Basic Data Transfer

TCP is responsible for packaging the data stream received from the upper layer process into segments that have as the fundamental components a series of 8-bit data octets. Usually the upper layer data stream is also based upon some multiple of 8-bit data octets. But the upper layer data stream format is immaterial to the function of TCP. TCP considers the data received from the upper layer process as a bit stream. There is no concept of text, character, or record formatting of data. You could say all data are almost equal in the eyes of TCP, just binary ones and zeros.

TCP acts as the speed cop during the transmission between users. TCP accomplishes the speed cop duties by blocking or forwarding data segments to and from the IP as necessary to maintain the flow of data without overrunning the receive buffers at either user end of the connection.

When TCP sends a segment to the IP for transport across the medium, TCP attaches a sequence number and an acknowledgment number to the segment header. The combination of segment sequence and acknowledgment numbers serves to establish a reliable host-to-host connection between two user processes. UDP does not concern itself with such reliability features.

A sequence number uniquely identifies each TCP segment. All segments can be distinguishable from all other segments by its unique sequence number. The acknowledgment number is the value of the next expected sequence number. In other words, when a receiving TCP looks at the segment it will see a sequence number and an acknowledgment number that is equal to the sequence number plus one. Upon receiving a segment, the receiving TCP returns an "acknowledgment" segment back to the sending TCP with the sequence number equal to the acknowledgment number of the received segment, as shown in Figure 6-4.

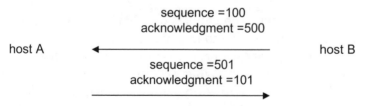

Figure 6-4 Reliable communications

When TCP sends a segment, it places a copy in a holding buffer and starts a time-out clock. If the TCP has not received an acknowledgment for a segment from the remote host before the time-out value, the TCP will resend the segment, again placing it back in the holding buffer and resetting the time-out clock. If an acknowledgment is received, TCP deletes the segment from the holding buffer.

PUSH

The PUSH function makes sure all the data received by the sending TCP from the upper layer process is transported to the remote host. The transmitting host sets the PUSH flag in the SEND call. A sending TCP can collect data from the upper layer process, sending the data to IP for transport when it is convenient. And the receiving TCP usually waits until the receive buffer is full before sending that data on to its upper layer process.

PUSH clears the data in the sending TCP buffer by pushing it all out to the IP, which must immediately package the data and place it on the data link layer for transport. The PUSH function appends a marker to the end of the data, so the receiving end has visibility that a PUSH occurred. The receiving TCP, upon receiving the segment with the PUSH flag set, immediately "pushes" that segment of data and any additional segments waiting in the receive buffer on to the upper layer process. What good is this?

In the beginning of time (circa late '60s), many different types of computers were (and still are) networked. These different computers operated at different speeds and had different size buffers for receiving and transmitting data. Since TCP causes the users to exchange buffer size information when the connection is first established, each user knows how much data can be sent before the receiver buffer overflows. This is called overflow control, which is one of the features of TCP that is lacking in UDP. The sending TCP buffer may be full because the receiving user's buffer is smaller and the receiving user's clock speed could be much slower than the transmitting end. So, there must be a traffic cop ready to make sure no one goes too fast.

Well, in the good old days when TCP/IP was primarily of use to the Department of Defense, buffers were large, data rates were slow in the hinterlands but reasonably fast at headquarters, and the high command wanted some assurance that if they needed to launch the BIG ONE, they could get the order off without waiting for some TCP buffer to clear. Or some such scenario. To put it in easy-to-understand terms, PUSH is the TCP laxative that flushes the system.

A locally issued call to close the connection (user CLOSE call) requires a PUSH call. All data in the sending buffer should be pushed out to the receiving TCP before the connection is closed.

Also, the reception of a segment with the FIN control flag set, indicating the remote TCP wants to close the connection, requires a PUSH call. All data in the local buffer should be pushed out to the receiving TCP before the connection is closed.

URGENT

The sending TCP has the ability to identify segments as "urgent," meaning the segments contain data that is of some special significance. When the sending TCP marks a segment as urgent, the sending TCP is telling the remote host that the data following the segment containing the Urgent flag is urgent. The idea is to give the receiving host time to prepare for the reception of the urgent data. The receiving host could then process all the current segments in the receive buffer, then wait for the urgent data. TCP itself does not take any particular action upon reception of the Urgent flag other than notifying the upper layer process of the flag reception. Rather, the receiving upper layer process must be able to specify what specific action must occur as a result of the urgent notification.

The sending TCP has the ability to identify to the receiving TCP the transmission of urgent data. TCP uses a "pointer" to identify the end of urgent data. The urgent mechanism uses an Urgent field in every segment. When the URG control flag is set, the receiving TCP understands the Urgent field is not empty or meaningless. The Urgent pointer is determined by adding the Urgent field value to the segment sequence number.

When the urgent pointer is ahead of the receive sequence number (RCV.NXT), the receiving TCP recognizes the data between the "pointer" and the receive sequence number as urgent and so notifies the higher level user process. When the urgent "pointer" and the receive sequence number are equal, TCP notifies the higher level user process of the end of urgent data. TCP makes no use of the urgent data and assumes the higher level user process makes productive use of the urgent data.

At least one data octet must be included in the segment for the Urgent field to be valid.

By combining the URGENT functionality with the PUSH function, data delivery to the end user process can be speeded up.

Segment Arrives

Now, we are in a position to diagram what happens when a segment arrives at a TCP/IP. The following flow charts describe the operations performed when a segment arrives and the TCP/IP is in the CLOSED state and when it is in the LISTEN state. The flow charts are self-explanatory (I think—but maybe not).

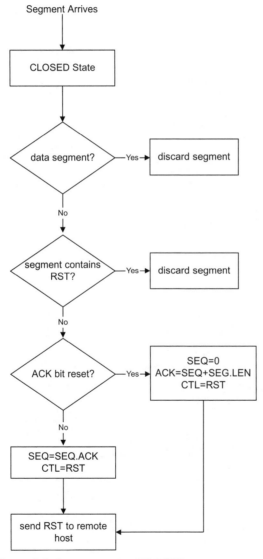

Figure 6-5 Segment arrives/CLOSED state

Figure 6-6
Segment
arrives/LISTEN
state

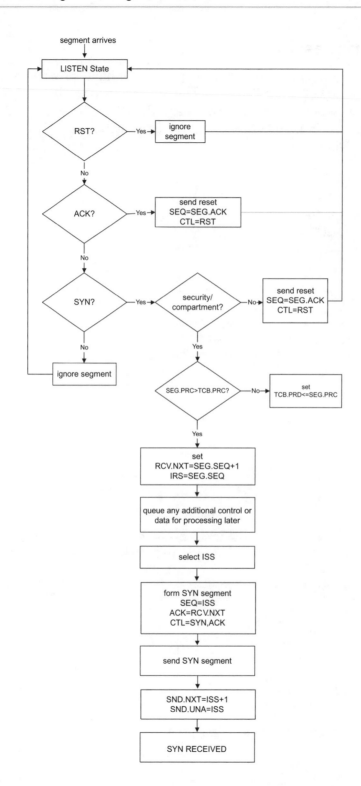

Closing a Connection

A connection is closed when either the source host or the destination host decides to terminate the communication. Closing a connection should be performed in an orderly manner so that both parties to the connection have the opportunity to gracefully terminate their underlying processes.

When a local user process initiates a CLOSE, the local host may continue receiving packets (stay in the RECEIVE status) until it receives a confirming CLOSE from the remote host. This is one of three possible scenarios for closing. Another scenario is when both hosts close simultaneously. The third closing scenario is when a host sends the remote host a FIN control signal. The three closing situations are summed up in the following figures.

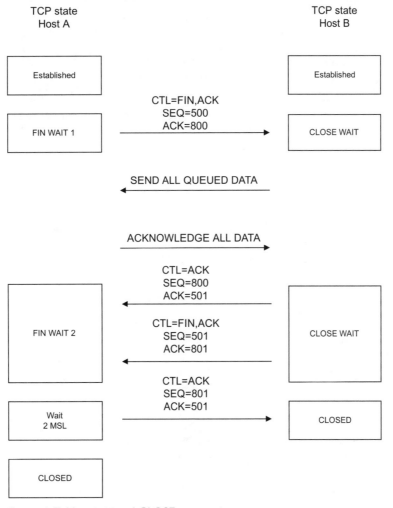

Figure 6-7 User-initiated CLOSE connection

Figure 6-7 illustrates the mechanism for managing a user process-initiated CLOSE connection request. In the user-initiated CLOSE connection request, the Host A user process sends a CLOSE request to its TCP. When the Host A TCP receives the CLOSE request, it places a FIN segment in the outgoing segment buffer and enters the FIN WAIT 1 state. At this point, the Host A TCP will not recognize any more SENDs initiated by the Host A user process. In the FIN WAIT 1 state, the Host A TCP may RECEIVE. If any previous segments are not acknowledged by Host B, including the FIN segment, the Host A TCP will retransmit the segments until acknowledged. The Host B TCP will RECEIVE the Host A FIN segment and will queue an ACK. In the meantime, all queued segments including ACKs are sent to Host A. Then, Host B will close its connection and send a FIN to Host A. Host A receives Host B's FIN and returns an ACK to Host B. When Host B receives the FIN ACK from Host A, it completes the CLOSE process by actually closing, or deleting, the connection.

As you may discern from the user-initiated CLOSE connection scenario, CLOSE does not really mean close in that the connection is disabled immediately. CLOSE state is the state of not accepting SEND segments from the user process anymore. The connection is closed when both TCPs have deleted the connection information. Remember the connection information is stored in a connection record called the TCB.

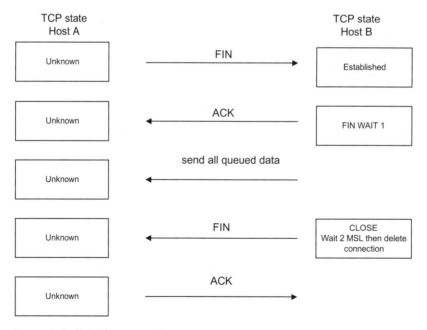

Figure 6-8 CLOSE source unknown

When a FIN of unknown origin arrives at Host B, the Host B TCP will ACK the FIN and inform its user process the connection is closing. This process is illustrated in Figure 6-8. The Host B user process will send a CLOSE request to its TCP and enter the CLOSE state. The Host B TCP now sends all queued data followed by a FIN to the Host A TCP. The Host B TCP now waits two MSLs (maximum segment lifetimes) to receive the FIN ACK. If the ACK is received, or if the two MSLs has passed, whichever occurs first, the Host B TCP will delete the connection.

When both hosts send a FIN simultaneously, all data queued by both hosts will be SENT and ACK. Then, each host will send a FIN and receive a FIN ACK. When each host receives the FIN ACK, it will delete the connection.

Figure 6-9 shows the sequence of events that occurs when both TCPs send a CLOSE simultaneously.

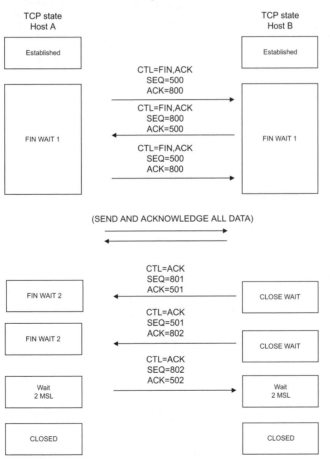

Figure 6-9 CLOSE simultaneously

Summary

TCP progresses through a series of defined steps, or states, to establish a connection, verify the authority of a user to use the connection or user process, receive data, send data, and gracefully close the connection upon the command of either TCP using the connection. When establishing the TCP connection, it is critical for each TCP to accurately inform the other TCP of the sequence numbers it will use. The use of sequence numbers to identify packets is crucial to the success of TCP's flow control and reliability features.

Point-to-Point Tunneling Protocol

Chapter 7

Questions answered in this chapter:

/// What is Point-to-Point Tunneling Protocol?

/// What is the relationship between VPNs and PPTP?

Introduction

Virtual private network is really just a couple of words that describe a particular type of network connection. The underlying software routines that realize the VPN connection are found in the Point-to-Point Protocol and Point-to-Point Tunneling Protocol, aided by the transmission technology of TCP/IP. We have discussed the enabling technologies PPP and TCP/IP. Now, our path to understanding VPNs leads us to the topic of PPTP.

Point-to-Point Tunneling Protocol (PPTP) is a network protocol that supports on-demand, multiprotocol, virtual private networking (VPN) over TCP/IP-based public data networks. The Internet is one such public data network. PPTP enables the secure transmission of data from a remote client to a private enterprise server by creating a virtual private network (VPN) between the two end points by encapsulating point-to-point packets into IP datagrams. PPTP is an extension of the remote access Point-to-Point Protocol defined in RFC 1661, The Point-to-Point Protocol (PPP), July 1994. RFC 1661 is a document produced and maintained by the Internet Engineering Task Force (IETF).

PPTP came about mainly due to the efforts of a consortium of private companies seeking to fulfill a business need. To further their cause, these companies formed the PPTP Forum and wrote the PPTP standards from which a draft was submitted to the IETF for consideration as an Internet standard. A draft of the PPTP extension of PPP document ("Point-to-Point Tunneling Protocol") was submitted to the IETF in June 1996 by the companies of the PPTP Forum, which included Microsoft Corporation, Ascend

Communications, 3Com/Primary Access, ECI Telematics, and US Robotics. From this effort we now have a Request for Comment defining PPTP. RFC 2637, Point-to-Point Tunneling Protocol, July 1999, is the defining PPTP document produced and maintained by the IETF.

Point-to-Point Tunneling Protocol (PPTP) is a software protocol that allows Point-to-Point Protocol (PPP) packets to be "tunneled" through a TCP/IP network. That is, TCP/IP is the pipeline through which the PPTP encapsulated PPP packets flow. PPTP does not change the PPP protocol or modify it in any way. So, PPTP is just a transport protocol for carrying PPP packets between a remote access user and a corporate gateway.

Perhaps a clearer picture of a VPN tunnel can be imagined if we look at Figure 7-1.

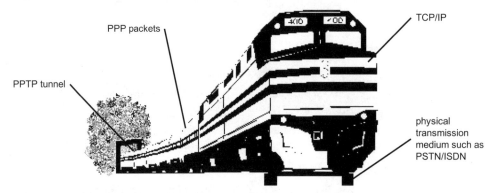

Figure 7-1 A realistic view of VPNs

The VPN "train," pulling PPP "cars," runs over a PSTN or ISDN "track." The engine pulling the train over the track is the TCP/IP "engine," which must change speed according to the varying right-of-way speed limit. The VPN train passes through the PPTP tunnel on its journey from remote access user (client-side) to corporate gateway (server-side). The corporate gateway may be managing numerous PPTP tunnels over various PSTN/ISDN tracks, and must switch the right VPN train to the proper destination on the corporate LAN.

The Big Three

A typical PPTP enterprise level application includes a mobile or remote access client, requiring access to a LAN via an ISP. Clients use some version of a point-to-point remote access protocol, such as Microsoft's Dial-Up Networking application, to connect to the ISP. The ISP provides a network access server (NAS) connection to the client upon the request of the client. That is, an NAS connection is provided when the client dials up the ISP. After the initial PPP connection is established with the ISP, a second Dial-Up Networking call is completed over the existing PPP connection. Data transmitted over this second connection consists of IP datagrams containing PPP packets. Such embedded PPP packets are called encapsulated PPP packets.

The second connection to the NAS creates the virtual private networking (VPN) connection to a PPTP server on the private enterprise LAN. The connection between the PPTP client and the PPTP server is referred to as a *tunnel*. *Tunneling* is, therefore, the process of embedding one PPP connection within another PPP connection. So, a VPN is really nothing more than a PPP connection embedded within another PPP connection with certain accompanying VPN management functions.

Note that other dial-up services, including the ubiquitous SLIP, are not designed to create PPTP connections.

Networks abound in the real world. Besides the commercial Internet, there are innumerable private networks owned by government, academia, business, and even individuals. Many of these private networks are connected to other private networks, now called an internetwork, as well as to the Internet. Regardless of the configuration of the network, every access portal to the network is through a gateway. A gateway is nothing more than a computer running the appropriate software programs to control access to the internal network, or intranetwork, and software to route datagrams to the proper destination. Such examples of a complex internetwork are the interconnections between a university, the Department of Defense (DOD), and a weapons manufacturer. See Figure 7-2.

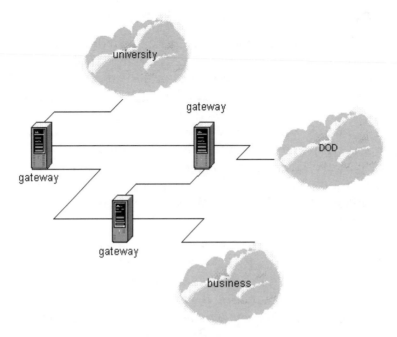

Figure 7-2 Network access through gateways

The data portal to any network is called a gateway. On one side of the gateway is the outside world, such as the Internet, and on the other is the inside world, such as a corporate LAN. The gateway is some type of computing device, running UNIX, DOS, Linux, etc., operating systems and connecting the internal LAN to the external internetwork. A gateway to the internetwork is called a network access server (NAS) in the literature. It is this NAS that will run the VPN software on the ISP site.

We are now ready to define the physical computing resources that form the elements of a VPN. Three computers, as illustrated in Figure 7-2, are involved in every PPTP deployment when the interconnect is via the PSTN, or public switched telephone network:

- A PPTP client—the mobile or remote client
- A network access server (NAS)—the ISP
- A PPTP server—the corporate mobile or remote access server

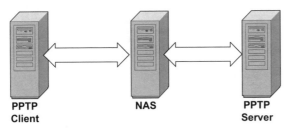

PPTP
Client

NAS

PPTP
Server

Figure 7-3 PPTP deployment

The PPTP client is a remote or mobile user. The network access server is the ISP interface between the client and the PPTP server. The network access server is also referred to as a front-end processor (FEP), dial-in server, or point-of-presence (POP) server. The PPTP server is the FEP of the private enterprise LAN. Once the client is connected to the NAS, the client may transmit and receive packets over the Internet via TCP/IP. The NAS uses TCP/IP protocol for all traffic to and from the private enterprise LAN. There is one instance when a PPTP application does not use a NAS. If the PPTP application is a LAN-LAN network, also called an IP-IP network, both the client and server PPTP software manage the PPTP tunnel connection without the need for an NAS, or for TCP.

The NAS is responsible for various functions in the performance of routing packets.

A client/server architecture is useful when discussing PPTP in order to separate functions existing in current network access servers. The server is referred to as the PPTP Network Server, or PNS. The client is referred to as the PPTP Access Concentrator (PAC). The PNS runs on any general purpose operating system, while the PAC operates on any dial-in access platform.

PPTP separates the traditional NAS functions and assigns them to the PAC and PNS, as appropriate. Separating the NAS functions into PAC and PNS functional areas of responsibility provides additional protocol functionality and robustness. As an example, a remote access user dialing into a PNS may contact different PACs using a single IP address. While a single IP address may not seem like such a major issue to the uninformed, it is of great concern to the Internet and networking community. The IP address space is finite and since it is available for use by the whole world, protocol developers must give consideration to its eventual depletion. A closer look at the separation of functions is worthwhile and even necessary to understanding how a VPN connection is managed.

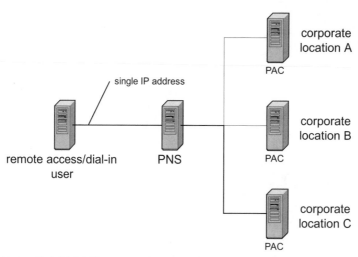

Figure 7-4 Multiple corporate campuses

PAC Functions

▶ connect

The PAC physically connects the computing device, also known as a computer, client, etc., to the PSTN through dial-up or ISDN. In order to accomplish the connection task, the NAS attaches either directly or via an external modem or terminal adapter and controls external modems and terminal adapters.

The connection may be either an analog or a digital connection. The circuit-switched connection is accomplished with either modem control for an analog circuit or DSS1 ISDN call control protocols for a digital circuit. In additional to connecting to the PSTN, the NAS, working with the modem or terminal adapter, performs rate adaptation, analog to digital conversion, digital to analog conversion, synchronous to asynchronous conversion, asynchronous to synchronous conversion, and any other data conversions and manipulations required by both the internal and external systems.

▶ terminate

The PAC must logically terminate the Point-to-Point Protocol (PPP) Link Control Protocol (LCP) session.

Shared PAC and PNS Functions

▶ authenticate

Both the PAC and PNS must participate in PPP authentication protocols.

PNS Functions

▶ multilink management

Channel aggregation and bundle management for Multilink Point-to-Point Protocol, used to aggregate, or collect, ISDN B channels, requires all of the channels composing a multilink bundle to be grouped at a single NAS. Since a Multilink PPP bundle can be handled by a single PNS, the channels comprising the bundle may be spread across multiple PACs.

▶ terminate

PNS provides for logical termination of various PPP network control protocols (NCP).

▶ route

PNS allows multiprotocol routing and bridging between NAS interfaces.

There are several different operating systems, running several different protocols, all wanting to interconnect to exchange data for various reasons. There must be a device capable of translating one protocol to another for all the diverse computing devices to interconnect over networks without freezing the network. The NAS is responsible for converting all protocols to the native protocol used in the internal network.

▶ Flexible IP address management

Dial-in users may maintain a single IP address as they dial into different PACs as long as they are served from a common PNS. If an enterprise network uses unregistered addresses, a PNS associated with the enterprise assigns addresses meaningful to the private network.

▶ Support of non-IP protocols for dial networks behind IP networks

This allows Appletalk and IPX, for example, to be tunneled through an IP-only provider. The PAC does not need the capability to process these protocols.

The protocol used to carry PPP protocol data units (PDUs) between the PAC and PNS, as well as call control and management, is addressed by PPTP. The PPTP protocol details a call control and management methodology providing the software routines for the PNS server to control access for inbound PSTN or ISDN originated dial-in, circuit-switched connections or to initiate outbound, circuit-switched connections. The call control and management methodology is presented later in this chapter.

Regardless of the system configuration, only the PAC and PNS implement the PPTP software. No other system device is aware of the existence of PPTP. The usual PPP client software will operate normally on tunneled PPP links.

PPTP is also used to tunnel a PPP session, with the caller acting as the PNS, over an IP network. In this configuration, the PPTP tunnel and the PPP session both operate between the same two computing devices. Such a configuration is the embodiment of a PPTP connection between a remote access user and a PPTP server over a public data network, such as the Internet.

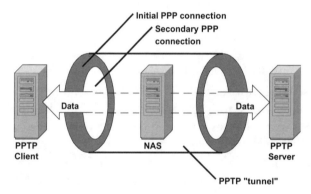

Figure 7-5 The PPTP tunnel

A PAC may provide connection service to many PNSs. An Internet service provider that supports PPTP connections for a number of private network clients is such an example of a PAC providing service to many PNSs. Each private network will operate one or more PNSs. Conversely, a single PNS may have connections to many PACs. Such an example of PNSs multi-linking is a large bank with many branch sites.

Tunneling enables the network routers to access the PPTP server when routing the encapsulated data packets from the remote or mobile client to the PPTP server. When the PPTP server receives the encapsulated data packet from the routing network, the PPTP server transmits the packet across the private network to the destination computer. The PPTP server accomplishes the routing of the packet by processing the PPTP packet, thereby obtaining the private network computer name or address information contained within the encapsulated PPP packet. The encapsulated PPP data packet may contain multiprotocol data such as IPX, TCP/IP, or NetBEUI protocols since the PPTP server is configured to send and receive multiprotocol packets.

There is an orderly sequence of steps the remote user, the NAS, and the PPTP server follow to establish the PPTP connection. The necessary steps, assuming TCP/IP protocol is used, to create a virtual private network connection are:

- Establish a PPP connection (use a PPP-enabled dialer such as Microsoft's Dial-up Networking) between the PPTP client (remote user) and the NAS.

- Establish a GRE/TCP connection between the PPTP client and the PPTP server.

- Establish a PPP connection between the PPTP client and the PPTP server.

- Transmit IP datagrams between the PPTP client and the PPTP server.

The VPN is the sum of the connection elements that consists of the PPP, TCP, IP, and PPTP protocols forming the connection between the PPTP client and the PPTP server.

Table 7-1 lists the networking protocols used to establish a VPN between a remote client and a PPTP server connected to a private network or LAN. During the establishment of the VPN, the protocols are exercised in sequence from left to right and top to bottom. That is, a PPP connection is established first between the remote user and the NAS (ISP), then a GRE connection is established between the remote user and the PPTP server, over the Internet, then a PPP connection is established between the remote user and the PPTP server, and finally data is exchanged via IP packets.

Table 7-1 Networking protocols and sequence used to establish a VPN

Communications Security	Protocol from Remote User to NAS	Protocol from NAS to PPTP Server	Protocol from PPTP Server to Private Network
unsecure	PPP/TCP		
unsecure	GRE/TCP	GRE/TCP	
secure	PPP/TCP	PPP/TCP	
secure	data (IP IPX IPSEC NetBEUI)	data (IP IPX IPSEC NetBEUI)	data (IP IPX IPSEC NetBEUI)

Note: lighter shaded cells denote valid internet addressing; darker shaded cells denote valid internal addressing

When establishing the VPN connection, secure communication does not occur until the remote user is connected to the PPTP server via encrypted PPP.

PPTP is responsible for encapsulating the encrypted and compressed PPP data packets into IP datagrams preparatory for transmission over the Internet. The encapsulated PPTP packet/IP datagrams are transmitted over the Internet until they reach the destination PPTP server. The destination PPTP server disassembles the encapsulated PPTP packet/IP datagram into a PPP packet and then decrypts the PPP packet using the network protocol used by the private network.

PPTP connections are supported in either of two ways:

- Using an ISP's NAS to connect a remote PPTP client (the remote access user we have been discussing) to the PPTP server (the corporate gateway we have been discussing) over the public data network
- Using a physical TCP/IP-based LAN connection to connect a PPTP server to a PPTP client over a LAN-LAN data network

What the above points say is the NAS must support the incoming TCP/IP connections and PPP packets, whether from the remote access user or the corporate PPTP server.

The mechanics of supporting a PPTP connection via the NAS is not the same as supporting the connection when the PPTP client and PPTP server are connected via a LAN. PPTP clients connecting via a NAS must utilize a modem and a VPN device to make the separate connections to the ISP and the PPTP server.

PPTP packets are placed on the physical media for transmission to the intended destination. For PPTP packets originating from a remote access PPTP client, i.e., connected via the public data network, the packets are placed on the telecommunication device physical media (the modem or VPN device) for transmission to the intended destination.

PPTP data packets originating from a LAN PPTP client are placed on the network adapter physical media, also known as a networking card. Connection via the LAN-LAN requires a networking device and a VPN device.

Establishing the VPN connection, or tunneling, via the NAS involves making two connections from the PPTP client to the PPTP server. The first connection made is a dial-up connection using the PPP protocol over the modem to an ISP. The second connection is a VPN connection using PPTP, over both the modem and the ISP connection, to tunnel across the Internet to a VPN device configured on the PPTP server. The tunnel between the VPN devices is established via the modem and PPP connection to the Internet.

To summarize, the public data network VPN connection process requires a dial-up connection via PPP from modem to ISP and a VPN connection via PPTP from modem to PPTP server.

The method of establishing PPTP connections when connected via LAN is somewhat different. When using PPTP to create a VPN between computers that are physically connected to the private enterprise LAN, the client is already connected to the network and only uses a method of connecting the physical computing device, such as Dial-Up Networking, with a VPN device to create the PPTP connection that terminates at a PPTP server connected to the LAN.

To summarize, the LAN-LAN VPN connection process requires a VPN connection via PPTP from PPTP client to PPTP server using PPTP-enabled connection protocol.

PPTP consists of two integrated components (given in order of their creation):

- A TCP-enabled control connection that is established between each PAC-PNS pair

   The existence of a control connection is called a control session.

- An IP tunnel operating between the same PAC-PNS pair

   The existence of an IP tunnel is called a tunneled (or tunneling) session.

As stated earlier, the IP tunnel is used to transport GRE encapsulated PPP packets between the PAC-PNS pair. And this is it. This is the famous VPN.

The LAN-LAN PPTP topology is simpler than the dial-up topology. Recall the LAN-LAN topology does not use TCP or dial-up, but packet transference is IP-IP. So, for the remainder of this book, we focus on the dial-up topology.

Control Connections

The control connection must be established between the PAC-PNS pair before PPP tunneling can be initiated. The control connection is established via the usual TCP. The TCP connection passes PPTP call control and management information between the PAC-PNS pair. The control connection is responsible for establishing, managing, and releasing sessions carried through the tunnel. It is the method used to notify a PNS of an incoming call at an associated PAC, as well as the method used to instruct a PAC to place an outgoing dial call. The establishment of a control and management connection initiates the control and management session. While the control and management session is logically associated with the PPTP tunneled sessions, it is nevertheless separate and distinct from the tunneled sessions. Both sessions, the control management and tunneled sessions, exist simultaneously.

Each PNS-PAC pair requires a dedicated control connection to be established. A control connection must be established before any other PPTP messages can be issued. The establishment of the control connection can be initiated by either the PNS or PAC. A procedure that handles the occurrence of a collision between PNS and PAC Start Control Connection Requests is described later in this chapter.

Either the PNS or the PAC may establish the control connection. In other words, either the client side or server side may initiate the creation of a PPTP connection.

When the PPTP connection is established, a TCP connection is created between the PPTP client and the PPTP server. The TCP connection is used to exchange control messages between the PPTP client and the PPTP server to establish, maintain, and end the PPTP connection. After the required TCP connection is established, the PNS and PAC establish the control connection using the Start Control Connection Request and Start Control Connection Reply messages. These two messages are also used to exchange information about basic operating capabilities of the PAC and PNS. Once the control connection is established, either the PAC or PNS may initiate tunneled sessions by requesting outbound calls or responding to inbound requests. The control connection may communicate changes in operating characteristics of an individual user session with a Set Link Info message. Individual tunneled sessions may be released by either the PAC or PNS via the Control Connection messages.

The control connection is maintained by echo messages which serve to "keep alive" the connection. This approach to managing the connection ensures that a connectivity failure between the PNS and the PAC will be detected within some time frame considered suitable. Other failures are reported via the control connection Wan Error Notify message. The design of PPTP is such that additional message types can be defined in the future. It can be said that PPP is robust in this respect.

To clarify terminology somewhat, a session is defined as the existence of a PAC, PNS, and a Call(er) ID.

PPTP Control Message Types

It almost seems trivial to point out that the use of control messages is necessary to properly manage the VPN connection. However, not only must it be pointed out, but we need to discuss those control messages in some detail. Toward that end, PPTP includes several types of control messages. The PPTP protocol specifies a set of control messages transmitted between the PPTP-enabled client and the PPTP server. The control messages establish, maintain, and release the PPTP tunnel in an orderly manner. Table 7-2 lists the primary PPTP control message types and their purpose.

Table 7-2 PPTP control messages

Message Type	Purpose
PPTP START SESSION REQUEST	Starts PPTP session
PPTP START SESSION REPLY	Reply to start session request
PPTP ECHO REQUEST	Maintains PPTP session
PPTP ECHO REPLY	Reply to maintain session request
PPTP WAN ERROR NOTIFY	Reports errors on the PPP connection
PPTP SET LINK INFO	Configures the connection between PPTP client and PPTP server
PPTP STOP SESSION REQUEST	Ends the PPTP session
PPTP STOP SESSION REPLY	Reply to end PPTP session request

All PPTP control messages are transmitted in packets encapsulated within a PPP datagram. A PPP datagram contains a PPP header, a TCP header, a PPTP control message, and appropriate trailers, as shown in Table 7-3. The control messages are discussed in much greater detail in the following sections.

Table 7-3 A PPP datagram

PPP header
TCP header
PPTP control message
trailers

After the PPTP tunnel is established, data may be transmitted between the client and PPTP server. The sequence of events is:

▸ Establish tunnel

▸ Transmit data

Data is transmitted between the PPTP client and the PPTP server in IP datagrams within PPP packets. PPTP utilizes an enhanced Generic Routing Encapsulation (GRE) mechanism. The GRE service provides a flow and congestion-controlled encapsulated datagram service for carrying PPP packets in IP datagrams between the remote user and the ISP. (GRE is defined in RFCs 1701 and 1702.) The IP datagram header includes the routing information necessary to route the datagram across the Internet to the destination PPTP server. The GRE header encapsulates the PPP packet, created by the NAS, within the IP datagram. The now-encrypted PPP packet becomes an unintelligible block of data bits. If the IP datagram should be intercepted, it is difficult to decrypt the data. Users who transmit sensitive data should be aware there are some security leaks which concerned vendors who supply PPTP products are attempting to rectify and may have by the time this book is printed.

PPTP Protocol Details

PPTP requires the existence of a tunnel for each communicating PNS-PAC pair. This PPTP tunnel is used to carry all PPP user session packets for sessions involving a particular PNS-PAC pair. A user session packet identifier, present in the GRE header, indicates which session, or instance of a PPTP connection, a particular PPP packet belongs to.

With the identification of individual session packets, PPP packets can be multiplexed, combined with other PPP packets from other sessions, and demultiplexed, separated from other session packets, through a single tunnel between a given PNS-PAC pair. The value used in the packet identifier field is determined by the call establishment procedure that takes place using the control connection.

The control connection is used to determine data rate and buffering values used to control and regulate the flow of PPP packets for each tunnel session. The GRE header contains acknowledgment and sequencing information that is used to perform some amount of congestion control and error detection over the PPTP tunnel. The PPTP specification does not specify any particular algorithms to use for congestion control and flow control. However, suggested algorithms for determining adaptive time-outs useful for allowing recovery of dropped data or acknowledgments on the PPTP tunnel are included in the specification.

Message Format and Protocol Extensibility

PPTP defines a set of control and management messages sent as TCP data on the control connection between a PAC-PNS pair. The TCP session for the control connection is established by initiating a TCP connection to port 1723. The source port is assigned to any unused port number. Each PPTP control connection message begins with a fixed header that is eight octets in length. This fixed header contains:

▶ The message length

▶ The PPTP Message Type indicator

▶ A "magic cookie"

The message length is the total number of bits in the message.

Two control connection message types are specified in the PPTP Message Type field:

▶ Control message

▶ Management message

　Currently, management messages are not defined.

The "magic cookie" is always sent as the constant 0x1A2B3C4D. The magic cookie's purpose is ostensibly to provide an initial synchronization function between the receiving system and the TCP data stream. A wise programmer will not attempt to use the magic cookie for reestablishing synchronization in the event an improperly formatted message is received. The TCP session should be closed (see Chapter 4) in the event synchronization is lost.

Control Connection Messages

Control Connection messages establish and release user sessions. The first set of Control Connection messages maintains the control connection itself. Recall the control connection can be initiated by either the PNS or PAC after establishing the TCP connection. Control Connection messages are transmitted as user data on the TCP connection between the PNS-PAC pair forming the connection. Control Connection messages can be grouped together, or categorized, by related function and responsibility. They are responsible for:

▶ Control connection management

▶ Call management

▶ Error reporting

▶ PPP session control

There are several control messages that endeavor to fulfill the obligations of the various categories of control messages as defined above. Each control message is assigned a unique integer value to distinguish it from other control messages. The currently defined control messages are:

Table 7-4 Control messages

Control Connection Management	Identifier
Start Control Connection Request	1
Start Control Connection Reply	2
Stop Control Connection Request	3
Stop Control Connection Reply	4
Echo Request	5
Echo Reply	6
Call Management	
Outgoing Call Request	7
Outgoing Call Reply	8
Incoming Call Request	9
Incoming Call Reply	10
Incoming Call Connected	11
Call Clear Request	12
Call Disconnect Notify	13
Error Reporting	
WAN Error Notify	14
PPP Session Control	
Set Link Info	15

Now, we will proceed to look into the control message formats in greater detail. For clarity, all control connection message templates in the next section include the entire PPTP control connection message header.

Note: Values preceded by 0x are hexadecimal numbers.

Control Connection Management

Table 7-5 lists the control connection management messages.

Table 7-5 Control connection management messages

Control Message	Message Code
Start Control Connection Request	1
Start Control Connection Reply	2

Table 7-5 (cont.) Control connection management messages

Control Message	Message Code
Stop Control Connection Request	3
Stop Control Connection Reply	4
Echo Request	5
Echo Reply	6

The Start Control Connection Request and Start Control Connection Reply messages determine the Control Connection protocol version used. The version number field contained within these control messages consists of a version number in the high octet portion of the field and a revision number in the low octet portion of the field. The value of the version number field for the latest version is 0x0100 for version 1, revision 0.

The Stop Control Connection Request and Stop Control Connection Reply messages provide an orderly means of closing the PPTP connection, allowing both client-side and server-side to process any pending messages.

Echo Request and Echo Reply are used to "keep alive" the connection.

The MTU for user data packets encapsulated in GRE is 1532 octets. This MTU value does not include the IP and GRE headers.

Start Control Connection Request

The Start Control Connection Request is a PPTP control message used to establish the control connection between a PNS and a PAC. Since the connection may be initiated by either PAC or PNS, the Start Control Connection Request may be sent by either one.

Note: The format of the control connection messages is high-order words, double words, etc., on the left and low-order words on the right.

A word about PPTP conventions: Word (2-octet) and long word (4-octet) values begin on 16-bit or 32-bit boundaries, as appropriate. Data is transmitted in high-order octets first. All reserved fields must be sent as a value of 0.

length = 32 bits	PPTP message type = 32 bits
magic cookie = 64 bits	
control message type = 32 bits	reserved = 32 bits
protocol version = 32 bits	reserved = 32 bits

framing capabilities = 64 bits	
bearer capabilities = 64 bits	
maximum channels = 32 bits	firmware revision = 32 bits
host name = 64 octets (256 bits)	
vendor string = 64 octets (256 bits)	

Figure 7-6 Start Control Connection Request format

Table 7-6 Start Control Connection Request format defined

Field	Meaning
Length	Total length in octets of this PPTP message, including the entire PPTP header.
PPTP Message Type	Type 1 for a control message.
Magic Cookie	Always set to hexadecimal 0x1A2B3C4D. This constant value is used as a benchmark for received messages.
Control Message Type	Type 1 for Start Control Connection Request.
Reserved	This field is set to 0.
Protocol Version	The version of the PPTP protocol that the sender wants to use.
Reserved	This field is set to 0.
Framing Capabilities	Indicates the type of framing the sender of this message can provide. The currently defined bit settings are: 1—Asynchronous framing supported 2—Synchronous framing supported
Bearer Capabilities	Indicates the bearer capabilities that the sender of this message can provide. The currently defined bit settings are: 1—Analog access supported 2—Digital access supported
Maximum Channels	The total number of individual PPP sessions this PAC can support. In Start Control Connection Requests issued by the PNS, this value should be set to 0. It must be ignored by the PAC.
Firmware Revision	When issued by the PAC, contains the firmware revision number of the issuing PAC. When issued by the PNS, contains the firmware revision number of the issuing PNS. **Note**: Firmware is the PPTP driver.
Host Name	Contains the DNS name of the issuing PAC or PNS. If the actual length is less than 64 octets, the remaining octets of this field should be set to 0.
Vendor Name	When issued by the PAC, contains a vendor-specific string describing the type of PAC being used. When issued by the PNS, contains the type of PNS software being used. If the actual length is less than 64 octets, the remaining octets of this field should be set to 0.

Start Control Connection Reply

The Start Control Connection Reply is a PPTP control message sent in reply to a received Start Control Connection Request message. This message contains a result code indicating the result of the control connection establishment attempt.

length = 32 bits	PPTP message type = 32 bits	
magic cookie = 64 bits		
control message type = 32 bits	reserved = 32 bits	
protocol version = 32 bits	result code = 16 bits	error code = 16 bits
framing capabilities = 64 bits		
bearer capabilities = 64 bits		
maximum channels = 32 bits	firmware revision = 32 bits	
host name = 64 octets (256 bits)		
vendor string = 64 octets (256 bits)		

Figure 7-7 Start Control Connection Reply format

Table 7-7 Start Control Connection Reply format defined

Field	Meaning
Length	Total length in octets of this PPTP message, including the entire PPTP header.
PPTP Message Type	Type 1 for a control message.
Magic Cookie	0x1A2B3C4D
Control Message Type	Type 2 for Start Control Connection Reply.
Reserved	0
Protocol Version	The PPTP protocol version the sender wants to use.
Result Code	Results of attempting to establish the command channel. Current valid Result Code values are: 1—Established channel successfully 2—General error (returned error code indicates the problem) 3—Command channel already exists 4—Requester is not authorized to establish a command channel 5—The protocol version of the requester is not supported
Error Code	Always set to 0 unless an error exists, in which case Result Code is set to 2 and this field is set to the value corresponding to the general error condition as specified in the General Error Codes section.
Framing Capabilities	The type of framing the sender of this message will provide. The currently defined bit settings are: 1—Asynchronous framing supported 2—Synchronous framing supported

Table 7-7 (cont.) Start Control Connection Reply format defined

Field	Meaning
Bearer Capabilities	Indicates the bearer capabilities the sender of this message will provide. The currently defined bit settings are: 1—Analog access supported 2—Digital access supported
Maximum Channels	The total number of individual PPP sessions this PAC will support. In a Start Control Connection Reply issued by the PNS, this value is set to 0 and must be ignored by the PAC. The PNS cannot use this value to track the remaining number of PPP sessions that the PAC will allow.
Firmware Revision	This field contains the firmware revision number of the issuing PAC or, if issued by the PNS, the version of the PNS PPTP driver.
Host Name	Contains the DNS name of the issuing PAC or PNS. If less than 64 octets in length, the remainder of this field is filled with octets of value 0.
Vendor Name	Contains a vendor-specific string describing the type of PAC or PNS being used. If less than 64 octets in length, the remainder of this field is filled with octets of value 0.

Stop Control Connection Request

The Stop Control Connection Request is a PPTP control message sent by one participant of a PAC-PNS control connection to inform the other participant that the control connection will be closed. Either participant in a PPTP session may initiate a Stop Control Connection Request. In addition to closing the control connection, all active user calls are cleared.

length = 32 bits		PPTP message type = 32 bits	
magic cookie = 64 bits			
control message type = 32 bits		reserved = 32 bits	
reason = 32 bits		reserved = 16 bits	reserved = 16 bits

Figure 7-8 Stop Control Connection Request format

Table 7-8 Stop Control Connection Request format defined

Field	Meaning
Length	Total length in octets of this PPTP message, including the entire PPTP header.
PPTP Message Type	Type 1 for a control message.
Magic Cookie	0x1A2B3C4D
Control Message Type	Type 3 for Stop Control Connection Request.
Reserved	0

Table 7-8 (cont.) Stop Control Connection Request format defined

Field	Meaning
Reason	Reason why the control connection is being closed. Valid values are:
	1—General request to clear control connection
	2—Can't support participant's version of the protocol
	3—Requester is being shut down
Reserved	This field is set to 0.
Reserved	This field is set to 0.

Stop Control Connection Reply

The Stop Control Connection Reply is a PPTP control message sent by one participant of a PAC-PNS control connection upon receipt of a Stop Control Connection Request from the other participant. Either participant of the PPTP connection may send a Stop Control Connection Reply.

length = 32 bits		PPTP message type = 32 bits	
magic cookie = 64 bits			
control message type = 32 bits		reserved = 32 bits	
result code = 32 bits		error code = 16 bits	reserved = 16 bits

Figure 7-9 Stop Control Connection Reply format

Table 7-9 Stop Control Connection Reply format defined

Field	Meaning
Length	Total length in octets of this PPTP message, including the entire PPTP header.
PPTP Message Type	Type 1 for a control message.
Magic Cookie	0x1A2B3C4D
Control Message Type	Type 4 for Stop Control Connection Reply.
Reserved	0
Result Code	Result of the attempt to close the control connection. Valid values are:
	1—Control connection closed
	2—Control connection not closed for reason indicated in Error Code
Error Code	Set to 0 unless an error occurs. If a general error occurs, Result Code is set to 2 (see above) and this field is set to the value corresponding to the general error condition as specified in the General Error Codes section.
Reserved	0

Echo Request

The Echo Request is a PPTP control message sent by either participant of a PAC-PNS control connection. This control message is used as a keep-alive message for the control connection. The receiving PPTP participant issues an Echo Reply to each Echo Request received. If the sender does not receive an Echo Reply in response to an Echo Request, it will clear the control connection after a predetermined time-out.

length = 32 bits	PPTP message type = 32 bits
magic cookie = 64 bits	
control message type = 32 bits	reserved = 32 bits
identifier = 64 bits	

Figure 7-10 Echo Request format

Table 7-10 Echo Request format defined

Field	Meaning
Length	Total length in octets of this PPTP message, including the entire PPTP header.
PPTP Message Type	Type 1 for a control message.
Magic Cookie	0x1A2B3C4D
Control Message Type	Type 5 for Echo Request.
Reserved	0
Identifier	Value is set by the sender of the Echo Request and is used to match the Echo Reply with the corresponding request.

Echo Reply

The Echo Reply is a PPTP control message sent by either participant of a PAC-PNS connection in response to the receipt of an Echo Request.

length = 32 bits	PPTP message type = 32 bits	
magic cookie = 64 bits		
control message type = 32 bits	reserved = 32 bits	
identifier = 64 bits		
result code = 32 bits	error code = 16 bits	reserved = 16 bits

Figure 7-11 Echo Reply format

Table 7-11 Echo Reply format defined

Field	Meaning
Length	Total length in octets of this PPTP message, including the entire PPTP header.
PPTP Message Type	Type 1 for a control message.

Table 7-11 (cont.) Echo Reply format defined

Field	Meaning
Magic Cookie	0x1A2B3C4D
Control Message Type	Type 6 for Echo Reply.
Reserved	0
Identifier	The identifier value is set by the sender of the Echo Request. It is used to match the reply with the corresponding request and is copied from the received Echo Request field.
Result Code	The result of the Echo Request reception. Valid values are:
	1—The Echo Reply is valid
	2—Echo Request not accepted for the reason indicated in Error Code
Error Code	This field is set to 0 unless an error condition exists, in which case the Result Code is set to 2 and this field is set to the value corresponding to the general error condition as specified in the General Error Codes section.
Reserved	0

Call Management

Table 7-12 lists the call management messages.

Table 7-12 Call management messages

Control Message	Message Code
Outgoing Call Request	7
Outgoing Call Reply	8
Incoming Call Request	9
Incoming Call Reply	10
Incoming Call Connected	11
Call Clear Request	12
Call Disconnect Notify	13

Outgoing Call Request

The Outgoing Call Request is a PPTP control message sent by the PNS to the PAC to indicate that an outbound call from the PAC is to be established. This request provides the PAC with information required to make the call. It also provides information to the PAC that is used to regulate the transmission of data to the PNS for this session once it is established.

length = 32 bits	PPTP message type = 32 bits
magic cookie = 64 bits	
control message type = 32 bits	reserved = 32 bits
call ID = 32 bits	serial number = 32 bits

minimum BPS = 64 bits	
maximum BPS = 64 bits	
bearer type = 64 bits	
framing type = 64 bits	
receive packet window size = 32 bits	packet processing delay = 32 bits
phone number length = 32 bits	reserved = 32 bits
phone number = 64 octets	
subaddress = 64 octets	

Figure 7-12 Outgoing Call Request format

Table 7-13 Outgoing Call Request format defined

Field	Meaning
Length	Total length in octets of this PPTP message, including the entire PPTP header.
PPTP Message Type	Type 1 for a control message.
Magic Cookie	0x1A2B3C4D
Control Message Type	Type 7 for Outgoing Call Request.
Reserved	0
Call ID	A unique identifier assigned to a particular PAC-PNS pair by the PNS in this session. The Call ID is used to multiplex and demultiplex data transmitted between the PAC-PNS pair in this session.
Call Serial Number	The PNS and PAC pair associate the same Call Serial Number with a particular PPTP session. It is assigned by the PNS for identifying this session in logged session information. The IP address and call serial number combination is a unique session identifier.
Minimum BPS	The lowest suitable line speed (in bits/second) for this session.
Maximum BPS	The highest suitable line speed (in bits/second) for this session.
Bearer Type	Indicates the bearer capability required for this outgoing call. The values are:
	1—Call to be placed on an analog channel
	2—Call to be placed on a digital channel
	3—Call can be placed on any type of channel
Framing Type	Indicates the type of PPP framing to be used for this outgoing call. The values are:
	1—Call to use asynchronous framing
	2—Call to use synchronous framing
	3—Call can use either type of framing
Receive Packet Window Size	The number of received data packets the PNS will buffer, or temporarily store, for this session.
Packet Processing Delay	A measure of packet processing delay imposed on data sent to the PNS from the PAC. The value is specified in tenths of seconds. For a PNS, this number should be very small.
Phone Number Length	The number of valid digits in the Phone Number field.

Table 7-13 (cont.) Outgoing Call Request format defined

Field	Meaning
Reserved	0
Phone Number	Number dialed to establish the outgoing session. For ISDN and analog calls, the Phone Number field is an ASCII text string. If the Phone Number is less than 64 octets in length, the remainder of the field is filled with zeros.
Subaddress	Specifies additional dialing information. If the subaddress is less than 64 octets long, the remainder of this field is filled with zeros.

Outgoing Call Reply

The Outgoing Call Reply is a PPTP control message transmitted to the PNS from the PAC in response to a received Outgoing Call Request message. The reply indicates the result of the outgoing call attempt. It also provides information to the PNS about particular parameters used for the call. It provides information to allow the PNS to regulate the transmission of data to the PAC for this session.

length = 32 bits	PPTP message type = 32 bits	
magic cookie = 64 bits		
control message type = 32 bits	reserved = 32 bits	
call ID = 32 bits	participant call ID = 32 bits	
result code = 32 bits	error code = 16 bits	cause code = 16 bits
connect speed = 64 bits		
receive packet window size = 32 bits	packet processing delay = 32 bits	
physical channel ID = 64 bits		

Figure 7-13 Outgoing Call Reply format

Table 7-14 Outgoing Call Reply format defined

Field	Meaning
Length	Total length in octets of this PPTP message, including the entire PPTP header.
PPTP Message Type	Type 1 for a control message.
Magic Cookie	0x1A2B3C4D
Control Message Type	Type 8 for Outgoing Call Reply.
Reserved	0
Call ID	A unique identifier assigned to a particular PAC-PNS pair by the PNS in this session. It is used to multiplex and demultiplex data transmitted between the PAC-PNS pair in this session.

Table 7-14 (cont.) Outgoing Call Reply format defined

Field	Meaning
Participant Call ID	This field is set to the value received in the Call ID field of the corresponding Outgoing Call Request message. It is used by the PNS to match the Outgoing Call Reply with the Outgoing Call Request it issued. It also is used as the value sent in the GRE header for muxing/demuxing.
Result Code	This value indicates the result of the Outgoing Call Request attempt. Currently valid values are:
	1 (Connected)—Call established with no errors
	2 (General Error)—Outgoing call not established for the reason indicated in Error Code
	3 (No Carrier)—Outgoing call failed due to no carrier detected
	4 (Busy) — Outgoing call failed due to detection of a busy signal
	5 (No Dial Tone)—Outgoing call failed due to lack of a dial tone
	6 (Time-out)—Outgoing call was not established within time allotted by PAC
	7 (Do Not Accept)—Outgoing call administratively prohibited
Error Code	This field is set to 0 unless a "General Error" condition exists, in which case Result Code is set to 2 and this field is set to the value corresponding to the general error condition as specified in the General Error Codes section.
Cause Code	This field provides additional failure information. The value of the Cause Code will vary depending upon the type of call attempted. For ISDN call attempts it is the Q.931 cause code.
Connect Speed	The connection speed used in bits/second.
Receive Packet Window Size	The number of received data packets the PAC can buffer for this session.
Packet Processing Delay	A measure of the packet processing delay that might be imposed on data sent to the PAC from the PNS. This value is specified in units of 1/10 seconds. For the PAC, this number is related to the size of the buffer used to hold packets to be sent to the client and to the speed of the link to the client. This value should be set to the maximum delay that can normally occur between the time a packet arrives at the PAC and is delivered to the client.
Physical Channel ID	This field is set by the PAC in a vendor-specific manner to the physical channel number used to place this call. It is used for logging purposes only.

Incoming Call Request

The Incoming Call Request is a PPTP control message sent from the PAC to the PNS to indicate that the PAC wishes to establish a call. This would be an inbound call for the PNS and an outbound call for the PAC. This request provides the PNS with call set-up and parameter information for the incoming call.

This message is the first message in the "three-way handshake" used by PPTP for establishing calls. The PAC may defer attempting to further process the call connection attempt until it has received an Incoming Call Reply from the PNS indicating that the call will be accepted by the PNS. This mechanism allows the PNS to obtain sufficient information about the call originator to determine if the call should be established.

length = 32 bits	PPTP message type = 32 bits
magic cookie = 64 bits	
control message type = 32 bits	reserved = 32 bits
call ID = 32 bits	call serial number = 32 bits
call bearer type = 64 bits	
physical channel ID = 64 bits	
dialed number length = 32 bits	dialing number length = 32 bits
dialed number = 64 octets	
dialing number = 64 octets	
subaddress = 64 octets	

Figure 7-14 Incoming Call Request format

Table 7-15 Incoming Call Request format defined

Field	Meaning
Length	Total length in octets of this PPTP message, including the entire PPTP header.
PPTP Message Type	Type 1 for a control message.
Magic Cookie	Always set to hexadecimal 0x1A2B3C4D. This constant value is used as a benchmark for received messages.
Control Message Type	Type 9 for Incoming Call Request.
Reserved	This field is set to 0.
Call ID	A unique identifier for this tunnel, assigned by the PAC to this session. It is used to multiplex and demultiplex data sent over the tunnel between the PNS and PAC involved in this session.
Call Serial Number	An identifier assigned by the PAC to this session for the purpose of identifying this particular session in logged session information. Unlike the Call ID, both the PNS and PAC associate the same Call Serial Number to a given session. The combination of IP address and call serial number should be unique.

Table 7-15 (cont.) Incoming Call Request format defined

Field	Meaning
Call Bearer Type	A value indicating the bearer capability used for this incoming call. Currently defined values are:
	1—Call is on an analog channel
	2—Call is on a digital channel
Physical Channel ID	This field is set by the PAC in a vendor-specific manner to the number of the physical channel this call arrived on.
Dialed Number Length	The actual number of valid digits in the Dialed Number field.
Dialing Number Length	The actual number of valid digits in the Dialing Number field.
Dialed Number	The number that was dialed by the caller. For ISDN and analog calls this field is an ASCII string. If the Dialed Number is less than 64 octets in length, the remainder of this field is filled with octets of value 0.
Dialing Number	The number from which the call was placed. For ISDN and analog calls this field is an ASCII string. If the Dialing Number is less than 64 octets in length, the remainder of this field is filled with octets of value 0.
Subaddress	A 64-octet field used to specify additional dialing information. If the subaddress is less than 64 octets long, the remainder of this field is filled with octets of value 0.

Incoming Call Reply

When the PNS receives an Incoming Call Request message, it will respond to the PAC with an Incoming Call Reply. The reply contains the result of the incoming call attempt.

The Incoming Call Reply Message also contains information concerning the PNS's ability to process packets, thereby providing a means for the PAC to regulate the data transmission rate. This control message is the second message in the three-way handshake used by PPTP for establishing incoming calls. Incoming in this context means calls initiated by the PAC. The message informs the PAC whether or not the call should be established.

length = 32 bits	PPTP message type = 32 bits	
magic cookie = 64 bits		
control message type = 32 bits	reserved = 32 bits	
call ID = 32 bits	participant call ID = 32 bits	
result code = 16 bits	error code = 16 bits	receive packet window size = 32 bits
packet transmit delay = 32 bits	reserved = 32 bits	

Figure 7-15 Incoming Call Reply format

Table 7-16 Incoming Call Reply format defined

Field	Meaning
Length	Total length in octets of this message, including the entire PPTP header.
PPTP Message Type	Type 1
Magic Cookie	0x1A2B3C4D
Control Message Type	Type 10 for Incoming Call Reply.
Reserved	0
Call ID	A unique identifier for this tunnel assigned by the PNS to this session. It is used to multiplex and demultiplex data sent over the tunnel between the PNS and PAC involved in this session.
Participant Call ID	This field is set to the value received in the Call ID field of the corresponding Incoming Call Request message. It is used by the PAC to match the Incoming Call Reply with the Incoming Call Request it issued. This value is included in the GRE header of transmitted data packets for this session.
Result Code	This value indicates the result of the Incoming Call Request attempt. Current valid Result Code values are:
	1 (Connect)—The PAC should establish the call
	2 (General Error)—The call should not be established due to the reason indicated in Error Code
	3 (Do Not Accept)—The PNS will not accept the call; it should hang up or issue a busy indication
Error Code	This field is set to 0 unless a "General Error" condition exists, in which case Result Code is set to 2 and this field is set to the value corresponding to the general error condition as specified in the General Error Codes section.
Receive Packet Window Size	The number of received data packets the PNS will buffer for this session.
Packet Transmit Delay	A measure of the packet processing delay that might be imposed on data sent to the PAC from the PNS. This value is specified in units of tenths of seconds.
Reserved	0

Incoming Call Connected

The Incoming Call Connected message is sent by the PAC to the PNS in response to a received Incoming Call Reply. It provides PAC parameter information to be used for the call to the PNS. It also provides data transmission information to allow the PNS to regulate the transmission of data to the PAC. This control message is the third in the three-way handshake used by PPTP for establishing incoming calls.

length = 32 bits	PPTP message type = 32 bits
magic cookie = 64 bits	
control message type = 32 bits	reserved = 32 bits
participant call ID = 32 bits	reserved = 32 bits
connect speed = 64 bits	
receive packet window size = 64 bits	packet transmit delay = 64 bits
framing type = 64 bits	

Figure 7-16 Incoming Call Connected format

Table 7-17 Incoming Call Connected format defined

Field	Meaning
Length	Total length in octets of this message, including the entire PPTP header.
PPTP Message Type	Type1
Magic Cookie	0x1A2B3C4D
Control Message Type	Type 11 for Incoming Call Connected.
Reserved	0
Participant Call ID	This field is set to the value received in the Call ID field of the corresponding Incoming Call Reply message. It is used by the PNS to match the Incoming Call Connected with the Incoming Call Reply it issued.
Reserved	Not used; reserved for future use.
Connect Speed	The actual connection speed used in bits/second.
Receive Packet Window Size	The number of received data packets the PAC will buffer for this session.
Packet Transmit Delay	A measure of the packet processing delay that might be imposed on data sent to the PAC from the PNS. This value is specified in units of tenths of seconds.
Framing Type	A value indicating the type of PPP framing being used by this incoming call.
	1—Call uses asynchronous framing
	2—Call uses synchronous framing

Call Clear Request

The Call Clear Request is transmitted by the PNS to the PAC specifying a particular call is to be disconnected. The call being cleared can be either an incoming or outgoing call and can be in any state. The appropriate PAC response to this message is a Call Disconnect Notify message.

length = 32 bits	PPTP message type = 32 bits
magic cookie = 64 bits	
control message type = 32 bits	reserved = 32 bits
call ID = 32 bits	reserved = 32 bits

Figure 7-17 Call Clear Request format

Table 7-18 Call Clear Request format defined

Field	Meaning
Length	Total length in octets of this message, including the entire PPTP header.
PPTP Message Type	Type 1
Magic Cookie	0x1A2B3C4D
Control Message Type	Type 12 for Call Clear Request.
Reserved	0
Call ID	The Call ID assigned by the PNS to this call. This value is used instead of the Participant Call ID because the latter may not be known to the PNS if the call must be aborted during call establishment.
Reserved	0

Call Disconnect Notify

The Call Disconnect Notify message is transmitted by the PAC to the PNS. The message is issued whenever a call is disconnected either due to the PAC's receipt of a Call Clear Request or for any other reason such as a dropped connection. The message's purpose is to inform the PNS of the disconnection and the reason the connection is being disconnected.

length = 32 bits	PPTP message type = 32 bits	
magic cookie = 64 bits		
control message type = 32 bits	reserved = 32 bits	
call ID = 32 bits	result code = 16 bits	error code = 16 bits
cause code = 32 bits	reserved = 32 bits	
call statistics = 128 octets		

Figure 7-18 Call Disconnect Notify format

Table 7-19 Call Disconnect Notify format defined

Field	Meaning
Length	Total length in octets of this PPTP message, including the entire PPTP header.
PPTP Message Type	Type 1
Magic Cookie	0x1A2B3C4D

Table 7-19 (cont.) Call Disconnect Notify format defined

Field	Meaning
Control Message Type	Type 13 for Call Disconnect Notify.
Reserved	0
Call ID	The value of the Call ID assigned by the PAC to this call. This value is used instead of the Participant Call ID because the latter may not be known to the PNS if the call must be aborted during call establishment.
Result Code	This value indicates the reason for the disconnect. Current valid Result Code values are:
	1 (Lost Carrier)—Call disconnected due to loss of carrier
	2 (General Error)—Call disconnected for the reason indicated in Error Code
	3 (Admin Shutdown)—Call disconnected for administrative reasons
	4 (Request)—Call disconnected due to received Call Clear Request
Error Code	This field is set to 0 unless a "General Error" condition exists, in which case the Result Code is set to 2 and this field is set to the value corresponding to the general error condition as specified in the General Error Codes section.
Cause Code	This field gives additional disconnect information. Its value varies depending on the type of call being disconnected. For ISDN calls it is the Q.931 cause code.
Reserved	Not used; reserved for future use.
Call Statistics	This field is an ASCII string containing vendor-specific call statistics that can be logged for diagnostic purposes. If the length of the string is less than 128, the remainder of the field is filled with octets of value 0.

Error Reporting

Table 7-20 lists the error reporting messages.

Table 7-20 Error reporting messages

Control Message	Message Code
WAN Error Notify	14

WAN Error Notify

The WAN Error Notify message is transmitted by the PAC to the PNS to indicate WAN error conditions, that is, conditions which occur on the interface supporting PPP. This control message is a diagnostic tool useful for checking the health of the connection. The message includes several counters which are cumulative. This message should only be sent when an error occurs, and not more than once every 60 seconds. The counters are reset when a new call is established.

length = 32 bits	PPTP message type = 32 bits
magic cookie = 64 bits	
control message type = 32 bits	reserved = 32 bits
participant call ID = 32 bits	reserved = 32 bits
CRC errors = 64 bits	
framing errors = 64 bits	
hardware overruns = 64 bits	
buffer overruns = 64 bits	
time-out errors = 64 bits	
alignment errors = 64 bits	

Figure 7-19 WAN Error Notify format

Table 7-21 WAN Error Notify format defined

Field	Meaning
Length	Total length in octets of this PPTP message, including the entire PPTP header.
PPTP Message Type	Type 1
Magic Cookie	0x1A2B3C4D
Control Message Type	Type 14 for WAN Error Notify.
Reserved	0
Participant Call ID	The Call ID assigned by the PNS to this call.
Reserved	Not used; reserved for future use.
CRC Errors	Number of PPP frames received with CRC errors since session was established.
Framing Errors	Number of improperly framed PPP packets received.
Hardware Overruns	Number of receive buffer overruns since session was established.
Buffer Overruns	Number of buffer overruns detected since session was established.
Time-out Errors	Number of time-outs since call was established.
Alignment Errors	Number of alignment errors since call was established.

PPP Session Control

Table 7-22 lists the PPP session control messages.

Table 7-22 PPP session control messages

Control Message	Message Code
Set Link Info	15

Set Link Info

The Set Link Info message is transmitted to the PAC by the PNS to establish PPP required link options. These options may change at any time during the life of the connection. Therefore, the PAC must be able to update its internal call information dynamically and perform PPP negotiation on an active PPP session.

length = 32 bits	PPTP message type = 32 bits
magic cookie = 64 bits	
message type = 32 bits	reserved = 32 bits
call ID = 32 bits	reserved = 32 bits
send ACCM = 64 bits	
receive ACCM = 64 bits	

Figure 7-20 Set Link Info format

Table 7-23 Set Link Info format defined

Field	Meaning
Length	Total length in octets of this PPTP message, including the entire PPTP header.
PPTP Message Type	Type 1
Magic Cookie	0x1A2B3C4D
Control Message Type	Type 15 for Set Link Info.
Reserved	0
Participant Call ID	The value of the Call ID assigned by the PAC to this call.
Reserved	0
Send ACCM	The send ACCM value the client should use to process outgoing PPP packets. The default value used by the client until this message is received is 0XFFFFFFFF.
Receive ACCM	The receive ACCM value the client should use to process incoming PPP packets. The default value used by the client until this message is received is 0XFFFFFFFF.

General Error Codes

General error codes are used to convey protocol or message format errors between the two connection participants. The error codes specify types of errors that are not related to any particular PPTP request but are applicable to all message requests. If a PPTP reply indicates in the Result Code of the reply that a general error occurred, the General Error value is examined to determine what the error is. The currently defined general error codes and their meanings are given in the following table:

Table 7-24 General error codes

Error Code	Meaning
0 (None)	No general error.
1 (Not Connected)	No control connection exists yet for this PAC-PNS pair.
2 (Bad Format)	Length is wrong or Magic Cookie value is incorrect.

Table 7-24 (cont.) General error codes

Error Code	Meaning
3 (Bad Value)	One of the field values was out of range or reserved field was non-zero.
4 (No Resource)	Insufficient resources to handle this command now.
5 (Bad Call ID)	The Call ID is invalid in this context.
6 (PAC Error)	A generic vendor-specific error occurred in the PAC.

Control Connection Protocol Operation

The operation of various PPTP control connection functions and the control connection messages that are used to support those functions are described in this section, including the various connection states that are supported by PPTP.

The operation of the control connection is simplified due to the use of TCP as the transport mechanism. TCP is very reliable and removes from PPTP the burden of managing the connection. Since TCP may close the connection due to various failure mechanisms without the permission of PPTP, an appropriate mechanism within PPTP must be available to manage this situation. Error recovery procedures, including appropriate logging of connection issues, is necessary for ease of connection management including problem resolution.

Typically, if an expected reply is not received within 60 seconds, PPTP will close the connection. Also, receipt of an invalid or corrupted message will result in the connection being closed, appropriate logging of the reason for closing, and subsequent restart so PPTP may recover into a known state.

The Control Connection Protocol is responsible for the following connection management tasks:

- Control Connection Originator
- Locally Terminate Connection
- Receive Stop Control Connection
- Receive Control Connection
- Start Control Connection Initiation Request Collision

The following sections examine the control connection management tasks in some detail.

Control Connection States and Message Sequences

Before we get into the control connection details, a short sidebar on the topic of machine states and message sequences is necessary to ensure a clear understanding of the flow charts describing the various control connection functions.

Messages are exchanged between the PAC and PNS during the establishment and teardown of connections. The messages are necessary to ensure the successful operation of the PPTP connection. In the business of establishing and managing a connection, the PAC and PNS will inhabit one of three possible states. The identification of specific connection states is useful for understanding the flow of messages between the PNS and the PAC. Whether opening or closing a PPTP connection, control messages will flow back and forth between the PNS and PAC until one of the defined machine states is realized. The PPTP control connection states are:

- idle
- established
- wait reply

"idle" state is the machine state of waiting for an attempt to open a TCP connection.

"established" state is the machine state of an open TCP connection ready to process PPP packets.

"wait reply" state is the machine state of waiting for a reply from the peer (PAC or PNS) attempting to establish the TCP connection. There are two wait states, wait_ctl_reply and wait_stop_reply. The wait_ctl_reply state occurs when the originating device, the PAC or PNS, is waiting for the peer to send a message informing the originating unit if a TCP collision has occurred. The wait_stop_reply state occurs when a PAC or PNS is waiting for a close connection response from a peer.

To further our understanding of the message flow between the PAC and PNS, flow charts are diagrammed to display the sequence of the messages exchanged between the PAC and the PNS. The following flow charts are not "states" but the sequence of events to set up and tear down PPTP connections. However, the purpose of all PPTP messages is to drive the machine into one of the three possible states. Now we are ready to delve into the control connection functions and their message sequences.

Control Connection Originator

The Control Connection Originator describes how to open a PPTP connection. The originator of the connection may be PAC or PNS. The Control Connection Originator state diagram is shown in Figure 7-21.

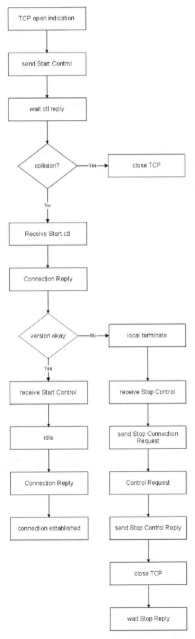

Figure 7-21 Control Connection Originator format sequence

The four states associated with the Control Connection Originator are idle, wait_ctl_reply, wait_stop_reply, and established.

idle

The Control Connection Originator may attempt to open a TCP connection to the participating peer during idle state. If the TCP connection is open, the originator transmits a Start Control Connection Request and enters the wait_ctl_reply state.

wait_ctl_reply

The originator checks to see if another TCP connection has been requested from the same participant, and if so, handles the collision situation described earlier in the section titled "Start Control Connection Request."

When a Start Control Connection Reply is received by the PAC or PNS, it is compared to the version running in the PAC or PNS. If the version of the reply is different than the version sent in the request, the older version will be used, provided it is supported, of course. If the version in the reply is supported, the originator moves to the established state. If the version is not supported, a Stop Control Connection Request will be transmitted to the participating peer, and the originator moves to the wait_stop_reply state.

established

The established state is the "working" state of the PPTP protocol. In the established state, PPP packets are transmitted and received between the two participating hosts. An established connection may be terminated by either a local condition or the receipt of a Stop Control Connection Request from the participating peer. In the event of a local termination, the originator will send a Stop Control Connection Request to the participating peer and enter the wait_stop_reply state.

wait_stop_reply

When a Stop Control Connection Reply is received, the TCP connection is closed and the control connection becomes idle.

Locally Terminate Connection

Locally Terminate Connection is the Control Connection protocol for closing a connection. If the peer receives a Stop Control Connection Request, it will send a Stop Control Connection Reply and close the TCP connection. Immediately prior to closing the connection, the peer ensures the final TCP information has been properly "pushed" to the participating peer. See the

TCP protocol for a detailed description of the PUSH operation. Either the PAC or PNS may initiate the Locally Terminate Connection.

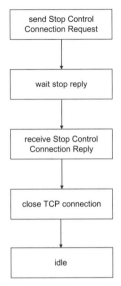

Figure 7-22 Locally Terminate Connection format sequence

wait_stop_reply

When a Stop Control Connection Reply is received, the TCP connection is closed and the control connection becomes idle.

idle

The Control Connection Originator may attempt to open a TCP connection to the participating peer during idle state. If the TCP connection is open, the originator transmits a Start Control Connection Request and enters the wait_ctl_reply state.

Receive Stop Control Connection

Receive Stop Control Connection is the Control Connection protocol for closing a connection when the remote peer has initiated the close connection request. If the local host receives a Stop Control Connection Request, it will send a Stop Control Connection Reply and close the TCP connection. Immediately prior to closing the connection, the local host ensures the final TCP information has been properly "pushed" to the participating peer. See the TCP protocol for PUSH operation. Either the PAC or PNS may initiate the Stop Control Connection.

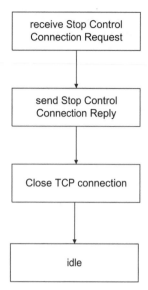

Figure 7-23 Receive Stop Control Connection request sequence

idle

> The Control Connection Originator may attempt to open a TCP connection to the participating peer during idle state. If the TCP connection is open, the originator transmits a Start Control Connection Request and enters the wait_ctl_reply state.

Receive Control Connection

The Receive Control Connection originator may be either a PAC or PNS.

The recipient of the Receive Control Connection waits for a TCP open attempt on port 1723. When notified of an open TCP connection, the recipient prepares to receive PPTP messages. When a Start Control Connection Request is received its version field is examined. If the version is earlier than the recipient's version and the earlier version can be supported by the recipient, the recipient will send a Start Control Connection Reply. If the version is earlier than the recipient's version and the version cannot be supported, the recipient will send a Start Connection Reply message, close the TCP connection and remain in the idle state. If the recipient's version is the same as or earlier than the originator's, the recipient will send a Start Control Connection Reply with the recipient's version and enter the established state.

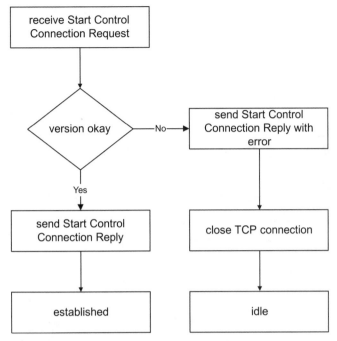

Figure 7-24 Receive Control Connection format sequence

established

> The established state is the "working" state of the PPTP protocol. In the established state, PPP packets are transmitted and received between the two participating hosts. An established connection may be terminated by either a local condition or the receipt of a Stop Control Connection Request from the participating peer. In the event of a local termination, the originator will send a Stop Control Connection Request to the participating peer and enter the wait_stop_reply state.

idle

> The control connection originator may attempt to open a TCP connection to the participating peer during idle state. If the TCP connection is open, the originator transmits a Start Control Connection Request and enters the wait_ctl_reply state.

Start Control Connection Initiation Request Collision

A PAC and PNS may have only one control connection between the pair. As stated several times previously, the control connection depends upon a standard TCP connection for its operation. The PPTP control connection

protocol is not distinguishable between the PNS and PAC, but is distinguishable between the originator of the session and the recipient. Either
the PAC or PNS may be the originator of the session and the other system
is then the recipient. The originating participant is the host that first
attempts the TCP open. Since either PAC or PNS may originate a connection, it is possible for a TCP collision to occur. Collisions occur when two
hosts originate a Start Control Connection Request (SCCR) with the
intended recipient the other host. Of course, each Start Control Connection
Request is initiated on its own TCP connection.

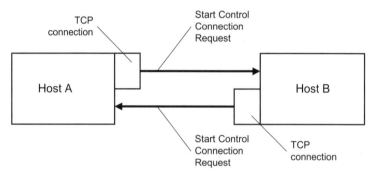

Figure 7-25 Simultaneous SCCR = Collision

The collision conflict is an easily managed situation. PPTP arbitrarily
selects the connection request on the TCP with the higher IP address. The
IP addresses of the two competing hosts are compared as 32-bit unsigned
values with the network number the more significant value. Each host will
compare the IP addresses and will independently close or ignore the appropriate TCP connection.

The host with the lower IP address, now called the recipient, will immediately close its TCP connection without sending any further PPTP control
messages on it. After closing its TCP connection, the recipient will respond
to the host with the higher IP address, now called the originator, with a
Start Control Connection Reply message. The originator will wait for the
Start Control Connection Reply on the connection it initiated and the originator will wait also for a TCP termination indication on the connection the
recipient opened. Obviously, the originator cannot send any messages on
the TCP connection the recipient initiated and subsequently closed.

Suppose two hosts with IP addresses of 198.090.250 and 250.100.065
simultaneously try to connect to each other. Two TCP connections will be

initiated, one by each host. The Start Control Connection Initiation Request of both hosts will select the TCP connection with the higher IP address, 250.100.065 in this case, to initiate the PPTP connection. The TCP connection opened by host 198.090.250 will be immediately closed by both hosts.

Incoming Calls

The next sections focus on what happens when a PAC (remote user) calls a PNS (corporate LAN). In the normal course of events, there will be many more calls placed from a PAC to a PNS than from a PNS to a PAC.

Incoming calls are received by a PNS (corporate LAN) from a PAC (remote user).

A word about something called low-level drivers. *Low-level drivers* are those software modules that connect computers to the physical devices, which in turn are connected to the telephone lines. A low-level driver provides a software interface between a modem or other physical medium of some type and the PPTP software. Connecting to or disconnecting from the telephone network is the dirty duty of low-level drivers. So, a PNS and a PAC function will be associated with a low-level driver.

The PAC host's low-level driver associated with the PAC function will initiate an Incoming Call Request message when one of the telephone lines associated with the PAC rings. The PAC will select a Call ID and serial number indicating the call bearer type, i.e., ISDN (digital) or analog, and create an Incoming Call Reply message.

Of course, analog modems will always indicate an analog call type. Yes, even so-called "digital modems" such as cable and DSL modems are really analog and will be designated as such. The only true digital calls are those calls originated as ISDN calls. ISDN calls may be unrestricted or rate adaptation may be employed. If the features dialing number, dialed number, and subaddress are available from the telephone network, they are included in the Incoming Call Reply message.

Once the PAC low-level driver sends the Incoming Call Request to the PPTP, it does not answer the call from the network until told to do so by the PPTP.

The PAC may choose not to accept the call if:

▸ No resources are available to handle this session.

▶ The dialed, dialing, or subaddress fields do not specify an authorized user.

▶ The bearer service (digital or analog) is not authorized or supported.

If the PAC chooses to accept the call, it will respond with an Incoming Call Reply. The reply indicates the maximum acceptable Receive Packet Window size the PAC can process. When the PNS receives the Incoming Call Reply, it attempts to connect the call, assuming the called party has not hung up. A final call connected message from the PNS to the PAC indicates that the connection states for both the PAC and the PNS should enter the established state.

PAC Incoming Call States

The states associated with the PAC for incoming calls are:

idle
  The PAC detects an incoming call on one of its PSTN (or LAN) interfaces.

  Usually an analog line is ringing or an ISDN TE detected an incoming Q.931 SETUP message. The PAC responds by replying with an Incoming Call Request message, then moves to the wait_reply state.

wait_reply
  The PAC receives an Incoming Call Reply message from the PNS indicating non-willingness to continue the connection attempt (general error or didn't accept). The PAC returns to the idle state. If the PNS reply message indicates that the call is accepted, the PAC sends an Incoming Call Connected message to the PNS and enters the established state.

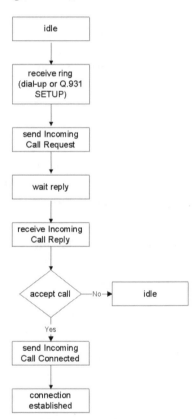

Figure 7-26 PAC Incoming Call sequence

PNS Incoming Call States

The PNS Incoming Call sequence is the same as previously detailed for the PAC. For the purpose of clarity, the following state diagram is provided.

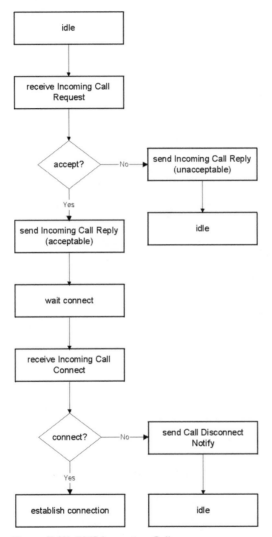

Figure 7-27 PNS Incoming Call sequence

The states associated with the PNS for incoming calls are:

idle

The wait for an incoming call on one of its PSTN (or LAN) interfaces.

An Incoming Call Request message may be received by the PNS. If the request is not appropriate, an Incoming Call Reply is transmitted to the PAC and the PNS remains in the idle state. If the Incoming Call Request message is appropriate, an Incoming Call Reply is transmitted indicating acceptance of the call attempt in the result code. The PNS then moves to the wait_connect state.

wait_connect

If the PAC accepts the call and establishes a session, the PAC will send an Incoming Call Connect message to the PNS. The PNS then moves into an established state. However, if the PNS receives a Call Disconnect Notify from the PAC to indicating the incoming call could not be connected, the PNS sends a Call Disconnect Notify message and enters the idle state.

established

Data is exchanged over the tunnel.

Terminating Connections

Either the PAC or the PNS may terminate a session. Sessions may be terminated due to user initiation or events outside the control of users such as PSTN "events." A PSTN event may be anything that disrupts the telco service between the PAC and PNS, such as a ditch digger cutting the phone lines between the two.

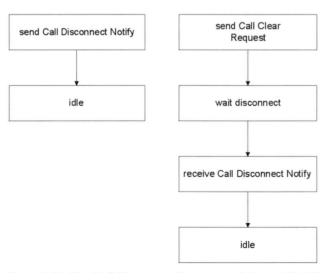

Figure 7-28 The PAC Terminates Connection (left) and PNS Terminates Connection (right)

If the PNS terminates the connection, the PNS sends a Call Clear Request to the PAC which responds with a Call Disconnect Notify. If the PAC terminates the connection, it sends a Call Disconnect Notify, then enters the idle state. The following state diagrams illustrate the process.

wait_disconnect

Once a Call Disconnect Notify is received, the session moves back to the idle state.

idle

The PAC or PNS waits for an incoming call on one of its PSTN (or LAN) interfaces.

PAC Close Connection States

When the PAC host disconnects, the PAC sends a Call Disconnect Notify message to the PNS and clears, or disconnects, the call. If the PNS wants to clear a call, it sends a Call Clear Request message to the PAC, then waits for a Call Disconnect Notify from the PAC.

While the following discussion is PAC specific, the same process is applicable to PNS-originated calls. Just replace PAC with PNS.

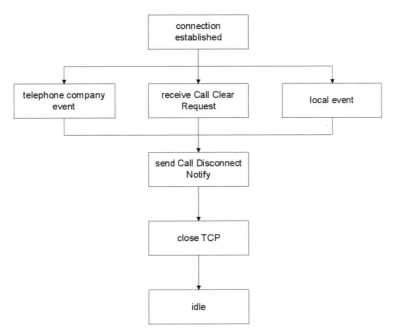

Figure 7-29 PAC Close Connection sequence

The connection may be disconnected following any of these events:

- An event on the PSTN (or LAN) connection

  The PAC sends a Call Disconnect Notify message.

- Reception of a Call Clear Request

  The PAC sends a Call Disconnect Notify message.

- A local reason

  The PAC sends a Call Disconnect Notify message.

established
> Data is exchanged over the tunnel.

idle
> The wait for an incoming call on one of its PSTN (or LAN) interfaces.

Outgoing Calls

Outgoing messages are initiated by a PNS and instruct a PAC to place a call on a PSTN interface to a remote user. There are only two messages for outgoing calls: Outgoing Call Request and Outgoing Call Reply. The PNS sends an Outgoing Call Request specifying the dialed party phone number and subaddress as well as speed and window parameters. The PAC will respond to the Outgoing Call Request message with an Outgoing Call Reply message once the PAC determines either the call was successfully connected or not. Reasons for an unsuccessful connection include, but certainly are not limited to the following:

- No interfaces are available for dial-out
- The called party is busy or does not answer
- No dial tone is detected on the interface chosen for dialing

PAC Outgoing Call States

Figure 7-30 details the states the PAC assumes when it receives an Outgoing Call Request from the PNS.

The states associated with the PAC for outgoing calls are:

idle
> The PAC receives the Outgoing Call Request message. If the message is received in error, the PAC responds with an Outgoing Call Reply with the error condition set. Otherwise, the PAC allocates a physical channel to dial the remote user. Then the PAC places the outbound call, waits

for a connection to the remote user, then moves to the wait_cs_ans state.

wait_cs_ans

If the call to the remote user is incomplete, the PAC sends an Outgoing Call Reply to the PNS with a non-zero error code. If a timer expires on an outbound call, the PAC sends back an Outgoing Call Reply with a non-zero error code. If a circuit-switched connection is established, the PAC sends an Outgoing Call Reply, which indicates a successful connection was established.

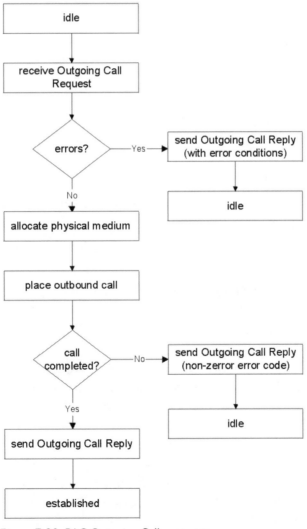

Figure 7-30 PAC Outgoing Call sequence

established

If the PAC receives a Call Clear Request, the PSTN connection is released and the PAC sends a Call Disconnect Notify message to the PNS. If the call is disconnected by the remote user or by the PSTN interface, a Call Disconnect Notify message is sent to the PNS.

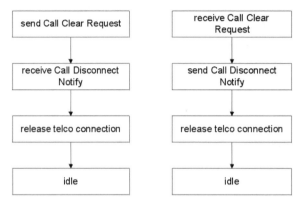

Figure 7-31 PAC Terminates Connection (left) and PNS Terminates Connection (right) sequences

PNS Outgoing Call States

Figure 7-32 details the states the PNS assumes when it receives an Outgoing Call Request from the PAC.

The states associated with the PNS for outgoing calls are:

idle

The PNS sends an Outgoing Call Request message to the PAC, then enters the wait_reply state.

wait_reply

The PNS receives an Outgoing Call Reply that indicates an error. The session returns to an idle state. No PSTN connection is active. If the Outgoing Call Reply does not indicate an error, the PAC establishes the PSTN connection and the session moves to the established state.

established

If the PNS receives a Call Disconnect Notify, the PSTN connection is terminated for the reason indicated in the result and cause codes. The session moves to the idle state. If the PNS chooses to terminate the session, it sends a Call Clear Request to the PAC, then enters the wait_disconnect state.

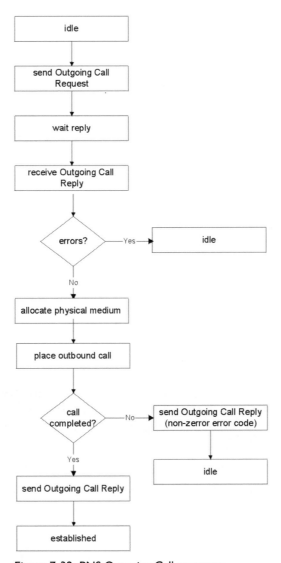

Figure 7-32 PNS Outgoing Call sequence

wait_disconnect
> The PNS is waiting for the PAC to confirm a session disconnect. Once the PNS receives the Call Disconnect Notify message from the PAC, the session enters the idle state.

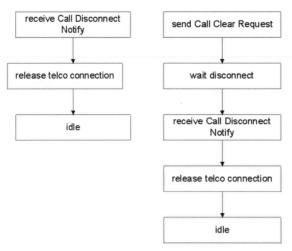

Figure 7-33 PAC Terminates connection (left) and PNS Terminates Connection (right)

Tunnel Protocol Operation

PPP data packets are transmitted between hosts by the PPTP protocol, which includes the following elements. The PPP data packets represent the "packetized" user data. Between the PAC and PNS, the PPP packets are "encapsulated" within GRE packets. IP is the protocol selected to actually carry the packets between hosts. However, the IP is a modified IP, as HDLC flags, bit insertion, control characters, control character escapes, and CRCs are not included in the IP header.

The form of the PPTP IP header includes the media header, IP header, GRE header, and the PPP packet, as shown in the following illustration.

Table 7-25 The PPTP IP header

Media Header
IP Header
GRE Header
PPP Packet

Enhanced GRE Header

The GRE header used in PPTP is modified somewhat from the format specified in the GRE protocol specification. The most significant difference is the definition of a new Acknowledgment Number field. This Acknowledgment Number field is used to determine if a specific GRE packet or set of packets arrived at the other host, or recipient. This Acknowledgment Number capability is not used in conjunction with the retransmission features supported by TCP or any other retransmission of user data packets. The capability is used to determine the rate user data packets will be transmitted over the tunnel for any particular user session. It is used as a flow control mechanism.

The PPP data packet contains a payload section without any media-specific framing elements.

The format of the enhanced GRE header is:

control word = 16 bits	protocol type = 16 bits
high word key = 16 bits	low word key = 16 bits
sequence number = 32 bits	
acknowledgment number = 32 bits	

Figure 7-34 Enhanced GRE header format

Table 7-26 Enhanced GRE header format defined

Field	Meaning
Control Word	Contains management information.
Protocol Type	Always set to 880Bx.
(High/Low) Key	Payload Length (high key word)—size of the payload, excluding the GRE header
	Call ID (low key word)—the participant Call ID for the session to which this packet belongs
	Key field use is optional.
Sequence Number	The payload sequence number (see TCP/IP for sequence numbering usage).
	Present if Sequence Number bit (bit 3) is one (1).
Acknowledgment Number	Sequence number of the highest numbered GRE packet received by the sending participant for this user session.
	Present if A bit (bit 8) is one (1).

The 16-bit Control Word includes various control bits including flags and tunnel management bits. The Control Word field is shown with an explanation for each bit.

Control Word Field

The following tables explain the Control Word field.

Table 7-27 Control Word field

0	1	2	3	4	5	6	7	8	9	10	11	12	13	14	15
C	R	K	S	s		recur		A			flags			version	

Table 7-28 Control Word field defined

Bit	Bit Number	Meaning
C	(Bit 0)	Checksum present. Reset to zero (0).
R	(Bit 1)	Routing present. Reset to zero (0).
K	(Bit 2)	Key present. Set to one (1).
S	(Bit 3)	Sequence Number present. Set to one (1) if a payload (data) packet is present. Reset to zero (0) if payload is not present (GRE packet is an Acknowledgment only).
s	(Bit 4)	Strict source route present. Reset to zero (0).
Recur	(Bits 5-7)	Recursion control. Reset to zero (0).
A	(Bit 8)	Acknowledgment sequence number present. Set to one (1) if packet contains Acknowledgment Number to be used for acknowledging previously transmitted data.
Flags	(Bits 9-12)	Must be reset to zero (0).
Ver	(Bits 13-15)	Must be set to 1 (enhanced GRE).

Sequence numbers uniquely identify each packet. Sequence numbers are initialized to zero at session startup. Each payload containing a packet sent for a given user session and has the S bit (Bit 3) set to one (1) is assigned the next consecutive sequence number for that session. This method of identifying individual packets provides a means for acknowledging received packets while not significantly increasing the overhead on PPTP. A more efficient protocol is the result. TCP/IP contains a good example of using sequence numbers to acknowledge the receipt of packets. However, acknowledgments may be transmitted independently of data packets. Such a need arises when one host receives a data packet from the other and the receiving host has no data to send.

PPTP is able to acknowledge multiple packets with a single acknowledgment. All outstanding packets with a sequence number equal to or lower than the acknowledgment number are considered acknowledged.

Sliding Window Protocol

The intention of the sliding window is to prevent one host from overloading another host. Both the PAC and PNS use a sliding window protocol for flow control. Such a mechanism is necessary to ensure neither host overloads the other's incoming data buffer. Each machine may, and probably does, operate with different size buffers and different machine clock speeds. Most likely, each machine's ability to clear its buffer is different from the other.

Each session participant maintains a "transmit window," which is the number of packets that can be safely transmitted to the session participant.

Initial Window Size

Each participant indicates the maximum receive window size in the initial exchange of control messages. The initial window size of the session originator is set to half the maximum size the other participant requested. A one-packet minimum window size is necessary, else the host cannot receive any packets.

Out-of-sequence Packets

There exist various reasons why packets may arrive at their intended destination in an order other than the order transmitted. Over the Internet, related packets may not transit the same path from source to destination.

PPP cannot process out-of-sequence packets. Therefore, if a PAC receives an out-of-sequence packet, it will be discarded. When the PNS does not receive an acknowledgment for the discarded packet, it will retransmit it, hopefully arriving at the PAC in the order intended.

Time-Outs

Basically, each packet has a time-to-live value associated with it. If the sender does not receive acknowledgment from the recipient that it has received the packet within the time-out period, the sender will resend the packet. Various "adaptive" approaches to managing the time-outs and the buffer window are used. A detailed discussion of these approaches is saved for a more advanced study of PPTP.

Packing the Mail

The MTU (maximum transmission unit) for user data packets encapsulated in GRE is 1532 octets. This MTU value does not include the IP and GRE headers. There is an optimal relationship between the MTU, the MSS (maximum segment size), and the RWIN (receive window).

Table 7-29 A full mailbag

Acronym	Full Name	Sample Value
MTU	Maximum Transmission Unit	1,532 bytes
MSS	Maximum Segment Size (MTU − 40)	1,492 bytes
RWIN	Receive Window (MSS * Z)	14,920 bytes

Where Z = 10 (this is an arbitrary number and is dependent upon the installation).

To ascertain the optimal relationship between MTU, MSS, and RWIN, suppose RWIN is a mailbag that can hold a maximum of ten letters (Z represents the size of the mailbag). Each letter in the mailbag represents an MTU. The address of the letter is the IP address of the MTU. The MSS represents the contents of each letter. MSS is usually set to the MTU − 40 to maximize the amount of data sent in each MTU. The value 40 is the number of bytes in the IP header.

Summary

PPTP is a useful means for connecting remote users to corporate intranets. Although the protocol is only several years old, it is mature since it is a conglomeration of existing protocols, adapted to the specific purpose intended. The result is an efficient and cost-effective means of securely exchanging data between a corporate location and its remote users. So, prospective users may avail themselves of the communication opportunities presented via a PPTP connection without fear of data loss, corruption, or hijacking.

The commercial implementation of the PPTP protocol, VPNs, are now found in widespread use in the corporate world and are beginning to find their way into the home as we push the Internet and our desire to communicate to new limits. Who knows what tomorrow will bring.

Appendix A RFC Listing

RFC 2153	PPP Vendor Extensions. May 1997
RFC 2152	UTF-7 A Mail-Safe Transformation Format of Unicode. May 1997
RFC 2151	A Primer On Internet and TCP/IP Tools and Utilities. June 1997
RFC 2150	Humanities and Arts: Sharing Center Stage on the Internet. October 1997
RFC 2149	Multicast Server Architectures for MARS-based ATM multicasting. May 1997
RFC 2148	Deployment of the Internet White Pages Service. September 1997
RFC 2147	TCP and UDP over IPv6 Jumbograms. May 1997
RFC 2146	U.S. Government Internet Domain Names. May 1997
RFC 2145	Use and Interpretation of HTTP Version Numbers. May 1997
RFC 2144	The CAST-128 Encryption Algorithm. May 1997
RFC 2143	Encapsulating IP with the Small Computer System Interface. May 1997
RFC 2142	Mailbox Names for Common Services, Roles and Functions. May 1997
RFC 2141	URN Syntax. May 1997
RFC 2140	TCP Control Block Interdependence. April 1997
RFC 2139	RADIUS Accounting. April 1997
RFC 2138	Remote Authentication Dial In User Service (RADIUS). April 1997
RFC 2137	Secure Domain Name System Dynamic Update. April 1997
RFC 2136	Dynamic Updates in the Domain Name System (DNS UPDATE). April 1997
RFC 2135	Internet Society By-Laws. April 1997

RFC 2134   Articles of Incorporation of Internet Society. April 1997

RFC 2133   Basic Socket Interface Extensions for IPv6. April 1997

RFC 2132   DHCP Options and BOOTP Vendor Extensions. March 1997

RFC 2131   Dynamic Host Configuration Protocol. March 1997

RFC 2130   The Report of the IAB Character Set Workshop held 29 February-1 March, 1996. April 1997

RFC 2129   Toshiba's Flow Attribute Notification Protocol (FANP) Specification. April 1997

RFC 2128   Dial Control Management Information Base using SMIv2. March 1997

RFC 2127   ISDN Management Information Base using SMIv2. March 1997

RFC 2126   ISO Transport Service on top of TCP (ITOT). March 1997

RFC 2125   The PPP Bandwidth Allocation Protocol (BAP) / The PPP Bandwidth Allocation Control Protocol (BACP). March 1997

RFC 2124   Cabletron's Light-weight Flow Admission Protocol Specification Version 1.0. March 1997

RFC 2123   Traffic Flow Measurement: Experiences with NeTraMet. March 1997

RFC 2122   VEMMI URL Specification. March 1997

RFC 2121   Issues affecting MARS Cluster Size. March 1997

RFC 2120   Managing the X.500 Root Naming Context. March 1997

RFC 2119   Key words for use in RFCs to Indicate Requirement Levels. March 1997

RFC 2118   Microsoft Point-To-Point Compression (MPPC) Protocol. March 1997

RFC 2117   Protocol Independent Multicast-Sparse Mode (PIM-SM): Protocol Specification. June 1997

RFC 2116   X.500 Implementations Catalog-96. April 1997

RFC 2115   Management Information Base for Frame Relay DTEs Using SMIv2. September 1997

RFC 2114   Data Link Switching Client Access Protocol. February 1997

RFC 2113	IP Router Alert Option. February 1997
RFC 2112	The MIME Multipart/Related Content-type. February 1997
RFC 2111	Content-ID and Message-ID Uniform Resource Locators. February 1997
RFC 2110	MIME E-mail Encapsulation of Aggregate Documents, such as HTML (MHTML). March 1997
RFC 2100	The Naming of Hosts. April 1997
RFC 2099	Request for Comments Summary RFC Numbers 2000-2099. March 1997
RFC 2094	Group Key Management Protocol (GKMP) Architecture. July 1997
RFC 2093	Group Key Management Protocol (GKMP) Specification. July 1997
RFC 2076	Common Internet Message Headers. February 1997
RFC 1886	DNS Extensions to support IP version 6. December 1995
RFC 1752	The Recommendation for the IP Next Generation Protocol. January 1995
RFC 1671	IPng White Paper on Transition and Other Considerations. August 1994
RFC 1563	The text/enriched MIME Content-type. January 1994
RFC 1542	Clarifications and Extensions for the Bootstrap Protocol. October 1993
RFC 1534	Interoperation Between DHCP and BOOTP. October 1993
RFC 1531	Dynamic Host Configuration Protocol. October 1993
RFC 1341	MIME (Multipurpose Internet Mail Extensions): Mechanisms for Specifying and Describing the Format of Internet Message Bodies. June 1992
RFC 1340	Assigned Numbers. July 1992
RFC 1271	Remote Network Monitoring Management Information Base. November 1991
RFC 1267	Border Gateway Protocol 3 (BGP-3). October 1991
RFC 1254	Gateway Congestion Control Survey. July 1991
RFC 1253	OSPF Version 2 Management Information Base. August 1991

RFC 1251   Who's Who in the Internet: Biographies of IAB, IESG and IRSG Members. August 1991

RFC 1250   IAB Official Protocol Standards. August 1991

RFC 1247   OSPF Version 2. July 1991

RFC 1246   Experience with the OSPF Protocol. July 1991

RFC 1245   OSPF Protocol Analysis. July 1991

RFC 1244   Site Security Handbook. July 1991

RFC 1243   AppleTalk Management Information Base. July 1991

RFC 1241   Scheme for an Internet encapsulation protocol: Version 1. July 1991

RFC 1240   OSI connectionless transport services on top of UDP: Version 1. June 1991

RFC 1239   Reassignment of experimental MIBs to standard MIBs. June 1991

RFC 1238   CLNS MIB for use with Connectionless Network Protocol (ISO 8473) and End System to Intermediate System (ISO 9542). June 1991

RFC 1237   Guidelines for OSI NSAP Allocation in the Internet. July 1991

RFC 1236   IP to X.121 address mapping for DDN. June 1991

RFC 1234   Tunneling IPX traffic through IP networks. June 1991

RFC 1233   Definitions of managed objects for the DS3 Interface type. May 1991

RFC 1232   Definitions of managed objects for the DS1 Interface type. May 1991

RFC 1231   IEEE 802.5 Token Ring MIB. May 1991

RFC 1230   IEEE 802.4 Token Bus MIB. May 1991

RFC 1229   Extensions to the generic-interface MIB. May 1991

RFC 1228   SNMP-DPI: Simple Network Management Protocol Distributed Program Interface. May 1991

RFC 1227   SNMP MUX protocol and MIB. May 1991

RFC 1224   Techniques for managing asynchronously generated alerts. May 1991

RFC 1222   Advancing the NSFNET routing architecture. May 1991

RFC 1220   Point-to-Point Protocol extensions for bridging. April 1991

RFC 1219   On the assignment of subnet numbers. April 1991

RFC 1215   Convention for defining traps for use with the SNMP. March 1991

RFC 1214   OSI internet management: Management Information Base. April 1991

RFC 1213   Management Information Base for Network Management of TCP/IP-based internets: MIB-II. March 1991

RFC 1212   Concise MIB definitions. March 1991

RFC 1209   Transmission of IP datagrams over the SMDS Service. March 1991

RFC 1208   Glossary of networking terms. March 1991

RFC 1207   FYI on Questions and Answers: Answers to commonly asked "experienced Internet user" questions. February 1991

RFC 1206   FYI on Questions and Answers: Answers to commonly asked "new Internet user" questions. February 1991

RFC 1205   5250 Telnet interface. February 1991

RFC 1201   Transmitting IP traffic over ARCNET networks. February 1991

RFC 1198   FYI on the X window system. January 1991

RFC 1196   Finger User Information Protocol. December 1990

RFC 1195   Use of OSI IS-IS for routing in TCP/IP and dual environments. December 1990

RFC 1188   Proposed Standard for the Transmission of IP Datagrams over FDDI Networks. October 1990

RFC 1187   Bulk Table Retrieval with the SNMP. October 1990

RFC 1184   Telnet Linemode Option. October 1990

RFC 1180   TCP/IP tutorial. January 1991

RFC 1179   Line printer daemon protocol. August 1990

RFC 1178   Choosing a name for your computer. August 1990

RFC 1175   FYI on where to start: A bibliography of internetworking information. August 1990

RFC 1173   Responsibilities of host and network managers: A summary of the "oral tradition" of the Internet. August 1990

RFC 1172   Point-to-Point Protocol (PPP) initial configuration options. July 1990

RFC 1171   Point-to-Point Protocol for the transmission of multi-protocol datagrams over Point-to-Point links. July 1990

RFC 1169   Explaining the role of GOSIP. August 1990

RFC 1166   Internet numbers. July 1990

RFC 1164   Application of the Border Gateway Protocol in the Internet. June 1990

RFC 1163   Border Gateway Protocol (BGP). June 1990

RFC 1157   Simple Network Management Protocol (SNMP). May 1990

RFC 1156   Management Information Base for network management of TCP/IP-based internets. May 1990

RFC 1155   Structure and identification of management information for TCP/IP-based internets. May 1990

RFC 1149   Standard for the transmission of IP datagrams on avian carriers. April 1990

RFC 1148   Mapping between X.400(1988) / ISO 10021 and RFC 822. March 1990

RFC 1147   FYI on a network management tool catalog: Tools for monitoring and debugging TCP/IP internets and interconnected devices. April 1990

RFC 1143   The Q method of Implementing TELNET Option Negotiation. February 1990

RFC 1142   OSI IS-IS Intra-domain Routing Protocol. February 1990

RFC 1136   Administrative Domains and Routing Domains: A model for routing in the Internet. December 1989

RFC 1129   Internet time synchronization: The Network Time Protocol. October 1989

RFC 1127   Perspective on the Host Requirements RFCs. October 1989

RFC 1125	Policy requirements for inter Administrative Domain routing. November 1989
RFC 1124	Policy issues in interconnecting networks. September 1989
RFC 1123	Requirements for Internet hosts—application and support. October 1989
RFC 1122	Requirements for Internet hosts—communication layers. October 1989
RFC 1119	Network Time Protocol (version 2) specification and implementation. September 1989
RFC 1118	Hitchhikers guide to the Internet. September 1989
RFC 1115	Privacy enhancement for Internet electronic mail: Part III. August 1989
RFC 1114	Privacy enhancement for Internet electronic mail: Part II. August 1989
RFC 1113	Privacy enhancement for Internet electronic mail: Part I. August 1989
RFC 1112	Host extensions for IP multicasting. August 1989
RFC 1108	U.S. Department of Defense Security Options for the Internet Protocol. November 1991
RFC 1104	Models of policy based routing. June 1989
RFC 1102	Policy routing in Internet protocols. May 1989
RFC 1101	DNS encoding of network names and other types. April 1989
RFC 1097	Telnet subliminal-message option. April 1989
RFC 1094	NFS: Network File System Protocol specification. March 1989
RFC 1091	Telnet terminal-type option. February 1989
RFC 1090	SMTP on X.25. February 1989
RFC 1089	SNMP over Ethernet. February 1989
RFC 1088	Standard for the transmission of IP datagrams over NetBIOS networks. February 1989
RFC 1086	ISO-TP0 bridge between TCP and X.25. December 1988

RFC 1085   ISO presentation services on top of TCP/IP networks. December 1988

RFC 1084   BOOTP vendor information extensions. December 1988

RFC 1080   Telnet remote flow control option. November 1988

RFC 1079   Telnet terminal speed option. December 1988

RFC 1074   NSFNET backbone SPF based Interior Gateway Protocol. October 1988

RFC 1073   Telnet window size option. October 1988

RFC 1072   TCP extensions for long-delay paths. October 1988

RFC 1070   Use of the Internet as a subnetwork for experimentation with the OSI network layer. February 1989

RFC 1069   Guidelines for the use of Internet-IP addresses in the ISO Connectionless-Mode Network Protocol. February 1989

RFC 1068   Background File Transfer Program (BFTP). August 1988

RFC 1058   Routing Information Protocol. June 1988

RFC 1057   RPC: Remote Procedure Call Protocol specification: Version 2. June 1988

RFC 1056   PCMAIL: A distributed mail system for personal computers. June 1988

RFC 1055   Nonstandard for transmission of IP datagrams over serial lines: SLIP. June 1988

RFC 1053   Telnet X.3 PAD option. April 1988

RFC 1044   Internet Protocol on Network System's HYPERchannel: Protocol specification. February 1988

RFC 1043   Telnet Data Entry Terminal option: DODIIS implementation. February 1988

RFC 1042   Standard for the transmission of IP datagrams over IEEE 802 networks. February 1988

RFC 1041   Telnet 3270 regime option. January 1988

RFC 1035   Domain names—implementation and specification. November 1987

RFC 1034   Domain names—concepts and facilities. November 1987

RFC 1033   Domain administrators operations guide. November 1987

RFC 1032   Domain administrators guide. November 1987

RFC 1027   Using ARP to implement transparent subnet gateways. October 1987

RFC 1014   XDR: External Data Representation standard. June 1987

RFC 1013   X Window System Protocol, version 11: Alpha update. June 1987

RFC 1011   Official Internet protocols. May 1987

RFC 1009   Requirements for Internet gateways. June 1987

RFC 1008   Implementation guide for the ISO Transport Protocol. June 1987

RFC 1006   ISO transport services on top of the TCP: Version 3. May 1987

RFC 1002   Protocol standard for a NetBIOS service on a TCP/UDP transport: Detailed specifications. March 1987

RFC 1001   Protocol standard for a NetBIOS service on a TCP/UDP transport: Concepts and methods. March 1987

RFC 995   End System to Intermediate System Routing Exchange Protocol for use in conjunction with ISO 8473. April 1986

RFC 994   Final text of DIS 8473, Protocol for Providing the Connectionless-mode Network service. March 1986

RFC 982   Guidelines for the specification of the structure of the Domain Specific Part (DSP) of the ISO standard NSAP address. April 1986

RFC 980   Protocol document order information. March 1986

RFC 974   Mail routing and the domain system. January 1986

RFC 959   File Transfer Protocol. October 1985

RFC 954   NICNAME/WHOIS. October 1985

RFC 951   Bootstrap Protocol. September 1985

RFC 950   Internet Standard Subnetting Procedure. August 1985

RFC 949   FTP unique-named store command. July 1985

RFC 946   Telnet terminal location number option. May 1985

RFC 941   Addendum to the network service definition covering network layer addressing. April 1985

RFC 933	Output marking Telnet option. January 1985
RFC 932	Subnetwork addressing scheme. January 1985
RFC 922	Broadcasting Internet datagrams in the presence of subnets. October 1984
RFC 920	Domain requirements. October 1984
RFC 919	Broadcasting Internet Datagrams. October 1984
RFC 911	EGP Gateway under Berkeley UNIX 4.2. August 1984
RFC 906	Bootstrap loading using TFTP. June 1984
RFC 905	ISO Transport Protocol specification ISO DP 8073. April 1984
RFC 904	Exterior Gateway Protocol formal specification. April 1984
RFC 903	Reverse Address Resolution Protocol. June 1984
RFC 896	Congestion control in IP/TCP internetworks. January 1984
RFC 895	Standard for the transmission of IP datagrams over experimental Ethernet networks. April 1984
RFC 894	Standard for the transmission of IP datagrams over Ethernet networks. April 1984
RFC 893	Trailer encapsulations. April 1984
RFC 888	"STUB" Exterior Gateway Protocol. January 1984
RFC 886	Proposed standard for message header munging. December 1983
RFC 885	Telnet end of record option. December 1983
RFC 879	TCP maximum segment size and related topics. November 1983
RFC 877	Standard for the transmission of IP datagrams over public data networks. September 1983
RFC 868	Time Protocol. May 1983
RFC 867	Daytime Protocol. May 1983
RFC 866	Active users. May 1983
RFC 865	Quote of the Day Protocol. May 1983
RFC 864	Character Generator Protocol. May 1983
RFC 863	Discard Protocol. May 1983

RFC 862	Echo Protocol. May 1983
RFC 861	Telnet Extended Options: List Option. May 1983
RFC 860	Telnet Timing Mark Option. May 1983
RFC 859	Telnet Status Option. May 1983
RFC 858	Telnet Suppress Go Ahead Option. May 1983
RFC 857	Telnet Echo Option. May 1983
RFC 856	Telnet Binary Transmission. May 1983
RFC 855	Telnet Option Specifications. May 1983
RFC 854	Telnet Protocol Specification. May 1983
RFC 827	Exterior Gateway Protocol (EGP). October 1982
RFC 823	DARPA Internet gateway. September 1982
RFC 822	Standard for the format of ARPA Internet text messages. August 1982
RFC 821	Simple Mail Transfer Protocol. August 1982
RFC 815	IP datagram reassembly algorithms. July 1982
RFC 814	Name, addresses, ports, and routes. July 1982
RFC 813	Window and Acknowledgment strategy in TCP. July 1982
RFC 799	Internet name domains. September 1981
RFC 793	Transmission Control Protocol. September 1981
RFC 792	Internet Control Message Protocol. September 1981
RFC 791	Internet Protocol. September 1981
RFC 783	TFTP Protocol (revision 2). June 1981
RFC 781	Specification of the Internet Protocol (IP) timestamp option. May 1981
RFC 779	Telnet send-location option. April 1981
RFC 775	Directory oriented FTP commands. December 1980
RFC 768	User Datagram Protocol. August 1980
RFC 749	Telnet SUPDUP-Output option. September 1978
RFC 736	Telnet SUPDUP option. October 1977

RFC 732	Telnet Data Entry Terminal option. September 1977
RFC 727	Telnet logout option. April 1977
RFC 726	Remote Controlled Transmission and Echoing Telnet option. March 1977
RFC 698	Telnet extended ASCII option. July 1975

Appendix B Well Known Ports

Port Number	Name	Service
0		Reserved
1	tcpmux tcp	Port Service Multiplexer
2-4		Unassigned
5	rje	Remote Job Entry
7	echo	Echo
9	discard	Discard
11	users	Active Users
13	daytime	Daytime
15		Unassigned
17	qotd	Quote of the Day
19	chargen	Character Generator
20	ftp-data	File Transfer (Data)
21	ftp	File Transfer (Control)
23	telnet	TELNET
25	smtp	Simple Mail Transfer Protocol
27	nsw-fe	NSWUser System FE
29	msg-icp	MSG-ICP
31	msg-auth	MSG Authentication
33	dsp	Display Support Protocol
35		Any Private Printer Server
37	time	Time
39	rlp	Resource Location Protocol
41	graphics	Graphics
42	nameserve	Host Name Server
43	whois	Who Is
49	login	Login Host Protocol
53	domain	Domain Name Server
67	bootps	Bootstrap Protocol Server
68	bootpc	Bootstrap Protocol Client
69	tftp	Trivial File Transfer
70	gopher	Gopher System
79	finger	Finger
80	http	World Wide Web

Port Number	Name	Service
101	hostname	NIC Host Name Server
102	iso-tsap	ISO TSAP
103	x400	X.400
104	s400snd	X.400 SND
105	csnet-ns	CSNET Mailbox Name Server
109	pop2	Post Office Protocol version 2
110	pop3	Post Office Protocol version 3
111	sunrpc	SUN RPC Portmap
119	nntp	Network News Transport Protocol
137	netbios-ns	NETBIOS Name Service
138	netbios-dgm	NETBIOS Datagram Service
139	netbios-ssn	NETBIOS Session Service
146	iso-tp0	ISO TP0
147	iso-ip	ISO IP
150	sql-net	SQL-NET
153	sgmp	SGMP
156	sqlsrv	SQL Service
160	sgmp-traps	SGMP TRAPS
161	snmp	SNMP
162	snmptrap	SNMPTRAP
163	cmip-manage	CMIP/TCP Manager
164	cmip-agent	CMIP/TCP Agent
165	xns-courier	Xerox
179	bgp	Border Gateway Protocol

Index

I don't have time for learning curves.

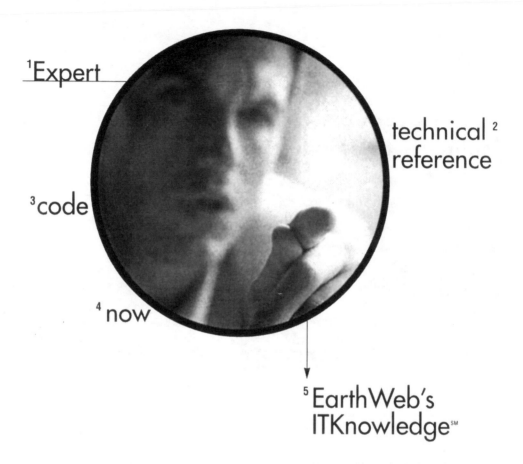

[1]Expert

technical [2]
reference

[3]code

[4] now

[5] EarthWeb's
ITKnowledge℠

They rely on you to be the **1** expert on tough development challenges. There's no time for learning curves, so you go online for **2** technical references from the experts who wrote the books. Find answers fast simply by clicking on our search engine. Access hundreds of online books, tutorials and even source **3** code samples **4** now. Go to **5** EarthWeb's ITKnowledge, get immediate answers, and get down to it.

Get your FREE ITKnowledge trial subscription today at itkgo.com.
Use code number 026.

EARTHWEB
Go further *faster*